AIR CARGO CLAIMS

AIR CARGO CLAIMS

by

REX C TESTER

LLP

LONDON HONG KONG
1998

LLP Reference Publishing
69–77 Paul Street
London EC2A 4LQ
Great Britain

EAST ASIA
LLP Asia
Room 1101, Hollywood Centre
233 Hollywood Road
Hong Kong

First published in Great Britain 1998

British Library Cataloguing in Publication Data
A catalogue record
for this book is available
from the British Library

ISBN 1 85978 846 7

Text set in 10/12 Plantin by
Mendip Communications Ltd
Frome
Printed in Great Britain by
WBC Limited
Bridgend, Mid-Glamorgan

ACKNOWLEDGEMENTS

One day I woke up to the astonishing fact that I had become regarded as some sort of authority on air cargo claims—not necessarily on the finer points of the law, although I hope a little of that comes into it somewhere, but certainly on the practical aspects of claims. However, like anyone else in a comparable position, I have an undischargeable debt to those whose generosity helped me reach such unexpected heights.

There have been a number of such people in my life, of course. Naturally, it is unlikely that any of them realised they were playing such a part, and, indeed, some of them may well eschew such mention!

Thus, first, the companies to which I owe a great deal were PanAm and Virgin Atlantic: the former of fond memory to me—they provided me with a job which led directly to my career—and the latter have supported me for many years and continue to be a source of stimulating work.

Cargosave—not too distant in memory—gave me a solid start in the freight industry in my early years as an independent consultant.

PBL Air Cargo—whose principal, Brian Lawrence, has become a great friend—have also provided me with many years of opportunity to sharpen my skills.

J. O. Sims Ltd.—whose principal, Christopher Sims, also has become a great friend—continue to provide me with varied and welcomely-difficult work in the perishables shipping world, not only in aviation, but also in a marine context.

I am also very grateful to insurers world-wide who have entrusted me with investigations, recoveries and liability-handling work on major cargo losses.

Among individuals, Peter East ranks first. A most loyal and trusted friend over many years, he oversaw my career, and indeed was primarily responsible for it. Of all those to whom I owe a debt, he may well have been the only one who actually had some inkling of what his original decision to appoint me PanAm claims supervisor—against my wishes as it happened—might lead to.

Sean Gates—now senior partner of Beaumont & Son—was responsible for pointing me in the right direction many years ago, when I was struggling to find out how to teach myself about air cargo liability, and undoubtedly he was a seminal influence on me.

Jonathan Barrett—late of Clyde & Co.—helped me to my first "thumping" success in litigation, and David Reynolds—presently of Clyde & Co.—rendered invaluable assistance for a long while and gave me the thrill of seeing one of my cases setting significant legal precedent. Jeremy Shebson—also of Clyde & Co.—has been of invaluable assistance in dealing with the fundamental changes in air law occurring just prior to publication, which required some radical revision of parts of this book.

I am immensely indebted to David Harris for reviewing this work: he has been a hard, able and honourable opponent for whom I have acquired the greatest respect over the years—and hopefully, his friendship. I do not see his peer as an airline claims handler, and British Airways should be proud of him. His solid experience in defence seems the perfect foil to my essentially plaintiff-oriented work. I was surprised to find us in general agreement, but where he disagreed with some of my conclusions, I found this only beneficial to the work as a whole.

Finally, Terry Gage of Davies, Lavery spent considerable time looking over the manuscript and has been kind enough to offer valuable suggestions, which have enabled me to extend my knowledge while completing this book.

R.C.T.

PREFACE

In 1974, I was thrust into a job within Pan American World Airways which I did not want: the airline was undergoing one of its periodic contractions (irreversible, as it turned out) and I was in no position to argue about my manager's decision. That in later years he turned out to be a most loyal and trusted friend in life and business is not actually a coincidence.

It took around six months for me to develop any enthusiasm in the work, and it arose from what I perceived to be an almost total lack of knowledge within the company of the disciplines involved in handling "cargo claims". It seems no-one within the company could guide me, and PanAm HQ did not seem willing to give me any help—they just handed down edicts, it seemed.

I burned to learn how to do my job. A friendly solicitor—well-known and highly respected in aviation circles now—gave me a "kick-start". That not only led me into enjoyment of my job, which seemed to become more like a vocation, but also it was responsible in 1983, against all sane advice apparently, for my becoming independent, and commencing a business life of great variety, not a few scares and, overall, tremendous satisfaction.

My experience, I believe, has been unique: neither loss adjuster in the traditional mould, nor lawyer, I developed my technical legal knowledge and combined it with practical operational knowledge. From my present viewpoint, it seems to have been inevitable that my sense of pragmatism would become highly developed: constantly searching for the truly practical way forward, without ignoring moral considerations completely, I hope; and operating on principle only when I was sure the client understood truly the position he was taking (and for which he was ultimately paying).

There is no doubt that the various parties involved in "air cargo claims" sometimes have difficulty in communicating; for instance, a solicitor, unavoidably ignorant of air cargo operational matters, can have a serious problem communicating with a junior clerk, charged by an airline with handling claims, who is unavoidably ignorant of the law.

I seek to promote understanding; hence this work tries to bridge the chasm—sometimes seemingly unbridgeable—between the party seeking compensation for losses sustained during carriage by air and the party of whom such compensation is demanded.

"Bridge builders" employed by claimants and respondents include insurers and insurance brokers who offer some ways out of the uncertainties of claiming for losses; forwarders and consolidators who, for commercial reasons, try to help their clients succeed in obtaining compensation; and lawyers, recovery agents and loss adjusters who often carry on the real fight to obtain recompense or to avoid paying it.

While it is intended primarily as a handbook for the claims handlers of exporters, importers, forwarders and carriers, both novices and the experienced among the interacting groups should derive benefit from this book which also bridges the chasm between the air cargo industry's operatives and those who concern themselves more with the technical side of liability.

This is not intended to be a "learned" work in the traditional sense, and few legal decisions are referred to in detail. Its thrust is one of practicality, distilled from a career of finding practical solutions, since none else would do.

March 1998 REX C TESTER

CONTENTS

Acknowledgements v
Preface vii
Glossary xvii
Table of Cases xxi
Table of Legislation xxiii
Table of Conventions xxv
Table of Trading Conditions xxvii

CHAPTER 1—INTRODUCTION 1

About this work 1
The work which has to be done 1
The breadth of the industry 2
The integrity and stature of the work 4
  Exporters and importers 5
  Forwarders (and consolidators) 5
  Airlines 6

CHAPTER 2—THE CONCEPT OF LIABILITY 7

CHAPTER 3—ABOUT INSURANCE 9

Insurance 9
Insureds 9
Insurance brokers 10
Insurers 10
  Underwriting 10
  Claims adjusters 11
Types of insurance 11
  Liability cover 11
  Transit or cargo cover 12
  What happens after claims settlements? 12
  Air waybill insurance 12

CHAPTER 4—RISK AND LOSS CONTROL 15

General risk control measures 16
Loss 16
Theft of entire packages or complete consignments: 16
Packaging 17
Description 17
Shipping arrangements 18
Pilferage 18
Mis-routeing 19
Damage 19
Wetting 20
Physical deformation 20
Delays 20
Loss control measures 21
Cargo owners 21
Mitigation 21
Claim notices 22
Carriers and forwarders 22
Documenting incidents 22
Loss 23
Tallying 23
Insurers 23
Missing on receipt 24
From another party 24
From another depot in the same company 24
From the inbound aircraft 24
Missing during bond-check 25
Missing on picking-out 25
Damage 26
Cameras 26
Damage reports 26
Insurers 26
Damage on receipt 27
From another party 27
From another depot in the same company 27
From the inbound aircraft 27
Damage noted at other times 28
Delay 28
Perishables 28
Theft 29
Pilferage 29
Whole packages or consignments 30
The police and insurance investigators 30
The police 30
Insurance investigators 31
Liability insurers 31

CHAPTER 5—CREATING AND ADMINISTERING THE CLAIM FILE 33

General principles 33
Assumption of future litigation 33
General construction of the file 34
File creation 34
A separate file and filing location 34
Claim number 34
Housekeeping 35
Chronology 35
Duplicated documents 35
Clarity of documents 35
Which records to maintain 36
Regular documents 36
Other documents 39
Ordinary 39
Special 40
Reviewing and progressing 40
Diary v. Database 41
Database spin-off 41
Correspondence standards 41

CHAPTER 6—LEGAL FRAMEWORK 43

Contract 43
Liability in bailment and transit 44
Bailment 44
Transit 44
The fundamental importance of incorporation 45
Agency 46
Evolution of Limited Liability 46
Regulation of Contracts 47
Civil regulation 47
Regulation by legislation 48

CHAPTER 7—CIVIL REGULATION—RHA AND BIFA 49

RHA 49
Condition 1—definitions 49
Condition 2—parties and sub-contracting 49
Condition 3—dangerous goods 50
Condition 4—loading and unloading 50
Condition 5—consignment notes 50
Condition 6—transit 50
Condition 7—undelivered or unclaimed goods 50
Condition 8—carrier's charges 51
Condition 9—liability for loss and damage 51

Condition 10—fraud 51
Condition 11—limitation of liability 51
Condition 12—insurance 52
Condition 13—indemnity to carrier 52
Condition 14—time limits for claims 52
Condition 15—lien 53
Condition 16—unreasonable detention 53
Condition 17—computation of time 53
Condition 18—loss adjustment 53
Condition 19—impossibility of performance 53
BIFA 53
Definition and application 54
Condition 1—definitions 54
Condition 2—application and overriding law 54
Condition 3—authority to accept contract conditions 54
Condition 4—further authority to accept conditions 54
The company 54
Condition 5—agency 55
Condition 6—acceptance of liability 55
Condition 7—contracts arranged by the company as an agent 55
Condition 8—freedom of choice for company 55
Condition 9—use of associates, etc. 55
Condition 10—liens 55
Condition 11—remuneration 55
Condition 12—frustrated delivery 56
Condition 13—(transit) insurance 56
Condition 14—special delivery circumstances 56
Condition 15—advice and information 56
Condition 16—special cargoes 56
Condition 17—dangerous goods or goods likely to cause damage 56
Condition 18—declarations of value 57
The customer 57
Condition 19—warranties 57
Condition 20—dangerous goods or goods likely to cause damage 57
Condition 21—against whom to claim? 57
Condition 22—the customer must indemnify the company 57
Condition 23—moneys owed to the company 57
Condition 24—customer guarantee of charges 58
Condition 25—general average 58
Liability and limitation 58
Condition 26—diligence 58
Condition 27—relief of liability 58
Condition 28—delay 58
Condition 29—limitations 58
Condition 30—time limits for claims 59
Condition 31—the applicable law 59

CHAPTER 8—STATUTORY REGULATION—AIR CARRIAGE 61

CHAPTER 9—THE WARSAW SYSTEM 63

Warsaw Legislation 64
Which version of Warsaw and why it is important 64
Major difficulties produced by recent U.K. legislation 64
Unamended Warsaw 65
Chapter I—Scope and definitions 65
Article 1 66
Article 2 66
Chapter II 66
Section I—pasenger ticket and Section II—baggage check 66
Section III—air waybill 66
Article 5—need for and absence of AWB 66
Article 6—number of copies, and signatures 67
Article 7—one AWB per package? 67
Article 8—AWB particulars 67
Article 9—effect of absence of particulars 67
Article 10—consignor's responsibility 68
Article 11—AWB particulars as evidence 68
Article 12—right of stoppage in transit 68
Article 13—acquisition of contract rights by consignee 69
Article 14—consignor's and consignee's respective rights 69
Article 15—limiting the effect of articles 12, 13 and 14 69
Article 16—consignor's responsibility for documents attached to AWB 69
Chapter III—liability of the carrier 69
Article 17—passenger liability 70
Article 18—damage and loss liability 70
Categories of road carriage 72
Article 19—delay liability 73
Article 20—carrier's defences 74
Article 21—contributory negligence 74
Article 22—limitation of liability 74
Basic liability limit 74
Raising the liability limit 75
Article 23—minimum levels of liability 75
Article 24—permitted context for claims 76
Article 25—deprivation of limitation 76
Article 26—delivery, and notices of claim 77
Article 27—"death" of carrier 79
Article 28—jurisdiction and legal proceedings 79
Article 29—time bar 80
Article 30—successive carriers 80
Chapter IV—Provisions relating to combined transportation—Article 31 80
Chapter V—general and final provisions 81
Warsaw/Hague 81
Relevant amended articles 82
Article 8—AWB particulars 82
Article 9—effect of absence of AWB particulars 82
Article 15—negotiable AWBs 82

Article 22—limitation of liability 83
Limitation amounts 83
Package weight 83
Litigation expenses 83
Article 23—minimum levels of liability 84
Article 25—intentional or reckless conduct 85
Article 26—delivery and notices of claim 85
Future Developments—Montreal Protocols Nos. 3 and 4 85
Simplicity 86
The air waybill 86
Liability of the carrier 86
Limit of carrier's liability 86
Loss of limitation 86
Complication 87
Guadalajara Convention 88
The forwarder/contracting carrier's liabilities 88
Notices of claim 90

CHAPTER 10—NON-WARSAW 91

CHAPTER 11—AIR WAYBILL CONDITIONS 93

Notice 93
Paragraph 1—definitions 93
Paragraph 2—applicability of rules 93
Paragraph 3—name and address on AWB 93
Paragraph 4—limitation of liability 94
Paragraph 5—special declaration of value 94
Paragraph 6—package weight limitation 94
Paragraph 7—protection of agents, and others 94
Paragraph 8—reasonable dispatch (avoidance of delay) 95
Paragraph 9—period of responsibility 95
Paragraph 10—shipper's guarantee and payment of freight 95
Paragraph 11—notice of arrival 96
Paragraph 12—notice periods 96
Paragraph 13—shippers' obligations 96
Paragraph 14—authority to vary air waybill conditions 97
Paragraph 15—transit insurance 97

CHAPTER 12—AIRLINE HANDLING AGREEMENTS 99

CHAPTER 13—CLAIMS DECISIONS 103

Which liability context? 103
Trucking of air cargo 104
Air transportation or not? 104

Worthy claimants and respondents, and "bad attitude" 105
Anger and aggression from claimants 106
Settlement criteria 107
Entitlement to claim 107
Freight 107
Title to goods 108
Subrogation 109
Notice of claim 109
Notice to contracting carrier only 110
Jurisdiction 110
Time-bars 111
Delays in pursuit of claims 112
Proving liability 112
Air carriage 112
Transhipments and successive or preceding carriers 113
Force majeure 113
Perceived force majeure 113
Undoubted force majeure 114
Continuing duty of care 114
Contributory negligence 115
Errors in documentation or handling instructions 115
Inadequate packing 115
Imprudent loading 115
Delivery signatures 116
ULDS and delivery circumstances 116
Perishables—damaged by delay 117
Inherent vice 118
Claim amount (quantum) 118
The measure of damages 118
Foreign currencies 119
Sound-arrived-value 119
Added value 119
Subrogated claims 119
Interest 120
Consequential losses 120
Proof 120
Foreseeability 121
Mitigation 121
Delayed perishables 122
Consequential losses 122
Damage 122
Reasonableness of mitigation 122
Accurate calculation and supporting documents 123
Personal effects and household goods 123
Settlement amount and limitation 123
Currencies 123
Weight basis 123
RHA 124
BIFA 124

Air carriage 124
Package limit under Warsaw/Hague and non-Warsaw 125
Volumetric variance under unamended Warsaw 125
Declared value for carriage 125
Limitation breaking 126
Interest 126
Undesirable settlement practices 127
Negotiation 128
Settlement 128
Lawyers and litigation 129

APPENDIX 1—ROAD HAULAGE ASSOCIATION LIMITED CONDITIONS OF CARRIAGE 1991 131

APPENDIX 2—BIFA STANDARD TRADING CONDITIONS 1989 139

APPENDIX 3—THE UNAMENDED WARSAW CONVENTION 1929 145

APPENDIX 4—THE WARSAW CONVENTION AS AMENDED AT THE HAGUE, 1955, AND BY MONTREAL ADDITIONAL PROTOCOL No. 2, 1975 155

APPENDIX 5—THE UNAMENDED WARSAW CONVENTION AS AMENDED BY MONTREAL ADDITIONAL PROTOCOL No. 1, 1975 165

APPENDIX 6—THE WARSAW CONVENTION AS AMENDED AT THE HAGUE IN 1955 AND BY PROTOCOLS Nos. 3 AND 4 SIGNED AT MONTREAL IN 1975 175

APPENDIX 7—GUADALAJARA SUPPLEMENTARY CONVENTION (1961) 185

APPENDIX 8—AIR WAYBILL CONDITIONS 191

Index 195

GLOSSARY

AWB	common abbreviation for air waybill
Air waybill	document evidencing a contract for carriage. This is usually issued by a company which is an actual carrier, *viz.* an airline. As opposed to a house air waybill, or master air waybill, it designates a consignment comprising one shipment for one shipper and one consignee
Back-to-back	a term designating a consolidation which comprises one house air waybill shipment only
BIFA	British International Freight Association. A trade organisation to which many forwarding agents belong
CAB	Civil Aviation Board—a US governmental organisation having responsibility for regulating the air transportation industry
Cargo	the actual consignment being moved
CCTV	closed circuit TV, used as a security measure
CIR	Cargo irregularity report, also known as a "damage and loss" report
CMR	Contrat de Transport International de Marchandise par Route. The international rules for the carriage of goods by road
Consequential loss	In this work, this term is used to denote any damages sustained following a delay to cargo or other event which causes the shipper or consignee to incur costs or losses which are not related directly to the cargo itself. It can also be defined as non-physical damage. An example would be the losses arising due to the shutting down of a factory because a vital part of machinery did not reach the factory on time, or pure loss of profit resulting perhaps from a delay to goods preventing a profitable sale

Consolidation	a shipment which consists of one or more individual consignments, each subject to a house air waybill. (Curiously enough, a consolidation can comprise one house air waybill only.)
Freight	usage 1—within the industry, this denotes the cargo itself usage 2—legally, and properly, this is the charge made by a carrier to its customer. (Within the industry, the term "freight charge" is used to differentiate the charges from the cargo.)
Guadalajara Convention	an international agreement additional to the Warsaw Convention
HAWB	common abbreviation for house air waybill
House air waybill	document evidencing a contract for carriage. This is usually issued by a company not itself an actual carrier
IATA	International Air Transportation Association, an international trade organisation to which most airlines belong, and which is highly influential in determining how civil aviation is organised world-wide
Jurisdiction	in effect this designates a sovereign country in terms of its legal system
MAWB	common abbreviation for master air waybill
Master air waybill	document evidencing a contract for carriage. This is usually issued by a company which is an actual carrier, *viz.* an airline. As opposed to an "air waybill", a master air waybill indicates that the consignment it covers is a consolidation
Montreal Protocols	a development of the Warsaw Convention
Negligence	for our purposes, "simple" negligence can be regarded as mistakes made innocently by one party who has a duty towards another
Prima facie	a principle applied herein to evidence which stands only in the absence of other evidence to the contrary. A Latin term, which literally means "at first sight", or "from a first impression"
Quantum	the correct legal term for a claim amount
Reserve	usage 1—within the industry to denote a notice of intended claim usage 2—within the insurance world to denote an accounting exercise, where an insurer sets aside a sum of money against the possibility of having to settle a claim

RHA	Road Haulage Association, a trade organisation to which many road haulage companies belong
SDR	Special Drawing Right—an "artificial" international currency used for various financial purposes. The relevance to us is that it is used as a means to express limited liability
SITA	the telex system used for operational messages by the airlines and larger forwarding agents and consolidators, which is still used in preference to facsimile. This system appears to show no signs of becoming obsolete and is "alive and well"
Subrogation	the principle that an insurer can settle a shipper's or consignee's claim for damage or loss of cargo arising under an insurance policy, and then acquire rights of claims allowing the insurer to pursue a claim against a respondent in order to attempt to recover the settlement paid out
ULD	Unit load device. The aircraft container or aircraft pallet, *viz.* that apparatus which is built specifically for loading cargo into or onto it, and once loaded to be placed on board the aircraft
Warsaw Convention	the international system of agreements governing the manner in which liability arises on air cargo, as well as passengers and their baggage
Warsaw/Hague	a development of the Warsaw Convention
Wilful misconduct	in general terms, this concept is met with where persons steal, and the term becomes obvious in meaning: this is the more common definition, involving criminal activity by the persons concerned. However, wilful misconduct can extend to the employee who is not acting dishonestly, but who, for instance, deliberately ignores a set procedure or instruction

TABLE OF CASES

Gatewhite Ltd *v.* Iberia Lineas Aereas de Espana SA (1988) 1 S & B Av. R V11/305, [1990] QB 326, [1989] 1 All ER 944, 1 Lloyd's Rep 160 .... 108, 127
Spectra International *v.* Hayesoak Limited & ors, unreported, *cited in* [1997] LMCLQ 478 52

TABLE OF LEGISLATION

STATUTES

Carriage by Air Act 1932 .... 48, 64
Carriage by Air Act 1961 .... 48, 64, 82
Carriage by Air and Road Act 1979 .... 64, 82, 85, 87
s. 2 85
Carriage by Air (Supplementary Provisions) Act 1962 88

STATUTORY INSTRUMENTS

Carriage by Air Acts (Application of Provisions) Order 1967 (as amended) ... 64, 91
Sched. 1 91
Carriage by Air Acts (Application of Provisions) (Fourth Amendment) Order 1998 64
Carriage by Air (Parties to Convention) Order 1988 64
Carriage by Air and Road Act 1979 (Commencement No. 2) Order 1997 83
Sterling Equivalent Order 1996 124

TABLE OF CONVENTIONS

(Page numbers in **bold** denote text reproduced)

Contrat de Transport International de Marchandise par Route (CMR) 71, 72, 81, 96, 103
Guadalajara Supplementary Convention 1961 (Guadalajara) 63, 88, 89, 110, **185**
Hague Protocol 1955 (Warsaw/Hague) 48, 63, 64, 65, 81, 82, 83, 85, 86, 87, 91, 96, 103, 124, **155**
arts 8, 9, 15 82
art. 20 84
22 83
(2)(a) 125
(b) 83, 94, 125
(4) 83, 84
23 84
arts 25, 26 .... 85, 86
Montreal Additional Protocol No. 1 1929 (Montreal 1) 63, 64, 65, 85, 87
Montreal Additional Protocol No. 2 1975 (Montreal 2) 48, 63, 64, 65, 82, 83, 85, 87, 91, 124, **155**
Montreal Protocols Nos. 3 and 4 1975 (Montreal 3 and 4) 63, 82, 85–86, 87, 91, 125, **175**
Warsaw Convention 1929 (Unamended) ..... 7, 48, 49, 50, 55, 59, 62, 63, 82, 83, 85, 87, 89, 93, 96, 103, 109, 121, 125, **145**, also amended at **155**, **165**, **175**
Chapter I 65
art. 1 66
2 66
Chapter II 66

Warsaw Convention 1929 (Unamended) —*cont.*
Chapter II—*cont.*
sections I, II 66
arts 3, 4 66
section III 66
arts 5–16 86
art. 5 66
6 67
7 67
8 .... 67, 93
9 67
10 68
11 68
12 .... 68, 69
arts 13, 14, 15, 16 69
Chapter III 69
art. 17 70
18 .... 70, 73, 74, 76, 95
(3) 70, 73, 80
19 .... 73, 74, 76
20 74
21 74
22 .... 74, 94, 125, 126
23 .... 73, 75, 94, 96, 118
24 76
25 .... 76, 85, 99, 126
26 .... 75, 77, 109, 110
(1) 116
arts 27, 28 79
art. 29 .... 80, 111
30 .... 80, 110
(3) 70
Chapter IV 80
Chapter V 81
art. 32 81
34 81

TABLE OF TRADING CONDITIONS

(Page numbers in **bold** denote text reproduced)

Air Waybill Conditions 71, 73, 78, 85, 93, 96, 104, 107, 115, 125, **191**
para. 1 93
2 93
(a) 93
(b)(iii) 71, 93
3 93
4 .... 71, 94
paras 5, 6, 7 94
8, 9 95
para. 10 95
(a) 95
11 96
12 96
(a)(i), (ii), (iii) 96
(iv) 71, 96
13 96
paras 14, 15 97

British International Freight Association Conditions 1989 (BIFA) 43, 49, 53, 54, 55, 71, 72, 80, 81, 89, 100, 103, 104, 109, 110, 112, 118, 124, 126, **139**
Conds 1–4 54
5–11 55
12–17 56
18–23 57
24–29 58
26–29 55
30–31 59

Road Haulage Association Conditions of Carriage 1991 (RHA) 43, 49, 81, 100, 103, 109, 110, 111, 112, 118, 124, 126, **131**
Conds 1, 2 49
3, 4, 5 50
Cond. 6 .... 50, 51
Conds 7, 8 50
9, 10, 11 51
12, 13, 14 52
15, 16, 17, 18, 19 53

CHAPTER 1

INTRODUCTION

ABOUT THIS WORK

First and foremost, this book must be regarded as a guide and not a definitive rule-book.

While many of the principles and procedures set down herein are undoubtedly accurate and true, other commentators and learned practitioners will have different ideas on procedure for claims handling, and indeed on interpretation of applicable rules and regulations. Accordingly, no matter how experienced you become in claims handling, and although your own judgement and experience are of great importance, do not be reluctant to seek other's views.

Finally, you must treat every case as a fresh one, considering it apart from all foregoing ones.

THE WORK WHICH HAS TO BE DONE

A claims handler, fully developed in his function, is using theoretical knowledge tempered with experience, extreme judgement, initiative, and administrative skills of no less merit than those of any other highly skilled professional. This is seldom recognised.

Examine the processing of a single claim. Detailed analyses of the paper trail and operational trail may be needed in order to reach an understanding of the incidents giving rise to the claim. Inquiries of varying complexity may be triggered. Analysis and verification of liability, entitlement to claim, and the claimed amount will be necessary, and each of these aspects is subject to complex rules of law, and each can generate further inquiries. Having completed the foregoing, the handler moves on to a decision (more usually a recommendation to superiors) on settlement or commitment to pursuit of the claim.

Settlement decisions range from outright repudiation of liability to full payments without demur. Decisions of less certainty are also necessary, where there seems to be a chance of forcing claimants to accept less than they are asking. The converse is also true and sometimes more poignant, because a cargo owner—having lost money already—must commit resources certainly, and more money probably, to achieve compensation. For the respondent, it is different: he has probably received his freight or other fees, and if he can sit tight without settling, he can preserve his profit, of course.

Overall, the claims handler must keep a crystal-clear file in case of litigation.

Does this cover all the functions of a claims handler operating at full potential? It does not. Over all the foregoing functions, our claims handler, more than likely, will have to liaise with the company's insurer. Not far away at any time from the exigency of pursuing or defending the claim will lurk the anxiety about the effect the claim may have on insurance premiums.

What follows from all these duties and concerns is an ever-growing fund of experience and knowledge, putting our claims handler in a unique position to advise on risks in order to avoid claims in the future, and to advise on losses to ensure that individual claims do not run out of control. This is an idealised job description for a claims handler, of course; some companies recognise this and accord claims handlers their dues, others demote the task, and occasionally suffer painful consequences unnecessarily.

THE BREADTH OF THE INDUSTRY

A claimant must determine against whom he should act and in what legal context, and, because the airfreight process is no less complex than any other, the claimant, whoever he is and wherever he is in the contract chain, can be severely challenged in identifying the correct "target".

★ ★ ★

The figure opposite illustrates the movement of cargo from shipper to consignee and the key illustrates the contractual relationships. Of course, it is illustrative only, and there are routinely many variations on this scheme.

KEY TO THE FIGURE

1 *The shipper* has a choice of acting against the forwarding agent, consolidator, or airline, depending on what went wrong.

2 *The trucker collecting goods from the shipper* is contracted to the forwarding agent to collect the goods, and thus is generally liable only to the forwarder and not directly to the shipper.

3 *The forwarder* is responsible to the shipper for any mistakes it makes, but usually finds itself attempting to pursue claims against a third party on behalf of the shipper.

4 *The consolidator* is liable to the shipper (and on rare occasions to the consignee).

5 *At the outbound airport* the cargo handling agent acting for the airline is generally liable only to the airline.

6 *The airline* is liable to the shipper or consignee.

In this case, the cargo is being trucked to a secondary airport, e.g. London Heathrow Airport to Manchester Airport.

7 *The airline's cargo handling agent* is liable generally only to the airline.

8 *The airline's trucker* is liable generally only to the airline.

9 *At the secondary airport* the cargo handling agent acting for the airline is generally liable only to the airline.

10 *The consolidator's break-bulk agent* is generally liable only to the export consolidator, although it may choose to assume liability to others.

11 *The customs/import agent* is responsible to the consignee for any mistakes it makes, but usually finds itself attempting to pursue claims against a third party on behalf of the consignee.

12 *The trucker acting for the customs/import agent* is generally liable only to the customs/import agent.

13 *The importer* can claim against the customs/import agent, the consolidator, or the airline, depending on what went wrong.

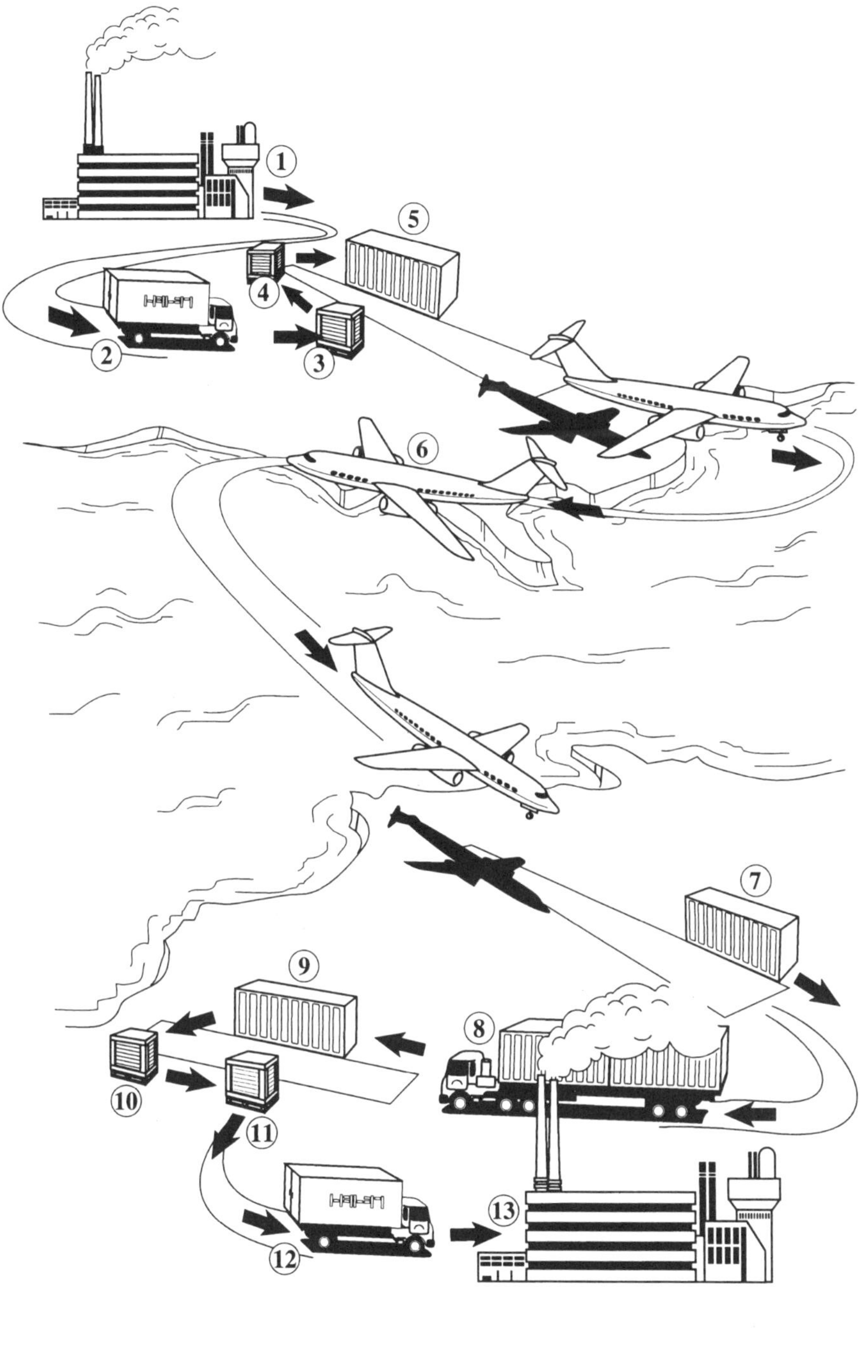
1
2
3
4
5
6
7
8
9
10
11
12
13

It is by no means the most complex arrangement that exists: although rare, it is certainly not unknown for four forwarders to be interposed between shipper and consolidator. Each forwarder is probably acting as a contracting carrier and will wish to avoid his or her immediate customer knowing of the next one "down the lines"—so the problems become more and more involved. Thus, if you are either the consignee whose vegetables are delayed, or at the other extreme—but rarely—the airline which has suffered a very expensive delay caused by a pallet collapse within the hold, probably brought about by a consolidator failing to stow correctly, you must think seriously about who is your opponent and why.

An attempt is made herein to show how the various contractual elements interlock. The system can appear to claimants to be a maze, seriously discouraging attempts at compensation, but with calm analysis ways forward can often be found.

The shipper should now be able to see who should be its target and in what legal context; the forwarder—as a pure agent—can see where it fits in, the consolidator can be sure of its location in the chain, and the actions it should take, and the airline can understand why a claim seems to have arrived on the claims handler's desk from an odd quarter.

THE INTEGRITY AND STATURE OF THE WORK

I must address a few words to the people to whom claims handlers report within commercial organisations. This book is aimed at the importer and exporter who tries to do the job himself, as well as organisations large enough to be able to deputise a clerk to handle the work. It is also aimed at the forwarder who feels that he must do everything possible to handle his clients' liability claims against third parties, even though there is seldom, if ever, written anywhere into the contract with the client that the forwarder must deal with such claims. Finally, this book is aimed at airlines whose claims work is almost exclusively concerned with claims against themselves.

Responsible executives have different approaches to the work, according to their perceptions of it. Some regard it as a necessary evil and a drain on resources; bosses in this frame of mind will probably put a junior in the role and give some vague instructions for overall administration of the task. It becomes unavoidable sooner or later for the boss to step in and do his best when the "chips are down"—this can be thoroughly uncomfortable. The other extreme is the boss who feels customers' complaints so keenly that he will not allow his staff to handle the claims at all: and this is such a waste of his revenue-earning time. These are repeated scenarios, but with a little calm thought and consideration, managers into whose lap the responsibility for claims handling falls can ease the burden on themselves and their staff—not least because, for forwarders and airlines, undeniably it has strong customer-relations implications.

Exporters and importers

The customers of carriers and forwarders sustain losses when something untoward happens while cargo is being carried; in the absence of insurance cover, some large organisations can withstand the impact on cash flow that such problems bring, but the viability of smaller operations can be seriously threatened. Always seek to insure your goods if you perceive a real chance of transit loss, damage or delay, causing you real hardship. Under normal circumstances, your insurance cover will alleviate the potentially serious problems which may follow a claim incident. In the absence of insurance, you must face the possibility that the carrier or forwarder will simply not settle quickly, and may seek to avoid settling at all.

The reality of the situation is that unless you are a regular client providing steady profitable business to the carrier or forwarder, then the carrier or forwarder will likely perceive the problem as a simple financial exercise. The question he will ask is: is the profit I am making out of this claimant sufficient in a reasonable period of time to make it attractive to me to settle his claim if I do not have to? If you do not do regular business with him, then he can simply delay until you lose interest or resort to legal proceedings: the decision to litigate can be excruciating, and it often discourages claimants from pursuing their claims, even when they seem strong.

Help can be at hand in the form of recovery agents—sometimes known as loss assessors. Most of these people work exclusively for insurance companies. They are reluctant to work directly for importers and exporters because such work is perceived as full of pitfalls and difficulties compared to insurers' work. However, there are a few assessors or recovery agents who will willingly act for you. Even when employing such people, do not expect early results. They are more likely to be able to bring about an eventual result—where you will probably not know how to proceed with confidence—rather than an early one.

Forwarders (and consolidators)

Forwarders often face exporters and importers refusing to pay their charges[1] if their claims are not settled immediately—and nearly always it is a third party who is responsible for the loss. The forwarder is hit from both sides: not only will his customer take the soft option and refuse to pay his charges but he will also feel duty-bound to carry out the claims task for his customer. Often there is no hope of reward for carrying out this duty, except perhaps to retain the customer's account if the forwarder is lucky. Stories abound of forwarders

1. The withholding of charges may well include freight, especially in the case of a consolidator. It is well understood that freight cannot be withheld legally, except in the most extreme circumstances. However, if a shipper or consignee does in fact do this, the forwarder/consolidator faces a difficult decision: does he exert the force of law, and certainly lose his client, or does he swallow his pride, hope to get the claim settled by the carrier, and—with luck—retain the client? There is good legal precedent for forcing a debtor to pay up, should it be necessary to take such matters to law.

doing all they know to get a claim settled, and still losing the customer. If forwarders must carry out this task, then it must be recognised as an important and respectable function. Firm and confident handling of a claim against a third party places the forwarder in a strong position with his client. Perhaps he can not only avoid the client withholding fees and freight, but even increase the client's dependence on him as his best hope of obtaining compensation.

Airlines

The withholding of freight charges is not really a problem, because of the existence of strict rules and procedures for payment of such charges.

The airline claims handler will from time to time find himself under pressure from the cargo marketing division, so he must integrate two goals which sometimes appear to be mutually exclusive. He must try to avoid both spending the company's money on settling the claim, and losing the customer. Either factor produces a loss for the company: paying the claim has an immediate impact on the company's funds,[2] and losing the customer has a cumulative adverse effect on profit.

Whether pursuing a claim for your client against a third party or defending one against your own company, finding the right solution is challenging. Whether the goal is to reject a claim but keep the customer or to make the customer understand that it is impossible to get compensation for him, the task can test the claims handler to the limit.

Powers of deduction and intuition when trying to work out how a loss occurred are indispensable. Imagination can really be put to the test when there is a defence, but there is need to work out how clearly to justify it.

2. Most, if not all, reputable airlines insure their liability, but because of the operation of an excess under their insurance policies, they must either pay in full those claims which fall below their excess, or contribute a maximum fixed amount (nowadays often US$ 10,000) towards the settlement, while their insurer pays the rest.

CHAPTER 2

THE CONCEPT OF LIABILITY

We are all familiar with "liability", although we do not always call it that. It stems from the simple principle that if you cause someone harm, whether it is loss of money, reputation or physical injury, then financially it may cost you dear.

In the transit world the reason for claims is that a shipper or consignee believes that a party acting for him in connection with the carriage has caused him to suffer monetary loss: it is obvious that if a shipment is lost or damaged, then the shipper or consignee certainly suffers a financial loss. If a delay occurs the shipper or consignee *may* sustain a loss. Also, if there is an error or omission—for instance, leaving documents behind, which hinders customs clearance at the destination, or mislabelling of cargo—that also can give rise to a claim.

In nearly every case the party sustaining the loss will make a claim. But liability seems so complex: why? Because human nature and corporate thinking combine to look instinctively for methods of avoiding paying compensation. For every type of claim ever made, a respondent has looked for a way out: many types of claim are now known not to have defences, and seldom if ever now result in disputes, *viz.* the question of liability itself will not be disputed, although other things, such as how much the claim is, may be.

Conversely, many claim situations are not so straightforward, and you can depend on those claimed against picking situations to bits looking for defences, which sometimes finish up in court being tested to see if they will succeed. Consequently, bodies of law have come into being. In the field of carriage, for instance, the law surrounding sea transit seems particularly extensive, but, then, the carrying of goods by sea has been going on for thousands of years. The body of air law continues to grow. Who knows? Perhaps someday it will rival that of the sea.

From time to time, governments seek to standardise law internationally and, while this is a laudable enterprise, it is doomed to be only partially successful. Not all governments join in the game, and those which are participants have different systems of law, which occasionally result in inconsistent decisions on the same point in different countries.

In air carriage, the Warsaw Convention system has grown up. Some commentators regard it as a shambles, but this is not really fair. It has produced a measure of consistency and some reasonable expectations for claimants and respondents alike, notwithstanding that there are repeated efforts to update and improve the system.

In a world where human beings routinely experience catastrophes because they disagree violently about how to live their lives, is it not a signal lesson that world-wide commerce often reaches a measure of international agreement without commercial bloodshed?

CHAPTER 3

ABOUT INSURANCE

Many parties involved in claims handling in the transit industry can be confused by the various niches occupied by and different roles played by those connected with insurance. This confusion has often led to a claimant submitting a claim to the wrong party, and consequently getting it off to a bad start. The implications of this can be horrendous and, accordingly, it seems appropriate to describe the different parties involved, and to discuss their different roles, commencing with an elementary exposition of insurance itself.

INSURANCE

Insurance is a sophisticated gamble. However, commerce—international and otherwise—could not survive without it: nonetheless, it remains a gamble. From the viewpoint of insurers, it is a form of betting in which the insurer maintains that if he charges a certain amount to those who wish to be insured (and if he charges enough insureds for the same risk) he will receive enough money in total not only to pay claims for the unlucky ones, but also ultimately to make a profit, after having paid all his business costs.

INSUREDS

Sometimes the insured is called the "assured"; this is not strictly correct, because the insured is insured against something undesirable which *may* happen, whereas an assured is "assured" that something *will* happen—it is the difference between being insured in case your shipment gets lost in transit and having a life assurance policy which is assured to be fully paid and mature at some time in the future, in which case you receive a sum of money.

Here we are concerned with insureds in the proper sense of the word, and we need to illustrate how insurance covers normally arise in international trade.

If a supplier sells something to a buyer, goods must be shipped from the one to the other. The supplier may be called an exporter or shipper now, and the buyer an importer or consignee. They will agree terms for the sale, and one of them will recognise that he or she runs a risk whilst the goods—now known as cargo—are travelling from the exporter to the importer. The "risk", in transit terms, generally concerns the whole of the time the cargo is out of the hands of either the exporter or the importer. Insurers and brokers usually refer to the period the cargo is out of the hands of either as the "voyage".

A significant number of shippers and consignees do not bother or consciously decide not to insure. However, many will want to insure themselves against the risk of loss or damage in transit and this introduces us to the next party in the procedure: the insurance broker.

INSURANCE BROKERS

Our shipper or consignee will approach an insurance broker, who will ascertain from his prospective client precisely what he fears may go wrong. Having understood the risk, the broker identifies the best insurer in his view who may be prepared to cover the risk. Alternatively, he will have a number of insurers who may be interested.

It is the broker's job to arrange a contract of insurance on behalf of his client with the insurer best suited to his client's needs; among the criteria for deciding who is the best insurer are the type of policy the insurer is prepared to offer, the cost of the insurance (the premium) and the insurer's claims-processing standards. (As with any service and market, there are differing standards. There are insurers who charge lower premiums than others, and insurers whose claims handling is better than others.) For this service, the broker charges a commission, which he normally deducts from the premium which the shipper or importer will pay.

INSURERS

Insurers are of two main types—the underwriter and the claims handler.

Underwriting

It is the underwriter's job to decide whether the risk being offered for cover by the broker is good business or not. While it is often said that you can be insured for almost anything if you are prepared to pay the appropriate premium, no matter how high, underwriters operating in the transit market are in an intensely competitive world, knowing that if they do not obtain the business—or "write" it, as the jargon goes—then some other underwriter will do so. The underwriter may sense that business which does not look particularly attractive to start with can—with a little effort—be made worthwhile: accordingly, he may spend time and effort with the broker, working out the wording of the policy contract, and fine-tuning the circumstances in which he will pay a claim, and for how much. He will try to agree a sensible premium with the broker, since, clearly, the underwriter must make a reasonable profit, the broker must achieve a reasonable commission and the potential insured must consider the premium he must pay as acceptable.

A good underwriter is a person of great skill and initiative. Daily, by covering traders' risks, he facilitates and promotes international and domestic trade. The largest international companies could not ship vast consignments around the world with confidence unless they had insurance cover against things going wrong.

Claims adjusters

Here we consider the claims adjuster working within an insurance company or within an underwriting syndicate, as opposed to an independent loss adjuster who is contracted by insurers on an *ad hoc* basis. This adjuster—fully developed—is as much a professional as the underwriter. His skill is in interpreting the insurance policy and making decisions about whether and how much to pay under the policy. He may have been consulted by the underwriters when the latter were agreeing the policy, but it is not certain that he will have been.

The word "adjust" is used because the claimant presents a claim valued at a certain amount, and that amount is "adjusted" to be consistent with what has been agreed for settlement under the policy in question.

TYPES OF INSURANCE

To complete the picture, we must understand how insurers "writing" business in our field line up on two recognisable sides—although, to confuse matters, it is not unusual for one insurer to be involved on both sides of the divide through two different departments.

Liability cover

Carriers and forwarders are liable for any losses caused to their customers through their mistakes—legally termed "negligence"—whether these mistakes are of commission or omission. Sometimes they find themselves liable for claims for reasons which are a surprise to them—few carriers or forwarders at the operations level, or even at the executive level, truly understand the legal provisions of statute law or legal precedent which may determine their liability. One major claim against which there is no defence could wipe a carrier or forwarder from the commercial map, as the plaintiff succeeds in his case and proceeds to strip the assets of the company in order to obtain the compensation ordered by the court. Even a series of smaller claims in one year of trading could seriously jeopardise viability. Thus there is the need for the carrier and forwarder to insure against their liability proving too much for them.

Consequently, insurers covering such risks are naturally known as "liability insurers", and since the liability insurer may wish to avoid paying a claim made against his client, naturally, the scene is set for confrontation: the liability insurer to all intents and purposes becomes the defender of the carrier or forwarder he insures. He defends against claims made by the cargo owner who has suffered a loss or, more often than not, the insurers of the cargo owner who has previously settled the cargo claim.

This brings us to the other category of insurers in the goods-in-transit field.

Transit or cargo cover

It is because exporters and importers seldom have confidence in forwarders or carriers settling their claims for missing, damaged or delayed goods, either quickly or in full, that they seek insurance cover. A less important but significant factor in persuading exporters and importers to insure is that carriers and others often limit their liability, and thus any claim successfully pursued may result in a settlement far below the actual value of the goods lost or damaged. Consequently, the exporter's or importer's broker goes to the transit or cargo insurer.

In these cases the insured will usually receive settlement reasonably quickly from the insurer—normally far more quickly than could be expected from a carrier or forwarder. (Cargo insurers normally cover only actual loss or physical damage. Delay seems very seldom to be covered, but on occasion transit policies are seen which cover physical damage as caused by delay to perishables.) If a settlement is reached, then the insured or receiver of the settlement assigns to the insurer his right of claim against the party which caused the losses. This introduces us to the final facet of goods-in-transit insurance cover.

What happens after claims settlements?

The insured who receives an insurance settlement is usually required to sign a form, known as a subrogation receipt, which evidences both receipt of the settlement from, and the passing of claim rights to, the insurer. Following this, the cargo insurer becomes empowered to seek reimbursement of the claim settlement from the carrier or forwarder and, more often than not, the liability insurers will take up the gauntlet on behalf of the carrier or forwarder.

Air waybill insurance

There is one other form of cargo cover which must be mentioned in passing. Many air waybill (AWB) and house air waybill (HAWB) forms include a box designated "amount for insurance". The original purpose of this was to provide easy access to insurance cover for shippers presenting cargo at an airline's or forwarders' office. This box has fallen largely into disuse, because most shippers of cargo will think first of going to a regular insurance broker. Additionally, the insurance offered on an AWB or HAWB is seldom cheaper than other more regular transit insurance cover as described above: it is always less generous in terms of how much of the risk or voyage can be covered. However, curiously enough, such cover is normally offered by the liability insurer of the carrier or of the forwarder whose AWB or HAWB is involved.

It follows that in such cases, if a settlement is made, then the settling insurer does not seek reimbursement from the defaulting party, who is nearly always his or her client in relation to liability insurance.

CHAPTER 4

RISK AND LOSS CONTROL

As the claims handler progresses in his career, it is clear that he will gradually acquire much knowledge about how losses are caused: he is very likely to develop definite views about how those losses can best be avoided. He will realise that risk and loss are two sides of the same coin: the *risk* is a "before" concept, and the *loss* an "after" concept.

The shipper, forwarder, carrier and importer all run risks—something could go wrong, involving them either in loss or in potentially having to compensate that loss. When they are regularly involved in transportation of goods, sooner or later a risk is realised and a loss[1] is sustained. There is no doubt that risk can be reduced to significantly low levels, although elimination seems impossible.

There is also no doubt that a loss can be controlled, in terms of ensuring that no more than absolutely necessary is claimed, whether it be by overseeing repairs, salvage or other means: the correct term for this process is mitigation, and it is a common law duty placed upon any person suffering a loss.

Indeed, it is clear that the shipper and importer must ensure the loss is as small as can be contrived, because they cannot ever be totally sure that the carrier, forwarder or insurer will compensate them in full, not to mention the time it will take to settle the claim. They must also put themselves in as good as possible a position to prosecute their claim against the perceived author of the loss.

Conversely, the carrier and forwarder must also place themselves in as good a position as possible to defend the forthcoming claim. Additionally, of course, it is in the carrier's and forwarder's interest to do all possible to assist in keeping the loss as low as can be contrived, because they will probably be called upon to settle the claim.

Specific professional expertise in various loss situations can be obtained, and in general such expertise is required where, for instance, a chronic theft problem cannot be solved or there are inexplicable repeated incidents of damage. Before such expertise needs to be contracted in, the cargo owner and carriers and

1. Use of the term "loss" depends on your orientation—insurance-related or freight industry-related. In the insurance world, "loss" means the financial loss which a physical loss, damage, delay incident or error or omission may have given rise to: within the industry, one tends to take the meaning narrowly as the disappearance of goods.

forwarders should be acting prudently and there are many general risk-control measures which can be applied easily.

Accordingly, we will look at the various stages of transit and ascertain:

- how losses can arise, and what responses there should be;
- how cargo owners' and carriers' and forwarders' actions should be determined in accordance with the situation in which they find themselves; but
- to begin with, we shall look at general overall measures which can be applied.

GENERAL RISK CONTROL MEASURES

I will set down various measures which can be taken, but it is clearly understood that each case will be different, and circumstances will determine which measures can be applied and to what extent. Although there are tried and tested procedures to follow, initiative and innovation will always have a pivotal role in such work.

In the final analysis, the cargo owner must accept that certain risks must be run, and that perhaps nothing can be done about them—and that is probably where insurance comes in. Some measures will be theoretically possible, but in financial terms not viable.

In each case, it seems that acceptable compromise must be the goal, with a clear and active recognition of the risks involved.

Loss

The first consideration will be whether the cargo is *vulnerable* to theft.

Clearly, precious stones, bullion, money and the like are extremely vulnerable and, in most cases, shipping is carried out by professional organisations specialising in this field. Losses of such consignments are few and far between, but they still happen. Such carriage is normally subject to exhaustive analysis and strong risk control.

We are more concerned with other commodities which are valuable or desirable, or both: examples are computers and their components, such as memory modules and processors, and luxury goods, including designer clothes and shoes. There are many other examples, of course.

Theft of entire packages or complete consignments

It must be recognised that if the cargo owner seeks to move his consignment within a consolidation, in order to minimise shipping costs, rather than to move it as a single consignment, subject to one airline AWB, then security for his cargo will not be a priority for either the forwarder or carrier. The cargo will travel with other goods and be regarded by the carrier as general cargo, and normally not given any specific level of security against theft.

Thus, if the supplier's and buyer's deal will stand it financially, it is nearly always better to ship the consignment as a single consignment on its own, in which case much can be done to focus the carriers' and forwarders' attention on security against theft.

Packaging

A positive measure to take is to "anonymise" the packaging and change it on a regular basis. A potential thief welcomes a package identifying its contents as computers or the latest trainers, etc. It is placing temptation in the cargo handler's way, and should be avoided.

Anonymity should also extend to labelling and addressing: having deleted the contents description from the outside of the package, there is no point if the consignee is identified as a known luxury goods supplier, or a well-known computer operation.

Description

We turn now to description of the goods on the shipping documents, which are normally seen by several different people. Some means of anonymising the shipping documents should also be sought. Of course, false, or otherwise deliberately misleading, descriptions must not be given, but there seems no bar to describing computers as electrical equipment, for instance.

Forwarders should always examine the documents in detail, of course, and are likely always to know what is being shipped, because they will have built a good working relationship with the shipper. However, cargo identified on the shipping invoice by a serial or catalogue number must always be better than, for instance, "gold-plated lighters".

Carriers must be aware of what they are carrying, but "electrical equipment" is usually an acceptable description in preference to "computer processor units".

(Those parties completing Air Waybills should be wary, however, in regard to some South American countries in view of reports received during 1997 and 1998. Where mobile phones were described as "electrical equipment", heavy fines were imposed by some Customs Authorities for "incomplete" description.)

These measures should all contribute to avoiding a dishonest cargo handler becoming fully aware of the nature of the goods, so there is every chance of his overlooking your goods and not being tempted. However, regular and routine shipping of similar goods will enable that potential thief to become familiar with the goods and pounce. Accordingly, unpredictable routeing changes or changes of carrier also should be a standing option.

Those making out AWBs, specifically forwarders, and entering descriptions of the cargo must take particular care in anonymising it. Straying too far from the true description may incur a liability on the forwarder if such description prevents the carrier from applying the handling regime which the commodity requires and, consequently, a loss occurs.

Shipping arrangements

The cargo owner must take the view that at all times goods are vulnerable to theft between collection from him and delivery into the hands of the consignee. This is not to damn the freight industry in general, but simply a prudent working premise for cargo owners. The general danger times are when cargo remains on hand in carriers' and forwarders' warehouses for periods of time: "dwell" time is the usual term denoting this. Most thefts of consignments occur at these times.

Accordingly, can the cargo owner arrange for delivery at the last possible moment? Can the cargo be picked up from his premises and taken straight to the airline shed for delivery just before the "cut-off" time publicised by the airline? If this is possible, then the opportunity for theft at the forwarder's premises is eliminated, and any dishonest cargo handler at the airline warehouse will have no or very little time to effect a theft. The cargo will not be left unattended for a long period, and there is likely to be significant activity in its vicinity. The activity discourages the thief, who usually needs to be undisturbed and unobserved to effect his theft. There will be weighing, palletising or stuffing into containers, documentary processing, and trucking to the aircraft occupying this limited time.

Can the consignee apply for collection at the first possible moment after customs clearance? Will he be able to have his customs broker expedite clearance at the earliest possible opportunity? Aim at reducing the time that the cargo remains in the airline shed to as short as possible.

For similar reasons, can the consignee's agent arrange for trucking direct from the airline warehouse to the final delivery address? Is there a transhipment point during the carriage? Can the carrier be persuaded to apply special measures at that location?

If dwell time cannot be avoided, then can special arrangements be made with the carrier to provide specific security for a particular consignment? Is there a lock-up in the warehouse? Can the cargo be placed in the strong-room? Will the carrier tally the goods into a container and seal it for the dwell time envisaged?

Pilferage

A determined and specific attack on a package with a view to stealing some or all of the contents is very difficult to counter. However, having done all possible and reasonable to anonymise the cargo, what can be done to discourage or foil an attack?

Pilferage is probably a spontaneous crime, and seldom planned: a petty thief may go equipped with a pocket knife, keeping a look-out for suitable goods to pilfer, but probably makes a spot decision to carry out the theft. He may contrive to break open packaging, perhaps forcing boxes to split open at corners or seams. He will probably pounce on cargo which arrives in his warehouse with split and broken packaging.

Thus, when it is impractical for a cargo owner to arrange special security to eliminate the chance of pilferage, he must counter it by using appropriate packaging. There are sound packaging experts to advise on this subject, but—and again with an eye to the value and desirability of the goods—if you must use cardboard cartons, then the materials from which they are made can be such that they hamper the attentions of a knife. Sealing tape is also available which is termed "tamper-proof". Stringing and plumbing, which seems to have fallen into virtual disuse in the developed world but are still routinely used elsewhere, remain a reasonable discouragement.

Mis-routeing

The only type of "innocent" loss is mis-routeing. If the consignment is never recovered, then the chance is that the loss goes unexplained. It is certain, however, that a good number of such losses occur.

The clearest possible labelling is always the priority—I would suggest that, whether printed or hand-written on the carton or labelled, the destination airport or city be shown in the boldest possible print. This measure alone promotes correct routeing. If labels are used, then they should be stuck on the package in such a way that they cannot be removed without considerable effort.

A carrier or forwarder loading a pallet or stuffing a container will occasionally load an incorrect package, and once it is hidden by other cargo that package does not surface until the unit load device (ULD) is unloaded at its destination. There is little that can be done, except for carriers and forwarders to be ever-vigilant against this error. However, the showing of the destination in bold should facilitate correction of the error.

Mis-routeing can sometimes result from re-use of old packaging, unless all old labels are removed or permanently covered, and all old markings are obliterated.

Damage

Again this is an expert field, well-served by sound packaging consultants, who for the appropriate cost could protect cargo from all risk of wetting and physical deformation. Seldom is packaging that good, as, again, all interested parties must adhere to their budget for the deal in hand.

The packing of perishables is also a well-developed discipline, but can seldom guard against a delay[2] in transit which allows the goods to deteriorate.

2. Delay to perishables is a two-fold problem: often they must reach a market on a specific day, because there are probably only two days a week when prices are high; delay also causes deterioration, which is properly to be considered physical damage, usually caused by omission of the carrier to cool store during the delay. This idea is developed below.

Wetting

There is no sound reason for expecting goods to be wetted during transit by air, because there is no excuse for exposing cargo to weather. There is no need to use open trucks to transport cargo from the shipper's premises to the airport, and from the airline warehouse to the aircraft, nor for the rest of the transit. However, some carriers still use open vehicles. Additionally, at times of peak traffic, both airlines and forwarders will store goods outside, and take little or no care to protect them from precipitation.

A cargo owner should keep this in mind, and if his cargo is vulnerable to wetting, and owing to practicality or cost it has not been totally protected, then he should be instructing his agent and the carrier not to expose the goods to weather unnecessarily.

Physical deformation

This term is intended to denote all types of physical damage, caused by impact, crushing or penetration by fork tines, and so on.

Packaging experts, or even common sense on the part of the cargo shipper, will eliminate most damage risks, but careless fork-lift truck operators, inadvertent over-stowage with heavy cargo which crushes, incorrect stacking and heavy landings and turbulence can take their toll.

Little can be done to avoid a fork-lift truck driver making an error—even the most experienced do so. Also, heavy landings and violent turbulence cannot be predicted. However, avoiding over-stowage and correct stacking can be promoted by the giving of specific instructions to the carrier.

Delays

Air cargo, by its nature and by reason of its relatively high cost in relation to other carriage modes, is time-sensitive. Clearly some cargoes such as perishables,[3] exhibition goods, machine parts for repair of plant breakdowns in manufacturing operations, and so on, are more time-sensitive than others. (Documents are seldom carried as simple cargo nowadays, but as "courier" items: since the courier companies are dedicated to speedy carriage already, there are few facets of transit which they have not looked at in order to avoid delays.)

When setting up carriage of urgent cargoes, shippers will have already given significant thought to speedy carriage, although it is not unknown for a shipper unaccustomed to regular air carriage to assume that it will be speedy and thus take no specific precautions.

The central principle should be that simple routeings, with all parties alerted to the need for speedy carriage, clearance and delivery, should be sought.

3. See the preceding note.

There is no substitute for all interested parties receiving written or faxed instructions concerning their part in the transit, and for them to be alerted in simple terms to consequential losses which delay will cause, and to insist on each party confirming in writing, or by fax or telex, that they can play the part demanded of them.

The measures urged above concerning clarity of the marking of destinations on the package apply as strongly here as anywhere, of course.

LOSS CONTROL MEASURES

There are a finite number of stages in transit when loss becomes apparent, and it follows that measures to deal with losses can reasonably be standardised. Since we are considering losses which arise in transit, it naturally follows that loss control measures will fall mainly within the province of the carriers and forwarders. However, there is a general word for cargo owners on this matter. The sooner you act following discovery of cargo having gone missing, the better are the chances of locating the missing consignment. Delay in acting allows the "trail to go cold" and, in the event of theft, the "waters to become muddied". If damage is noticed, then the sooner it is dealt with the less the potential damage to customer-relations.

Cargo owners

If your consignment is insured and it is lost or damaged, then urgently reporting the matter to your insurers (backed up in writing) is absolutely vital. Do not allow yourself to be lulled into not doing so by a carrier or forwarder who tells you that the cargo is bound to turn up shortly. Insurers could go so far as to deny settlement if late reporting to them of the claim creates difficulties in relation to the insurance policy, or jeopardises a subsequent recovery claim against the defaulting party.

In some cases, the insurer, or rather the loss adjuster or specialist investigator appointed by him, will take the matter over. He will investigate the loss, or oversee repairs, while maintaining contact with you as necessary. However, at all times, you are required to act as a "prudent uninsured", which means that, to the extent that your insurer or its adjuster has not taken over the matter, you must act as if you had no insurance, which brings us to the subject of mitigation.

Mitigation

Mitigation is the process of ensuring a loss is no greater than can be avoided. You are required to take all practical and reasonable measures to remedy the loss. If your consignment is damaged, then you cannot simply abandon it and claim for the complete value if there is something you can reasonably do to salvage or repair it. If you fail to mitigate your losses, then it is possible you will not obtain settlement under your insurance policy. If you have no insurance, then the carrier or forwarder against whom you claim is entitled to repudiate the claim, or to reduce any settlement in line with an amount which could have been saved if you had mitigated the loss.

Claim notices

Notices of claim must be given in writing immediately. In some contexts, you are obliged by law to give a notice in writing, in the absence of which you lose your right to claim. In other contexts, contract conditions may require a notice or may not: the best principle to follow is to issue your written claim notice to all parties who had anything to do with the transit. "Overkill" is better than loss of claim rights.

Carriers and forwarders

In recent years, cargo-handling companies (known as "GHAs" or simply "handling agents") have come more to the fore, and self-handling for airline cargo operations has reduced. Regrettably, the forwarding community seems to hold a general opinion that handling agents do not achieve high standards. Nevertheless, handling agents should be expected to accommodate their client companies' wishes concerning handling procedures and standards.

Until legislation concerning the hiring of personnel working with air cargo was introduced, hiring policy was lax, and the curricula vitae of a good number of staff employed by handling agents prior to this legislation would not stand close scrutiny. A number of such questionable employees remain employed by handling agents, who are unable legally to discharge them without proven cause. (Perhaps some sympathy should be felt for senior executives in handling companies who experience this problem.) Accordingly, standards may rise only slowly, and at the time of writing there seems to be no reduction in the losses reported within the possession of such handling companies.

Documenting incidents

It cannot be stressed too strongly that claims situations are always worsened by failure to document loss, damage and delay incidents. To illustrate the point, there is no substitute within an airline for a timed and dated statement made out by a warehouseman, wherein he reports discovering damage to a package or a shortage from a particular flight load on checking it in, followed by notes by a supervisor about conversations with cargo owners about the incident. Equally, documenting efforts to resolve a delay situation and get the cargo to the destination will save later wasteful and frustrating efforts by claims staff to ascertain why a delay occurred and what was done about it. Documentation of this nature tends to put matters beyond dispute, and enables a claim to proceed with minimum fuss and uncertainty.

Compare the discovery of damage or loss at the time of collection by the consignee's agent and unexplained delay. A claimant who may otherwise be a good customer will be most unimpressed by your inability to explain problems, but you have the chance to retain his custom if you can give a good account of how the mistake was made, so that you can ensure such an incident can be avoided in the future.

This point is developed further when we come to deal with physical damage to cargo.

Loss

Tallying

It is apparent that many truck drivers do not tally goods onto their trucks, and it is this circumstance which causes the greatest proportion of losses and masks earlier unnoticed losses. It cannot be stressed too strongly that drivers must be encouraged to tally goods diligently. No laxity in this rule should be permitted.

However, it is understood that there are circumstances where such tallying is onerous and undesirably time-consuming. Special arrangements should be made to deal with situations where a driver is collecting a very large number of pieces.

Suppose a busy airline at Heathrow has received many consignments during the day for Prestwick. A driver collecting that evening is faced with (say) 20 consignments, each comprising 20 or 30 pieces of different dimensions and appearance: it is self-evident that the driver should tally the pieces instead of allowing the cargo warehouseman simply to fork a number of stillage pallets on to his truck and then signing for the goods effectively "unseen". Signing unseen in this way will mask the fact that a loss of cargo may already have taken place: by the time the loss is noted in Prestwick, the following day, things have already moved on in the warehouse out of which the cargo came, and opportunities to resolve the loss are fast disappearing.

The truck operator may seriously resent the extra time spent by the driver tallying, but the loss of one piece containing (say) clothing worth £1,000 is a powerful argument in favour of such tallying.

Insurers

The value of the goods will be the criterion for deciding whether to notify the company's insurers, and the policy on this point should be set by management, who should seek guidance from their insurance broker. If reporting to the insurer is required, then you may find the insurer taking over the situation, with an appointment—in major losses—of a specialist investigator to look into the disappearance. The insurers will, of course, want the missing cargo found in order to avoid having to pay out a settlement.

Missing on receipt

The carrier or forwarder always receives cargo from a truck which has carried it from another party, from another depot within the same organisation or from the inbound aircraft. Obviously, tallying is of paramount importance, and the following measures should be taken.

From another party If tallying shows up a shortage on receipt then the best action to take is immediately to call the office of the company delivering the goods, following a thorough check of the delivery vehicle if there is cargo left on board with which the missing item(s) could have been mixed up. Such prompt action will ensure the best chance of locating missing goods left behind at the previous location.

Some receivers will simply sign the delivery note as "short", taking no other action. But calling the delivering office will not only perhaps solve the problem, but will raise your professional profile with the delivering trucker, and perhaps with the shipper—all likely to promote customer relations.

In some cases, of course, the missing piece(s) will not be found: signing for and accepting short loads may be the only option, but make sure the fact of the shortage is carefully documented. It is not unknown for consignments delivered short to be rejected in total by the receiver: circumstances may make this the only option.

By taking these measures, you will have prevented your company becoming embroiled in a claim situation and, if fortunate, will have enabled missing goods to be found with reasonable ease.

From another depot in the same company A shortage at this point is a serious matter for the receiver, since it is now not possible to avoid being involved in a claim situation. Urgent contact with the previous location of the goods is required, and you will hope to see positive co-operation from fellow company employees there in carrying out appropriate searches.

If however the lost carton(s) cannot be found, the right and proper action is to inform the shipper or consignee immediately. You may already be in trouble with your customer for the loss, but to allow it to surface at the final destination without warning will be a worse way for your client to learn of the loss, and will not endear you further to him.

From the inbound aircraft Loads from wide-bodied aircraft can be extensive, posing quite difficult problems of checking-in. The routine is for warehousemen to be supplied with a copy of the aircraft manifests, and for them to check the cargo against the lists. As cargo is checked in, it is removed from the check-in point and stored in the shed, with the shed location being inserted in the copy manifest. When the task is finished, the information now marked on the manifest is input to the central computer record.

Loss noticed at this stage, subject to double-checking the warehouse, can only have arisen from the cargo having been left off the aircraft at origin, mistakenly offloaded at a preceding station or not offloaded before the aircraft carried on to the next destination.

Positive tracing to each station must take place. Airline operatives often complain about out-stations not responding to their tracers, and airline executives must take control of this problem.

Again, notification of the loss to the customer at the earliest opportunity, rather than hoping the lost cargo will turn up, is the best customer-relations-oriented action. Consignees who learn of the loss when their trucker collects from you will be all the more incensed if you have known about the loss for several days and did not tell them.

Missing during bond-check

Most operations of integrity carry out a regular check of what is in their warehouse: this is routinely known as a "bond check". Some operations do it twice a week; others less often; and some never, but, frankly, it is indispensable and resolves many queries that would otherwise never be resolved.

Bond checks simply list what is on hand in the shed. It is seldom that the warehouse operative matches his list against what should be in the shed, so complete consignments disappearing are not always noticed immediately. In such circumstances, and in retrospect, it becomes possible only to determine the latest date on which the missing consignment was present in the shed.

The term "UTL" arises at this point, and means "unable to locate". Again, it is wiser in the long run to notify the cargo owner or his agent quickly of the shortage.

It is certainly feasible to check off shipments listed against the inventory revealed from the central cargo computer records, although you might suppose that to do so in operations of great size—mainly flag carriers' home bases—would be a very daunting task. However, it is usual for a bond-check to show up parts of consignments missing, and there is no reason to not try to deal with these.

Searches of the warehouse and double-checking of receiving documents should be carried out to see if any irregularities show up. Possibility of mix-delivery should be investigated and, if possible, contact should be made with all parties collecting between the last date the cargo was known to be in the shed and the date it was missed. Mis-loading to a departing aircraft is also a possibility, and should be considered.

All such actions should again be carried out as quickly as possible. (In the event that theft is assumed, please refer to the section on theft below.)

Missing on picking-out

Eventually the cargo is picked out for making up into an aircraft load, or for delivery to the collecting trucker. If a loss becomes evident at this point, then action should be very similar to that detailed in the preceding section. Searches of the warehouse should be made and double-checking of receiving documents should be carried out to see if any irregularities show up.

Questions of mis-delivery should be investigated, and if possible contact should be made with all parties collecting between the last date the cargo was known to be in the shed and the date it was missed. The possibility of mis-loading to a departing aircraft should again be considered, and tracing action carried out accordingly. Speed is essential as always, and certainly assumption of theft should be made with care. (In the event that theft is assumed, please refer to the section on theft below.)

Damage

Damage can be observed at any time, but is commonly noticed on receipt into the shed, during the bond check and at the time of delivery out.

Cameras

First, it is wise to keep an instant camera on hand at all times, charged with film: if it is the type of camera that prints date and time on the photographs, then even better. When damage is noticed, it is always worth taking a picture or two, as this tends to eliminate various questions at a later stage.

Damage reports

Secondly, it is common for carriers and forwarders to have a standard form for reporting damage. This form is often only partly filled in by warehousemen, and their superiors should encourage them to be diligent in completing it. In the absence of a standard form, staff should be ready to make a short written statement about the damage, giving as much detail as possible and identifying the goods in question.

Whereas gross and obvious damage to what may be an expensive machine may not require much judgement about whether to report it or not, there is also an unavoidable necessity for the person noticing the damage to exercise significant judgement in some situations. For instance, a loose sealing tape, if on a box of lamp parts, is superfluous, but if on a package of designer clothing, is vital, since it may indicate stealthy pilferage.

There is no easy way to decide how to set the guidelines for staff to report damage, and much will depend on the motivation of staff in general and the alertness of supervisory staff in particular.

Insurers

The value of the potential claim will be the criterion for deciding whether to notify the company's insurers, and the policy guidelines on this point should be set by management, who should seek guidance from their insurance broker. If reporting to the insurer is required, then you may find the insurer taking over the situation and appointing a surveyor/loss adjuster to handle things.

If the claim is one which falls below a certain amount set in your insurance policy (known as the "excess" or "deductible"), the insurer may have no interest in dealing with it. Since the excess can be a considerable amount—perhaps U.S.$ 10,000 or more—it may be prudent to instruct a surveyor yourselves. Such people are expected to be skilled in examining damaged goods, and liaising with claimants to ensure repairs are carried out or replacement is made in as economical a manner as possible.

Damage on receipt

From another party If you are handed a damaged consignment, then the choices are to reject the consignment or to hold the driver there while you telephone his office to report the problem and ask for instructions from them. They may require you to hold the cargo for inspection or may simply instruct you to re-load the cargo onto the truck for return.

Circumstances may require you to accept the cargo in a damaged condition, and the delivering party may appear not to want to deal with the damage problem. In this case, you must ensure that the delivery note is clearly and properly annotated with details of the damage—if you accept the cargo with a "clean" signature you may well be held liable for the damage.

A photograph or two is often prudent, together with a short written note by the warehouseman or supervisor to avoid the possibility of a later accusation of damage occurring while the goods were in your possession at or after the time of delivery.

If you are instructed to accept the cargo in a damaged condition, then photographs and a clear statement and description of the circumstances become, of course, vital.

From another depot in the same company Again, you are already into a claim situation which is unavoidable. Photographs should be taken and a short written note about the circumstances should be made. Urgent contact with the previous location should follow, and instructions should be obtained from the cargo owner or his agent. Reporting to your insurers should be considered.

From the inbound aircraft If damage is discovered at the time of checking-in, then photographs and a statement should again be made. Contact with the consignee or his agent should take place, again to obtain instructions about what to do with the cargo. Reporting to your insurers should be considered.

Damage noted at other times

Damage may also be noted for the first time during bond-check or at delivery out. Photographs and written records are again essential, of course. If the damage is noted at the time of bond-check the better customer-relations choice is to tell the client without delay and request his instructions. If the delivering warehouseman and/or collecting driver notes the damage, then judgement comes to the fore. Perhaps a supervisor should be called to make a decision on whether simply to accept a "claused" signature from the driver if the damage is not serious, or to make contact with the driver's company to determine what action is required. Reporting to your insurers should be considered.

Delay

Delays tend to be brought to the notice of a particular office of the carrier or forwarder by consignees and shippers who are already anxious and possibly irate. At that time, it is often unclear whether it is loss or delay in fact.

In the airfreight industry, it is usually the airline which is responsible for the delay: either an aircraft has experienced a mechanical problem, or a weather situation, or an unexpected reduction in available cargo capacity has occurred, or the carrier has simply made an error in loading. If you know where the cargo is, you may find there is little you can do to get it to its destination quickly, but what you must not do is nothing. Failure to try may negate a potential defence that the delay was beyond your control, a situation known properly as *force majeure*. Claims for delay often result in damages for what is classed as economic, indirect or consequential loss, *viz*., loss suffered not as a direct result of damage or loss to the cargo itself. These damages can be very high, often much higher than the intrinsic value of the cargo itself. Since at that stage it is not possible to know whether your company can defend itself against such a claim, you must do all you can to minimise the loss by cutting the delay as much as possible. In any case, the better customer-relations response is to do all possible to resolve or ameliorate the problem.

You may need to see if you can re-accommodate the cargo on another carrier whose flight will reach the destination earlier; although this seems bizarre when you are competing with other carriers for cargo, there is significant legal precedent for it, and cases have been lost by carriers who did not try this option.

Perishables

A special word about delayed perishables is required. Such delay involves two different possible claims: not only for delay in reaching a wholesale market on a particular day, but also potentially for damage. In combination or in the alternative, the cargo owner may sustain losses from both damage and missed markets.

Again, it is not possible at an early stage for cargo staff to know whether such a claim can successfully be defended, and thus measures to be taken involve not only resolving or ameliorating the delay, but also safeguarding the condition of the goods.

The principle is that if you as a carrier are prepared to carry perishable goods, you accept that you must do all possible to safeguard their condition. You are presumed to be aware generally of the requirements of perishables in transit, and thus, in a delay situation, if you fail to put the goods in cold storage overnight when they require it, you have no defence against a claim for damage to them brought about by that failure to cool store.

Many airports now have cool stores. Do your best to use them. If unavailable, then a good option is the urgent hiring of a reefer truck for the period of the delay.

Theft

If theft is suspected, carriers and forwarders have little choice but to try and solve the problem, but determining the effort to be put into this is not always simple. If you have a security department, bring it in at the first opportunity.

Strong and good administration of claims will be a discouragement to a thief anyway, because he usually wants to operate in an environment where little fuss is made about losses.

The value of the goods will always be a significant factor in your decision about how to treat a particular loss. After all, if a pair of shoes has gone from a box, and it is an isolated and single incident over a long period, then you need to consider carefully to what extent you need to act. However, the disappearance of a valuable consignment in circumstances indicating theft should always be reported to the police. It is not uncommon for carriers and forwarders to fail to do so, and even fail to take any action at all. It may be impossible to catch the thief, but leaving a thief in place without stirring things up significantly by making a clear and positive effort to resolve the problem will signal to that thief that his way is clear to try his luck again.

Pilferage

Pilferage tends to occur in warehouses overnight and at weekends, when there is a significant reduction in people moving about the warehouse. The pilferer requires undisturbed time to broach packages unobserved and take his pick. Old, dimly-lit warehouses without security guards patrolling are the most inviting targets: well-lit warehouses with patrolling guards or closed-circuit television (CCTV) are the least inviting.

Unfortunately, CCTV is not always managed properly. It tends to be well-monitored at its installation and for a while thereafter, but interest wanes and, when an incident occurs and a review of recordings is required, it is not uncommon to find that the vital camera has been repositioned or switched off for some time. Any operation using CCTV must ensure a means of checking the operation of the system on a daily or more frequent basis.

The answers to regular pilferage are not easy. If such a culture exists amongst warehouse staff it is difficult to root out. The police will advise and take action if the problem is serious enough or there is a real chance of catching thieves, but their co-operation cannot be guaranteed unless you show real commitment and do not hesitate to prefer charges against an individual who is caught.

Complete changes of warehouse staff have been made to solve such problems, but such options are open only to companies with significantly large operations to be able to absorb the considerable costs involved.

With the enforcement in recent years of measures under aviation security laws, hiring programmes now have real teeth, and this brings hope for the gradual improvement of levels of reliability and honesty of staff, as natural wastage and retirement remove older and longer-serving un-vetted staff.

Whole packages or consignments

This type of loss needs to be treated separately from pilferage, because there is often an element of conspiracy involved in the stealing of whole packages and consignments from a warehouse. The warehouseman cannot be seen to walk out with the cargo, and usually requires the co-operation of a collecting driver, appearing to act innocently in collecting goods, in order to achieve the theft. While the driver is receiving his proper load onto his truck, it is often possible for the attending warehouseman to pass him other, stolen, boxes; unless there is a security guard or supervisor checking the loading no suspicions are aroused, except by chance.

Again, the quality of staff lies at the root of the problem, and perhaps the application of well-maintained and monitored CCTV on the delivery doors is a strong discouragement to such theft. It is seldom financially viable routinely to provide a security guard to monitor deliveries, but random monitoring several times a day could be a reasonable measure.

The police and insurance investigators

The police In general terms, the majority of policemen in the U.K. are keen to do their job well, but those who have little interest will be encountered, and it must be recognised that any policeman will act purposefully only if he sees a chance of a result and if the matter is sufficiently serious.

The police must be convinced that a crime took place in the U.K., so, if you report a loss from a warehouse, they may consider after investigation that the missing item never arrived from overseas in the first place, and will then conclude that no crime took place in the U.K. and close their investigation. (Sadly, it does appear that less enthusiastic policemen will seize occasionally on an apparently unjustified assumption of no crime in the U.K. in order to avoid taking up a possibly difficult investigation.)

A loss of computer processor units worth many hundreds of thousands of pounds will attract their attention and effort, but a small pilferage incident may be worthy of note, but pointless to investigate.

Some elements in the police in the U.K. have little sympathy for an industry which—in their view—seems to take few precautions to protect itself. Carriage of very valuable consignments as general cargo within consolidations does not encourage them.

In recent years, one of the worst incidents was the arrival at Heathrow Airport of seven tons of gold bullion without any pre-arrangements for security or even pre-advice from the sending station. Adroit but irregular negotiations ensured an armed but unofficial police presence nearby, but their anger over the incident was evident.

Insurance investigators Insurance investigators will arrive on the scene regularly: many of these are ex-policemen with varying levels of ability and understanding of the transit world. They are normally instructed by cargo insurers, who want the missing cargo found or require to understand how the loss occurred, so that they can prepare their case against the culprit company for reimbursement of the settlement which they have to make.

Little or nothing within the carrier's file is allowed legally to be withheld, but only a court can finally force a carrier to yield up its records in full. Few documents can be classed as "privileged", but if you are being pressured hard by the "other side" to produce some document or other which you do not wish to, then speak to your insurance broker, or solicitor if appropriate.

While carriers and forwarders should co-operate fully with investigators, there is often a real fear that revealing too much information will seriously damage a company's interests—it is often true, but to counter this risk by simple non-co-operation and refusal to talk to investigators can bring about serious problems when and if claimants take legal action.

Liability insurers

The reporting of losses and damage incidents by carriers and forwarders to their liability insurers depends on the potential seriousness of the claim, and guidance must be obtained from the broker on what procedure to adopt. Carriers and forwarders must co-operate fully with insurers, and regard them as wholly on their side. The relevant insurance policy will require such co-operation, in the absence of which the insurer is entitled to dispute a claim and leave the carriers or forwarders to deal alone with the claimant.

A loss adjuster is often appointed to look into each claim reported under the insurance policy. If the right choice of adjuster has been made, then he will understand the air cargo business well, and generally be of considerable help to carriers and forwarders.

CHAPTER 5

CREATING AND ADMINISTERING THE CLAIM FILE

GENERAL PRINCIPLES

Some carriers and forwarders have regarded claims handlers simply as administrators in the broadest sense: just organisers of paperwork and administrative procedures who have no allegiance to a specific discipline. They fail to see that claims handlers must be specialised operational staff who deal with the more difficult facets of customer relations. This failure of perception has sometimes led to unsuitable personnel being assigned the task, and it seems very clear that the ideal person for this job is, in fact, one whose experience of the industry is wide and full.

Because losses during transit are more serious for exporters and importers, such companies have tended to be somewhat more alert to the real needs. Either a senior man (with some appreciation of the effect losses have on the company balance sheet) is likely to be assigned to the task, or a youngster is drafted in to assist such a person, who then aims at close supervision of the assistant.

The claims handler is actually an operational staff member. However, there are, of course, general principles of administration which seem of peculiar value in the claims-handling world.

Assumption of future litigation

It is a prudent working assumption that any claim may have to be pursued or defended in court at some stage, even if the vast majority never get anywhere near there. Many claimants shy away at the thought of court action, but the requirements for actions involving "small" claims are now relatively simple, and for a modest sum a claimant can issue a summons and force a reluctant respondent into court.

Scruffy and hard-to-understand papers presented either to support your claim or to defend your position will not facilitate your action or defence. If the judge who examines the papers has problems in understanding your position, but understands your opponent's, then you are in for probable disappointment. Accordingly, the highest standards of file maintenance are recommended: here, "fussiness" is a positive virtue.

Claims have a habit of becoming dormant for long periods: if you have to pick up a file you have not looked at for six months, give yourself a chance easily to re-familiarise yourself with it by having made sure it was tidy and easy to read in the first place.

General construction of the file

Having accepted the working assumption that your file may have to be produced in court at a later stage, you must recognise that alteration of original records may well be a contempt of court or fraud of some sort if detected. If such an alteration goes to the heart of the claims dispute, then your defence may simply disappear. Thus, the construction of the file, as it develops, becomes paramount, and your judgement is vital.

The claims handler may well be required to guide a warehouseman as he makes out his first report of an incident and, while positively avoiding untruths, the claims handler is entitled to guide the wording to place his company in the best possible light.

The general rule should be that all documents having any bearing on the matter in hand should be included in the file. The omission of any relevant document can, at the least, cause embarrassment, and, at the worst, destroy your case. Of course, if the case gets to court, should the court gain the impression that you have suppressed vital information or deliberately excluded it from your papers, then serious trouble can ensue.

Thus, it becomes clear that the integrity of the claims handler is fundamentally involved in this process.

FILE CREATION

A separate file and filing location

Whilst an exporter or importer is almost certain to create a separate file for each claim, the carrier or forwarder may not, because he will have file drawers full of AWBs, and it is not unusual for claims papers to be simply pinned to the relevant and put back in the drawer. This is unwise because such copy AWBs are usually on very light-weight paper and often get mixed up. The loss of an old copy AWB may not be a problem, but the loss of a claim file can produce serious problems and often an inability to defend a claim at all. Thus, a separate storage location for claims files is urged.

Claim number

Since air cargo claims can often have a life of two years or more, any carrier or forwarder builds up a significant portfolio of live, but possibly dormant, claims. Accordingly, provided the files are maintained separately from operation files, the Air Waybill number can be used as the filing reference. Alternatively, a different file numbering system may be felt appropriate.

At some stage, it is likely that an analysis of claims records will have to be carried out for insurers, or perhaps it is perceived that a reserve fund must be built into budgeting against claims which may have to be settled. If the numbers are sufficient a computer database may be appropriate.

HOUSEKEEPING

To echo earlier points in this chapter, there are three specific housekeeping principles to apply to file maintenance.

Chronology

Avoid simply bundling papers together in any order as they are received. A claim file should be a "moving picture": if the documents are in the strictest chronological order, it is possible for a newcomer to the file to read the papers in order and to develop a clear and precise understanding of how the claim arose, what efforts were made to resolve the problem and how the claimant's demand for compensation was dealt with. Chronology so strict that papers such as telexes and facsimiles with identical dates are filed in order of the time at which they were generated can be vital to understanding.

Such principles may be applied to matters other than claims, but the peculiarity of claims is that they "stutter": there are periods of great activity followed by periods of long inactivity. If after several months of dormancy a claim becomes active, it is always necessary for the handler to re-familiarise himself with the case. Chronology applied strictly to the file will always facilitate this.

Duplicated documents

Duplicate documents can be a curse and a serious obstacle to the understanding of a claim file. As parties involved in the claim correspond, they attach copies of AWBs, invoices and packing lists, and so on, to their communications. Simply including the attachments in the file can lead to serious confusion for anyone who needs to access the central file.

On receipt of correspondence with attachments, it is prudent to remove duplicated documents, after, of course, having made certain that there is no comment or legend thereon which justifies its inclusion at that point in the file. If there is, then it is wise to make an additional note on the duplicated document, which will remind you why it appears in the file at that point.

Clarity of documents

It seems clear that legible documents are vital to efficient claims handling. For example, claim submissions are often countered by sending a copy of a delivery signature, purporting to evidence no visible damage at the time of delivery. A third or fourth copy of such a document, faint and bearing alien comments caused by writing on an unrelated document placed over it at some earlier stage will cause more problems than it should solve, and the copy may in fact be unusable if it cannot successfully be photocopied or faxed.

It seems clear that claimants should bear in mind that respondents need clear copies of invoices and packing lists with which to work: nothing is more likely to hold up processing of claims than confused copies. If the copy you have is not good enough, then seek the best possible one available. Of course, it may simply be impossible to obtain an improved one, and it may be necessary to arrange to produce the actual poor original in your file to the company with which you are corresponding. This is all very awkward, and usually avoidable if action is taken early enough to obtain the appropriate clear and legible copy.

WHICH RECORDS TO MAINTAIN

The carrier or forwarder facing a claim, or even a forwarder seeking to have a carrier settle his client's claim, will need to keep the most detailed file. The claimant's file is unlikely to require such detail, if, indeed, the claimants' insurer has not settled with him and taken over the claim against the carrier or forwarder.

Accordingly, the guidance offered here is given from the carrier's point of view: forwarders and claimant exporters and importers can browse through a listing of the carrier's file and note which documents may be important to them.

If claimants take legal action, they eventually reach a stage of "discovery", where the court orders that documents from each side be exchanged. Claimants and legal representatives may obtain some guidance on the documents which may or should be in a carrier's or forwarder's file when turned over to them.

It will be evident to handlers with experience of the freight industry that the listed documents denote a strict chronology, paralleling the development of the transit history.

Useful comments are made on the documents listed. Their purposes, interpretation and use is also indicated where appropriate.

Regular documents

A. Packing list(s):

- (i) This should show the contents of each package and its weight. Important in inventorying packages which have been pilfered and confirming, together with the shipping invoice(s), that claim calculations are correct.
- (ii) Where a consignment comprises a single package, there may not be a separate packing list.

(iii) Consignments of perishables seldom have separate packing lists, even where there are different commodities within the same shipment.

B. Shipping invoice(s):

(i) This helps to establish and prove the claimant's right to pursue a claim.

(ii) In the majority of claims it proves the value or part of the value of the claim.

(iii) Values thereon do not apply where the claimant bases his claim on the market price at destination, in which case it will be necessary to provide some other document as evidence of value, *vide* sound-arrived-value in Chapter 13.

C. Booking sheet:

(i) This should evidence the taking of the booking by the carrier or forwarder when the exporter contacted him originally.

(ii) It may evidence what the original intentions of the exporter were with regard to carriage.

(iii) It may resolve disputes about incorrect bookings, where, for instance, a consignment of greater weight or dimensions than originally expected is presented for carriage, and is consequently delayed in some way.

D. Truck delivery notes (to carrier or forwarder):

These prove when and where consignments were delivered, and are *prima facie*[1] evidence that the goods were in sound condition at that time.

E. House air waybill (HAWB):

(i) This exists only if the consignment was to form part of a consolidation.

(ii) It is evidence of the contract of carriage made between the exporter and the forwarder.

(iii) Intended routeing should be apparent, and may be needed where the forwarder contracted for the whole movement, and then sub-contracted part only to an airline.

(iv) Booked flights should be shown, but do not necessarily appear.

F. Consolidation manifest:

(i) This exists only if the consignment is to form part of a consolidation.

(ii) It lists the different consignments within the consolidation.

(iii) Analysis of weights and numbers of packages can sometimes reveal whether the consignment or part of the consignment was omitted from the consolidation.

G. Airline master air waybill (MAWB) or air waybill (AWB):

(i) In the case of a consolidation, the airline's AWB is known as a MAWB: it is essentially no different from an ordinary AWB, except that it should name the forwarder issuing the MAWB as the shipper.

1. The term *prima facie* means "at first sight" or "on the first view". Thus, *prima facie* evidence is evidence which stands in the absence of other information disproving it. In this case, a "clean signature" is not valid if it is proved that damage could only have occurred prior to the giving of that signature.

(ii) If it is an MAWB, it evidences the contract of carriage made between the forwarder and the airline.
(iii) If it is an AWB, it evidences the contract made by the shipper with the airline, or made with the airline by the forwarder on behalf of the shipper.
(iv) It will show routeings, and should show booked flights, which will aid re-construction of transit history where delay occurred or mis-routeing may have been possible.

H. Pallet tags and/or pallet manifests:
(i) A forwarder building a pallet or pallets, or stuffing a container or containers for a consolidation should retain a form of record showing what was loaded on or in which ULD.
(ii) The study of such records should aid investigations into losses, including possible mis-routeings.

I. Flight manifests:
(i) These list the entire cargo load on an aircraft. There must be two sets: one lists cargo by AWB number only, and the other lists the ULD numbers, with cargo therein sub-listed by AWB number.
(ii) They should aid investigation of losses.
(iii) For some reason airlines are often reluctant to release these documents, although there seems no obvious rationale for this.

J. Check-in sheets:
(i) These are normally flight manifests listing the cargo by AWB number only. Destination warehousemen mark them to show receipt of cargo from flights. If the tallying of packages has been simple and straightforward the number of pieces on the manifest is usually ringed. If tallying has been difficult owing to the receipt of multiple pieces in different ULDs, traditional "gate" checking is often seen.
(ii) Shed storage location is normally shown.
(iii) Sometimes the warehouseman will add a remark about damage noted on arrival.
(iv) They should assist in confirming receipt of a consignment into an airline warehouse.

K. Out-turn report:
(i) A report should be telexed[2] back to the origin station, either confirming receipt of cargo in order, or noting irregularities. Both shortage and damage should be notified to the origin station.
(ii) Sometimes cargo received but not manifested on the flight is notified.
(iii) It sometimes assists in confirming irregularities relevant to the claim.

L. Tracing records:
(i) These are normally telexes and faxes to relevant stations requesting searches for missing cargo.

2. It is noted that the SITA telex system remains a regular means of communications within airlines, and that few regular operational cargo messages are sent by other means.

(ii) Airlines often have a tracing record sheet and, since sometimes dozens of tracing messages and answers arise, it is suggested that the strict rule of chronology be suspended for this one facet only. It makes good sense to attach all tracers and answers to the record sheet to avoid unnecessary complexity in the file, and because they are subset of the main file anyway.

M. Damage report:
  (i) This is usually made out by a warehouseman, usually a supervisor, on noting damage to cargo.
  (ii) It is a vital aid to confirming nature of and time and date of the damage incident.

N. Delivery note:
  (i) This is a vital document evidencing on a *prima facie* basis the number of pieces delivered and whether a consignment had visible damage at the time of delivery.
  (ii) May carry specific "clausing": comments about visible damage or simply a remark such as "see damage report" or "see CIR" (cargo irregularity report) or "see IRP" (irregularity report). It is noted that some airlines have been known to insist on such a signature, and then refuse to release the report referred to!

O. Notice of claim:
  (i) Notices of claim are required in most, but not all, claim situations, and are required to be given within a specific time.
  (ii) A respondent needs to confirm to its satisfaction that the notice has been given properly.
  (iii) A claimant needs to be able to prove beyond reasonable doubt that he has given such a notice of claim.

In general terms the above documents are basic requirements, subject to the needs of the case in question. They usually have to be sought and requested, to enable the claims handler to have a basic understanding of the claim situation. All other documents which go to make up the latter part of the file usually flow fairly naturally as the claim is prepared on a formal basis, submitted to the respondent, and the respondent considers the relevant papers.

Other documents

Ordinary

It is self-evident that, depending on the complexity of the cargo's movement, there may be intermediary but reasonably routine documents at the beginning of the transit and at the end, after delivery out of the airline. These will comprise such documents as receiving and delivery sheets peculiar to forwarders involved. Each claimant must assess the need to see these documents based on the particular circumstance of the subject claim.

Special

It is also clear that there are additional documents from the airline's point of view, having to do with the movement of cargo and the carrying aircraft, but, in general terms, the above items should be sufficient to enable a clear picture of a transit history and claims situation to emerge.

When documents additional to those above are sought, the likelihood is that the claim is a fairly serious one under significant dispute and being handled by people with expertise and special knowledge in this field. Deadload weight statements, notifications to the aircraft captain and loading sheets showing where ULDs and bulk cargo were loaded on the aircraft, among other documents, are included in this category.

REVIEWING AND PROGRESSING

A claimant exporter or importer tends to be a party who makes settlement of a claim a priority, and thus needs no encouragement to review the claim file on a regular basis or to chase respondents. Accordingly, it is the carrier or forwarder processing a claim made against him, or a forwarder pursuing his client's claim against a third party, who may benefit from suggestions on general monitoring of claims progression. Thus, the following observations are mainly for the benefit of the party claimed against.

However, claimant exporters and importers will be able to see what the respondent should reasonably be doing, and this may enable them to bring pressure to bear in a more effective way.

Each live file should be routinely checked every now and then to ensure that necessary action on it has not been overlooked. For example, a claims handler often promises to revert to a claimant after having carried out more than one inquiry to different locations and to different personnel. One or more of the persons who have been questioned may delay in responding, and it is not difficult to overlook completing the inquiry because of delayed responses.

When the claimant chases him up for a progress report, it is often very uncomfortable for the handler to discover that he had not ensured completion of the inquiry. An explanation that one of the inquiry lines has not responded falls flat if the claimant asks what has been done to expedite that inquiry, when perhaps only one letter or fax was ever sent.

It is preferable to be able to report to the claimant that the handler has pursued the inquiry line by various means on various occasions. Indeed, if the handler has done this, then the inquiry may have been answered anyway, or he may have been able to formulate a means for overcoming the lack of information in some other way.

Other examples of unpleasant situations which could have been avoided by efficient administration no doubt suggest themselves.

They always look bad and damage customer relations significantly. Thus, claims handlers should seek to avoid such situations and efficient reviewing techniques are indispensable.

Diary v. Database

The efficient maintenance of a "progress" diary—if the number of claims being handled is not large—may be adequate, depending on the company's requirements. If the numbers of claim handled are large, then the use of a computer database is indicated. It is simple to set up the programme to print out a list of files on a due date which can be reviewed for action. It even allows the claims handler to delegate routine chasing to his secretary or junior.

Database spin-off

A computer database can provide analysis of claims, providing a wealth of useful information. It can be ascertained whether there is an increase over a period of time in a certain type of loss, or an increase in the frequency of a particular claimant making claims, which will enable policies to be formulated to reduce or eliminate such claims. That is, of course, an aspect of risk control. Total aggregate exposure to claims settlements can be ascertained; the company's insurers will need to know this, as will the company accountant, in order to pay claims settlements which are agreed.

Other applications can be formulated, of course.

CORRESPONDENCE STANDARDS

The standard of letters and other communications from the claims handler reflects totally on the image of his company. The claims handler can at times find himself in the vanguard of customer relations. Competence in the written language is a prerequisite, and all communications leaving the office should be presented as well as possible. Sound grammar and punctuation demonstrate professionalism, and are undoubtedly vital aids to the clear expression of ideas.

It seems that many people sometimes adopt in business correspondence a verbose and slightly pompous tone, which may cause amusement or irritation in the receiver. A lack of respect is also a common reaction in the reader, the opposite of what the writer probably intended. The guiding principles should be simplicity, brevity and clarity. Friendliness, if the situation permits, is a worthwhile additional facet, but is often out of place when a dispute is under consideration. The ultimate guide which no-one should ever forget is "if you would not say it, then do not write it".

All originators of correspondence should read their draft letters out loud every now and then, and judge whether their words could reasonably be one half of a business conversation with the person who is going to receive the letter or fax. If the originator could imagine listening to someone saying those words to him and he squirms, then the letter needs revising.

CHAPTER 6

LEGAL FRAMEWORK

In Chapter 2, we dealt in general terms with the concept of liability, but a transit claims handler requires a good deal more information and background in order to make decisions and formulate recommendations about claims. Accordingly, we shall, in the broadest terms, cover more detailed overall concepts of how liability in transit arises: doubtless, this will enable the claims handler to understand how the different regimes and regulations interact. A broad idea of contract law is set out, and British International Freight Association (BIFA) contract conditions, Road Haulage Association (RHA) conditions, and Contracts for Carriage by Air will be covered. There will also be a few words on the law concerning international trucking contracts.

The common law concerning contract and bailment is extensive, and, in order to ensure simplicity and ease of understanding for the industry claims handler, it is set out herein in the broadest manner. Little more than what follows is needed to enable claims handlers to discharge their duties, but claims handlers desiring to increase their knowledge of contract and bailment should undertake further study of the subjects.

CONTRACT

We make contracts many times in a day, on a personal level and in business. There are marriage contracts, contracts of employment, contracts of sale, and so on, but, of course, we are interested here only in contracts in our industry.

For our purposes, a contract is an agreement between two people (or companies), where one agrees to do something for the other, and the other agrees (usually) to pay for it to be done.

There is a whole body of law which has arisen concerning the effect of contract, what happens if things go wrong, and so on, but we will try to develop these thoughts as we proceed.

LIABILITY IN BAILMENT AND TRANSIT

Bailment

The idea that a freight operator (be it an airline, forwarder or trucker) is liable to his customer arises primarily from a historic body of law known as bailment. If Smith gives something that belongs to him to Jones to look after, with the intention that Jones will return the goods to Smith in the future, then Smith has "bailed" the goods to Jones: a contract of bailment has been agreed. At its simplest, Jones (now legally the "bailee") may simply be storing the goods for Smith (now a "bailor") for a while. Since we are contemplating such a contract as one involving Jones being paid for his work in storing the goods, Jones has become a "bailee for reward".

A whole body of law has slowly evolved in the courts resulting from bailors attempting to recover goods from bailees who would not give them back, or attempting to obtain compensation if the bailee lost or damaged them.

As far as liability goes, the general principle is that the bailee is liable in full to the bailor for the value of the goods in his care, but it is always open to the parties to agree special terms about how they will deal with Jones losing or damaging the goods, or how Smith is to pay for Jones's services.

The most fundamental and important point about the making of such special arrangements is that they must be fully agreed prior to the contract commencing. Jones cannot round on Smith and tell him he has lost the goods, but that his conditions of contract allow Jones to avoid paying more than a nominal amount, unless Smith had full knowledge of this condition at the time the contract was agreed. This is an extremely important theme, and one to which we will return more than once.

Transit

Keeping the above principle in mind, let us see what happens when the central purpose of the contract is for Jones to re-deliver the goods to another party. He now has a two-fold duty: both to look after the goods as a bailee and to transport them to another location. Smith and Jones are now parties to a contract of carriage. The contract will deal with a number of points concerning how the goods are transported, how the charges are worked out, and to whom the goods are to be delivered, and perhaps how long it is to take, but Jones's liability is not obscured: as a bailee his duty is to look after the goods irrespective of any other duties agreed. How much he has to pay if something happens to the goods can be based on a formula agreed prior to commencement of the contract. This brings us to the legal principle of incorporation. It is common, of course, today for freight operators to work to a set of standard contract conditions.

The fundamental importance of incorporation

Since it is such a vital principle, all participants in the freight industry, from carriers and forwarders to exporters and importers, should be absolutely aware that, unless liability conditions have been brought to the attention of exporters and importers by carriers and forwarders at the time of making the contract, carriers and forwarders are not entitled to limit their liability. When the exporter or importer has accepted the liability conditions they are said to be incorporated into the contract. (Of course, as one might expect, where legislation specifically exists to control contracts of carriage, such as by air, there are rules set down about how incorporation is achieved, or assumed to have been achieved. Reference will be made to this below.)

Of course, in general terms a contract can have conditions incorporated into it verbally or in a written form. To incorporate verbally seems most imprudent in business, for if the contract goes wrong one is faced with the very difficult task of proving incorporation. Contracts in writing, or documents proving incorporation into an otherwise verbal contract, are indispensable.

Even today, freight operators do not give much priority to clear and definite agreement of contract terms with their customers. Some smaller operators constantly accept jobs over the telephone without mentioning any contract conditions, and no piece of paper going to the customer ever makes mention of them. Such operators are, accordingly, liable in full under any circumstances, but, in most cases when a claim arises, they simply tell the client that any settlement is subject to standard conditions. Often, the operator's ignorance is echoed by the client's ignorance, and the client accepts a settlement or not without questioning the situation.

However, some customers are aware of such matters, and the operator occasionally has a very nasty surprise when he learns from the customer's solicitor that the customer can with confidence pursue a claim for the full value. Legal actions of this sort from time to time wipe an operator from the commercial map, because in the worst cases the operator is forced into liquidation if its assets fall short of the court's award of damages.

The wisest and perhaps only safe course has to be for an operator taking a job from a customer for the first time to state clearly that all work is subject to conditions which will be sent to the customer. If the job is very urgent and cannot wait for the customer to receive and agree to the conditions by mail, then the fax can be used, of course. If the customer is accustomed to transporting goods anyway, he is likely to be familiar with the existence of standard contract conditions: his agreement to them is then an informed one on his part.

If there are operators reading this work who realise they have not dealt with this vital aspect of their business, then it is suggested that with all urgency they post a copy of their conditions to all existing customers, and keep a clear record of having done so. At least the next job from any of those customers should be subject to those conditions.

Agency

There is one way in which Jones can act which fundamentally alters his position with Smith: he acts purely as forwarding *agent*.

Smith can agree with Jones that Jones will—on his behalf—*arrange* to have goods carried to a destination for him. Jones will make a contract of carriage on behalf of Smith, and Smith will be one party to the contract and the carrier the other party to the contract: Jones will not be a party to the carriage contract. If the carriage goes wrong, Jones is not liable to Smith for the goods. He is liable to Smith only for any failure or shortcoming in his duties of arranging the contract. (In reality, this does not stop Smith acting as if Jones were liable and, if Jones is dependent on Smith for regular business, he may well go along with this in order to retain the business.)

EVOLUTION OF LIMITED LIABILITY

A little thought shows that unless a freight operator can find some way to ensure that he cannot be forced to pay compensation for the total value of the goods which he may carry, or arrange carriage for, he will be unlikely to stay in business for long.

The principle of limited liability has undoubtedly been a vital factor in allowing commerce to grow to its present size. Without it, one cannot envisage the numbers of goods which fuel our lifestyles being shipped around the world, because there would be few freight operators hardy enough or wealthy enough to withstand even one claim for total and strict liability.

One can see how efforts to limit losses have been made over history. For instance we have "general average" in sea-carriage affairs. (The word "average" has more to do with the French word "*avarie*", meaning loss, than its seemingly obvious English meaning.) General average appears to have been a legal principle in Ancient Greece and, while no written record survives, its existence was reported to the Ancient Roman Emperor Justinian. The principle is that if, in order to lighten a ship, merchandise is thrown overboard, then that which was thrown overboard for the benefit of all should be replaced by the contribution of all.

Insurance against loss of cargo was certainly well-established in the Roman Empire and the same Emperor Justinian established risk insurance premiums.

While the Dark Ages, after the fall of the Roman Empire, obscured developments in trade, a return to more ordered times eventually permitted, first, the firm establishment of general average in international law and, second, the rise of Lloyd's and other providers of insurance cover: both fundamentally underpin international trade for the sole purpose (so far as international trade is concerned) of traders avoiding catastrophic losses.

The return to more ordered times also permitted various organisations in different commercial spheres to seek to limit liability, and by present-day standards some of the things that, for instance, railways and shipping lines "got away" with were scandalous. Limited liability conditions would even avoid responsibility or compensation for death, or perhaps enforce an appallingly low level of compensation.

Those days seem to have passed now, as a result of two basic methods of ensuring limited liability: either governments have stepped in to regulate such contract conditions or trading associations have banded together to produce respectable conditions. (Self-regulation cannot always be expected to work, but with the development of legislation to deal with unfair contract terms, trade organisations know they cannot seek to impose unreasonable contract conditions on their customers.)

REGULATION OF CONTRACTS

Without some form of consensus or regulation, one could envisage all kinds of different contracts in use with senders and receivers of goods involved effectively in a form of lottery. Self-regulation of contracts has arisen in trucking and forwarding, whilst in air carriage governments have stepped in from the early days.

Civil regulation

Many groups trading in particular areas of commerce band together and, while they remain in competition with each other, they often recognise the benefits of working together on some aspects of their business.

In a market economy, as a general rule only, so long as trading groups and associations do not unfairly regulate competition or seek to undermine or weaken the position of their customers, who are forced to come only to them for the services they provide, such groups will not attract opprobrium, and will be left alone by governments to get on with their business without interference. From this point of view, the British International Freight Association and the Road Haulage Association have been success stories. BIFA is concerned with all aspects of its business, and has departments dealing with the various aspects of the business in which its members participate. Accordingly, in the air cargo world, BIFA will be active in discussing methods of working with airlines, and perhaps seeking to influence regulations concerning the handling of certain types of cargo. Unquestionably, the RHA has a parallel role in its corner of the commercial world which is comparable to that of the BIFA. An interesting point is that freight operators are often found to be members of both BIFA and RHA: this can cause some difficulty when their operatives make contracts with customers without being certain which terms are applicable.

Regulation by legislation

In the case of air carriage, the route to regulation has been different. From the early days certain aspects of developing air transportation were recognised by several governments as requiring attention on an international basis; for instance, determining which country's laws applied to a particular carriage: was a passenger's claim or the claim for a consignment being flown to France and lost during transit to be judged by French law or English law? If French law were generous to a claimant, and English law not, how did you reconcile the claimant's wish to bring his case in France and the carriers' wish to defend the case in England?

Of course, there was much more to the build-up to and reasons for the first Warsaw Convention in 1929, and the French law/English law issue above is really only to show the relevance of the Warsaw Convention, particularly to our industry. In Warsaw, representatives of governments agreed to a treaty, after doubtless considering representations from their countrymen involved in different aspects of air transportation. In the U.K., the treaty was given the force of law by the Carriage by Air Act 1932. Since then, there have been numerous attempts to improve the treaty, most of which have taken many years to reach the Statute Books.

A notable exception was the amended Warsaw Convention agreed at the Hague in 1955—known familiarly as the Hague Protocol—which was given the force of law by the Carriage by Air Act 1961. However, it is significant to note that the U.S.A. has never adhered to the Hague Protocol, and this creates some interesting differences between the two basic systems.

For the future, another version of the original Convention known as the "Montreal Protocol", agreed in 1975, is being urged by airlines, and at the beginning of 1996 they committed themselves to persuading their respective governments to agree it, so that Sovereign States would sign it and thus enable it to be adopted as law around the world. That will make a considerable difference to the way cargo liability by air is dealt with, but it still remains uncertain if it will ever become law generally throughout the world of air transportation.

CHAPTER 7

CIVIL REGULATION—RHA AND BIFA

The following are intended as general comments on the meaning and intention of the provisions in the different liability systems relating to the more common claims situations. For the majority of the time, claims handlers will be dealing with the points covered below, but there can be no substitute for thoroughly reading the RHA and BIFA conditions, and the Warsaw Convention Treaty and ancillary Protocols.

You must be very clear that there is no real shortcut: it is relatively simple to learn enough to deal with routine claims, but there is no substitute for a proper study of the bodies of rules with which you will be working. This exhortation will appear below more than once, and no apology is offered for its repetition.

RHA

The conditions are properly known as the Road Haulage Association Conditions of Carriage 1991. There are 19 separate conditions and, as with other comparable schemes, matters concerning how business is to be conducted are dealt with, and actually form the greater part of the set. Some of these conditions also have a bearing on liability, which is not immediately apparent on first studying them.

The reader is once again strongly cautioned that there is no substitute for a proper and thorough reading of the conditions.

Condition 1—definitions

This defines the meaning of the terms customer, contract, consignee, consignment and dangerous goods.

Condition 2—parties and sub-contracting

This deals with four different points. Point 1 deals with the entitlement of the customer to give instructions concerning the goods being moved, either through his ownership of the goods or through authority given by the owner;

points 2, 3 and 4 deal with the carrier sub-contracting the carriage, and are of importance in determining whom claimants should effectively act against.

(A note of caution for some carriers operating under RHA conditions, but arranging carriage by air on behalf of clients: despite the wording of point 4, carriers have found themselves classed as contracting carriers under the Warsaw Convention, having used consignment notes not in accordance with that Convention. This renders them vulnerable to unlimited liability, since the Convention has the force of statute law, which invariably overrides the RHA contract.)

Condition 3—dangerous goods

This provides that the customer has a very high degree of responsibility for the presentation of dangerous goods for carriage. (Echoing the foregoing note of caution, RHA operators who may become involved in moving dangerous goods by air should be very aware of the major penalties involved in contravening the regulations applicable to air carriage of dangerous goods. Familiarity with dangerous goods moved by road absolutely does not qualify an operator to deal with dangerous goods to be carried by air.)

Condition 4—loading and unloading

This deals with the manner of loading the goods on the vehicle, and who shall provide which equipment for the purpose of loading.

Condition 5—consignment notes

This deals with consignment notes and their effect. They can never be used as evidence of condition, correctness of declared nature, quantity, or weight of the goods on receipt by the carrier. If any of these points is disputed in a claim, then the claimant will have to adduce other evidence to prove his point.

Condition 6—transit

This defines when transit commences and when it ends, and what happens if the carrier is unable to deliver for one reason or another.

Condition 7—undelivered or unclaimed goods

This deals with what the carrier can or must do if he is unable to deliver the consignment.

Condition 8—carrier's charges

This deals with how carriage charges are to be calculated, and the interest penalty on charges remaining unpaid.

Condition 9—liability for loss and damage

This is the central condition relating to liability for loss, mis-delivery and damage, and is split into three sections. The condition first confirms that the customer has accepted this condition, unless it has been agreed previously that the carrier has no responsibility at all. Does the latter ever happen?

In its second part, it then goes on to look at liability in two ways. Certain goods are singled out for special consideration: livestock, bullion, money, securities, stamps and precious metals. In these cases, the customer is supposed to obtain specific written agreement from the carrier to carry the goods, must agree to indemnify the carrier for any extra expenses involved in the carriage of such goods and can expect a claim to be paid only in the event of a carrier's negligence or omission. This appears to mean that no claim will be settled in the event of, for instance, a vehicle being struck by another without fault of the carrier's driver which results in livestock being killed or maimed; or, perhaps, a robbery of precious metals, where the carrier's driver cannot be shown to be negligent or an accomplice. For all other claims, the grounds for repudiation are carefully enumerated in relation to factors outside the control of the carrier. If a claim cannot be explained away in these terms, then the carrier is liable for the loss.

In the third part, the carrier is declared to be not responsible for loss of or damage to goods when transit has ended and he still retains them—the ending of carriage is defined in condition 6. If this situation arises, then the contract purports to hold him blameless for anything that happens to the goods. It is supposed that he cannot, however, act in a negligent or reckless fashion, and if there should be any subsequent agreement for him to continue to look after the goods until they are required then a further duty of care with responsibilities will arise.

Condition 10—fraud

If the customer or other party commits a fraud with respect to the goods, then the carrier cannot be held liable for them, unless he—or his staff acting within the scope of their employment—is complicit in the fraud.

Condition 11—limitation of liability

This is the central provision dealing with the limitation of liability. It is divided into two sections: liability incurred through loss, mis-delivery or damage; and that incurred through indirect or consequential losses.

Where loss, damage or mis-delivery is concerned, the carrier's liability is £1,300 per tonne, unless the customer has given notice to the carrier in writing of his requirement for a higher limit—not exceeding the value of the cargo—seven days prior to the commencement of the transit. The limitation can be calculated on a volumetric basis,[1] if such was the basis for the carriage charges, and the carrier is entitled to proof of the value in the event of a claim. Finally, the minimum liability of a carrier is £10.00.

Where consequential or indirect loss is concerned the carrier is liable only for the carriage charges, unless at the time of agreeing the contract for carriage the customer has declared a special interest in delivery in the event of loss, damage or the exceeding of a time limit, and agrees to pay a surcharge.

It is also necessary for the customer to confirm in writing such special interest, the amount, and the time limit.

Condition 12—insurance

Here the carrier undertakes to insure his liability as it arises out of the carriage contract. It is not clear what happens if the carrier does not insure his liability.

Condition 13—indemnity to carrier

This deals with ways in which the customer must indemnify the carrier. If through the customer's failure in some way the carrier incurs a loss and the total claims from whatever quarter arising due to a loss—even one caused by the carrier—exceed the carrier's limitation, then the customer becomes responsible for the amount by which the total claims exceed the limitation. This applies if the loss is caused by dangerous goods, whether or not declared by the customer and to all claims by Customs in respect of dutiable goods whether or not transit has ended.

Condition 14—time limits for claims

This is divided into two sections: partial loss from package and loss of whole packages or consignments. The effect of the condition is that the carrier does not have to answer for a claim on which the time limits have not been observed, unless the customer proves that he was unable to comply with the time limits.

In the case of partial loss, notice in writing should be given within three days, which requirement should present no real administrative difficulty. However, the submission of the claim itself within seven days appears quite difficult in many circumstances.

1. At the time of writing, the recent case of *Spectra International plc* v. *Hayesoak Limited & ors* has confirmed that this is correct. This case was unreported officially at the time of writing but was commented on by David Glass at [1997] LMCLQ 478. It is understood that the RHA have set 1 July 1988 as the target date to issue a revised set of conditions amending this provision.

In the case of loss of packages of a consignment, the respective time limits are 28 days and 42 days, which seems reasonable.

There is no time bar other than, of course, the common law one of six years.[2]

Condition 15—lien

This empowers a carrier to hold onto goods in the event that his carriage charges are not paid.

Condition 16—unreasonable detention

The customer is responsible for costs arising out of any delay to the vehicle. This appears to suggest that the customer is responsible for delays caused to the vehicle by other parties as well.

Condition 17—computation of time

In calculating the time limits in condition 14, Saturdays, Sundays and statutory public holidays are not taken into account.

Condition 18—loss adjustment

This determines how claims shall be valued. The invoice value is to be used if the goods have been sold, and in all other cases it is the cost to the customer that has to be taken into account.

Condition 19—impossibility of performance

Finally, the carrier it not obliged to perform the contract of carriage if he is prevented by various factors beyond his control.

BIFA

Although an earlier version of these conditions is still in use with some forwarders, its use is so limited as to be of little interest. Accordingly, we will consider only the BIFA Standard Trading Conditions 1989. Their proper title is "British International Freight Association (BIFA)—Standard Trading Conditions 1989 Edition". There are 31 separate conditions and, as with other comparable schemes, matters concerning how business is to be conducted are dealt with, and actually form the greater part of the set. Some of these

2. The new set of conditions referred to in footnote 1 will also include a time bar of one year.

conditions also have a bearing on liability, which is not immediately apparent on first studying them. The conditions are divided into five sections:

1. the first deals with definitions used and how conditions apply to the contract;
2. the second concerns the company which is offering the conditions as its contract basis;
3. the third deals with matters concerning the customer;
4. the fourth concerns liability and limitation; and
5. finally, the fifth states which legal system applies to any disputes arising under these conditions.

The reader is once again strongly cautioned that there is no substitute for a proper and thorough reading of the conditions.

Definition and application

Condition 1—definitions

Company, person, the owner (of the goods) and customer are defined, so that each party knows what is meant in the rest of the conditions when the terms are used.

Condition 2—application and overriding law

The conditions apply to all business transacted—even gratuitously—by the company using the conditions as its basic contract terms. Also, if any legislation overrides any condition within the set, then it only affects that part and not the rest of the terms.

Condition 3—authority to accept contract conditions

This concerns the ability of the customer to accept the conditions. Either he warrants he is the owner (of the goods which are subject of the contract) or that he is empowered to accept the conditions on behalf of others.

Condition 4—further authority to accept conditions

Here the contract provides that where the owner and consignee authorise the customer to enter into the contract, then they accept the conditions themselves. Additionally, the company is authorised to pursue the customer, owner and consignee for unpaid charges.

The company

The company is the party seeking to do business under the BIFA conditions.

Condition 5—agency

This condition comprehensively deals with issues arising as a result of the company acting as a principal or agent. First, the company is authorised to act as principal or agent, and it is stated that an all-in charge for a service does not necessarily determine whether a company has acted as a principal or not. Unfortunately, a good number of companies operating BIFA conditions do not realise that very often they act as principals, which will involve them in different roles as, for instance, contracting carriers under the Warsaw system, with much higher liability. When he is acting as an agent, it is underlined that if a BIFA operator arranges (say) a contract for packing with an independent packer, then he arranges a contract between the customer and the packer. Finally, the company can be called upon to provide evidence of such contracts and, if it does not or cannot, then it can be presumed that it has acted as a principal.

Condition 6—acceptance of liability

If the company acts as a principal, it confirms that it accepts liability under clauses 26–29, as dealt with below.

Condition 7—contracts arranged by the company as an agent

When the company acts as an agent, then the customer authorises it to enter into contracts for variously defined services.

Condition 8—freedom of choice for company

The company is accorded a good deal of freedom in its choice and method of making contracts for the various services which it undertakes to provide.

Condition 9—use of associates, etc.

The company is allowed to use its parent, subsidiary or associated companies in making its various contracts.

Condition 10—liens

Obviously, a very important point for the company is where it is authorised to hold goods in circumstances where its charges and other sums remain unpaid.

Condition 11—remuneration

This authorises the company to retain brokerages, commissions or allowances that would customarily be paid to it.

Condition 12—frustrated delivery

This determines how the company is to deal with a situation where it is unable to deliver goods.

Condition 13—(transit) insurance

In the past, there were occasionally quite difficult situations, where a forwarder was considered to be under an obligation to arrange insurance for the transit on behalf of his customer. Sometimes the instruction would be given verbally and, if the insurance were not arranged for some reason, the forwarder could find himself liable outside his contract conditions. This measure solves the problem for the forwarder, by requiring the customer to confirm the instructions to insure in writing.

Condition 14—special delivery circumstances

A regular feature of a forwarder's work is to deliver subject to collection of moneys or documents, and this condition attempts to ensure that the forwarder is always an agent of the customer in such circumstances.

Condition 15—advice and information

A forwarder is often involved in giving advice, for instance, on how to handle and route a consignment. It also gives quotations on freight charges, and so on. The conditions provide that the information is exclusive to the customer and that the customer must indemnify the company if parties other than the customer rely on that information.

Condition 16—special cargoes

Certain types of cargo are specified, which require special arrangements to be made. Accordingly, a customer cannot simply present such cargo to the company without prior arrangement: however, the company can waive this provision if it wishes to. This means that if such cargo is presented without notice to the company, it can simply accept it without objection if it chooses to.

Condition 17—dangerous goods or goods likely to cause damage

Special arrangements are also necessary with these goods, and the authority for the company to deal with any goods which it considers likely to cause danger to goods or life.

Condition 18—declarations of value

If there is available a choice of rates which affect the liability levels available to the customer, then no declaration of value will be made to the carrier or other party, with whom the company is contemplating a contract for the customer, unless the customer previously arranges it with the company in writing.

The customer

Condition 19—warranties

The customer confirms that he has given all necessary information about the consignment accurately and completely. He confirms complete and proper packing and other preparation for carriage.

Condition 20—dangerous goods or goods likely to cause damage

The customer comprehensively indemnifies the company if it causes such goods to be handled by the company without the special arrangements required above.

Condition 21—against whom to claim?

The customer is not permitted to claim against an employee, director or servant of the company.

Condition 22—the customer must indemnify the company

The customer undertakes to indemnify the company against its incurring a liability as a result of complying with the customer's instructions; against all claims, costs and demands above the liability limits set by these conditions; and against general average claims, a matter relating only to sea carriage, and of no interest to us here.

Condition 23—moneys owed to the company

The customer undertakes to pay the company any money owed without deduction, which means that the customer cannot set off any claims it may have against the company. This principle is very strongly enforced in English law, and is common world-wide. Additionally, if such money is overdue, then an interest penalty is payable.

Condition 24—customer guarantee of charges

If the company is unable to collect money from a consignee, then the customer remains liable for those charges. Of course, the company has to do its best to collect the money, and must prove that it has tried.

Condition 25—general average

Again, general average is irrelevant to air carriage, and will concern BIFA operators only in ocean carriage business.

Liability and limitation

Condition 26—diligence

This sets the standard of performance which the company must apply to its activities. It is required only to be reasonably diligent. In practice, it is seldom that what this means is disputed.

Condition 27—relief of liability

The company is excused liability in various circumstances where the cause of a claim arising is one essentially outside its control.

Condition 28—delay

Unless previously agreed in writing, the company cannot be held liable for delay to goods. This is probably meant to cover a situation where the carriage is sub-contracted by the company where it has no direct control over the movement.

Condition 29—limitations

This topic is dealt with comprehensively, and leaves little room for misunderstanding. The condition is set out in four sections. It sets up detailed limits, but goes on to provide the freedom for the customer and company to agree higher limits.

A. Subject to any overriding legislation and the freedom to agree a higher limit than set down in the conditions, the company is liable to the following limits:
   (i) for loss or damage, two special drawing rights* (SDRs hereafter) per kilo of gross weight, or the invoice value,* whichever is less;
   (ii) for all other claims, two SDRs per kilo gross weight, or the invoice value, whichever is less, but subject to an upper limit of 75,000 SDRs.

* The value of the SDR is applied as at the date the claim is received in writing by the company, and invoice value is defined as the value when the goods were or should have been shipped.

B. In the case of delay, the maximum compensation is set at twice the company's charges for the relevant transaction. This is also subject to any overriding legislation and the freedom to agree a higher limit than set down in the conditions.

C. The company cannot be held liable for indirect or consequential losses; thus loss of profit, loss of market or the consequences of delay or deviation cannot be held to the company's account. (However, it must be noted that if the company is acting as a principal in air transportation, for instance, having issued its own house air waybill, then this condition will be over-ruled by the statutory provisions of the Warsaw Convention.)

D. This provides for the freedom for the company and customer to agree a higher limitation than that set down in the conditions.

Condition 30—time limits for claims

Two periods are covered: the time allowed for giving notice of claim, and the time allowed for the customer to complete his claim and obtain settlement.

First, a customer must give notice of intention to claim in writing within 14 days of its learning of a claim problem or of when it should have become aware of it. The company absolutely cannot be held liable for a claim in the absence of such notice, unless the customer can prove that it could not reasonably have given such notice, and gave notice as soon as it reasonably could.

Secondly, if a customer has not been able to persuade the company to settle its claim within nine months of the date of the event alleged to have caused the claim, then it must give notice in writing of intention to commence legal proceedings, and actually initiate proceedings—the phrase used is "unless suit be brought" and this is well understood to mean the issue of a writ.

In both cases, because the contract is a civil one, the company has the power to waive these time limits, if it chooses.

Condition 31—the applicable law

If any dispute arises on these conditions, then it has to be adjudged under English law and in the English courts.

CHAPTER 8

STATUTORY REGULATION—AIR CARRIAGE

The body of law constituting the rules on air carriage is far more comprehensive than the rules concerning the activities of forwarders. Whereas forwarders are generally responsible only to their customers in the country in which the forwarding contract is made, an air carrier has responsibilities arising across international boundaries, and that is bound to complicate issues. The comprehensiveness of the rules also reflects the interest that governments world-wide have taken in the development of the conditions under which air transportation is conducted. Conditions concerning the movement of cargo are no less comprehensive than those concerning the carriage of passengers.

The sources of such rules are international treaties agreed over a period of time, which have been incorporated into the laws of nations, plus a minor but definite effect that the air waybill contract conditions brings.

It must still be borne in mind that bailment lies at the very basis of liability which air carriers may have towards their customers. Consider that bailment law in the U.K. has been steadily built up as a result of legal precedent created by many cases being brought before the courts over many years. Those cases were decided one way or the other, and from then on, parties having a dispute of a kind which had been before the courts were obliged to follow those decisions, unless they could find new arguments which would overturn such decisions.

It is to be expected that each country has its own peculiar system for legally deciding issues of bailment (however the principle may be expressed in foreign jurisdictions): broadly, some nations create much of their law by testing cases in court and thus setting down principles to be followed for the future—so-called "common law", whilst other nations codify their laws—so-called "civil law". Consequently, it was also to be expected that when the prospect of regular carriage by air was recognised, it would be understood that if a consignment were lost in transit between two countries, then if the case were brought at origin a very different result might arise than if it were brought in the destination country.

The first attempt to provide some international uniformity was a set of conditions sponsored by the International Air Traffic Association, the forerunner of today's International Air Transport Association. Again, the conditions were likely to be interpreted differently in different countries' courts, and in 1925 CITEJA (Comité International Technique d'Experts Juridiques Aériens) was established, with its first major task to prepare what was to become the Warsaw Convention.

In 1929 the Warsaw Convention became a reality, and its full title—Convention for the unification of certain rules relating to International Transportation by Air—is indicative of its purpose.

The Warsaw system has undergone significant development since then, but we will not concern ourselves with that history other than to set down those developments which affect us today, and the one development which will affect us tomorrow.

Considering the potential that existed in the early days of air transportation for the results of identical cases to differ wildly from one country to another, there is no doubt that the Warsaw system succeeded significantly in "unifying" the rules, and until recently, was probably a reasonable system for regulating liability matters internationally.

However, with fundamental developments of the system brought into force at the end of 1997 and the middle of 1998, and with a further one about to go "live", the face of air cargo liability shows a distinctly different complexion.

Whilst, hitherto, the Warsaw system on balance had probably enabled the air transport business to progress, rather than restrained it, the new complexity may hold some serious difficulties for the industry as a whole.

CHAPTER 9

THE WARSAW SYSTEM

We concern ourselves with the following treaties:

The Warsaw Convention (1929)—Convention for the unification of certain rules relating to International Transportation by Air—known familiarly as "unamended Warsaw";

The Hague Protocol (1955)—Protocol to amend the Convention for the unification of certain rules relating to International Transportation by Air signed at Warsaw on 12 October 1929—known familiarly as "Warsaw/Hague";

Montreal Additional Protocol No. 1—Protocol to amend the Convention for the unification of certain rules relating to International Carriage by Air signed at Warsaw on 12 October 1929—known familiarly as "Montreal 1";

Montreal Additional Protocol No. 2 (1975)—Protocol to amend the Convention for the unification of certain rules relating to International Carriage by Air signed at Warsaw on 12 October 1929 as amended by the Protocol done at the Hague on 28 September 1955—known familiarly as "Montreal 2";

Montreal Protocols Nos. 3 and 4 (1975)—Protocols to amend the Convention for the unification of certain rules relating to International Carriage by Air signed at Warsaw on 12 October 1929, as amended by the Protocol done at the Hague on 28 September 1955—known familiarly as "Montreal 3 and 4"; additionally, "Montreal 4" is often taken to mean "Montreal 3 and 4"; and

The Guadalajara Supplementary Convention (1961)—Convention supplementary to the Warsaw Convention for the unification of certain rules relating to International Carriage by Air performed by a person other than the contracting carrier—known familiarly as "Guadalajara".

Hereafter, these will be referred by their familiar terms.

Again the reader is unapologetically reminded that there is no substitute for a thorough reading of the Conventions, although for the cargo claims handler, sections of Warsaw relating to the passenger ticket, baggage check and passenger liability may not need to be studied in detail. The general and final provisions also have little to do with everyday claims handling.

WARSAW LEGISLATION

The two main enactments in U.K. law are the Carriage by Air Act 1961, which enforces Warsaw/Hague, and the Carriage by Air Acts (Application of Provisions) Order 1967, enforcing Unamended Warsaw: the Order also repealed an earlier law, the Carriage by Air Act 1932, which applied the original Warsaw Convention.

Subsequent statutory instruments which modify these are: Warsaw/Hague—the "air" part of the Carriage by Air and Road Act 1979, which was drafted to give effect to the Montreal Additional Protocol No. 2; and unamended Warsaw—the Carriage by Air Acts (Application of Provisions) (Fourth Amendment) Order 1998, which was drafted to give effect to Montreal Additional Protocol No. 1.

We will deal with the original Convention, and then move on to the Hague amendments. This is a valid way to approach the matter, since as the U.S.A. is a signatory only to the original version, and since much air traffic to and from the U.K. involves the U.S.A., a good deal of claims handlers' work may be in this context. An important point to bear in mind, although it is seldom relevant for everyday claims work, is that the original text of Warsaw is in French, and if the English translation appears to be slightly different in meaning or—more likely—the French appears to make matters slightly more clear on any single point, then the French text is the authoritative one.

Which version of Warsaw and why it is important

How does one discover which countries are parties to which version of the Convention and why do we need to? The reason we need to know is that some fundamental principles in the two versions differ, with important implications for the amount of liability, for instance. Of course, it is also important to know whether Warsaw does not apply to the claim being considered, in which case "non-Warsaw" rules apply, and this is dealt with below.

The primary way to find out which version applies is to refer to the Carriage by Air (Parties to Convention) Order 1988. In it are listed all countries which have signed either or both basic versions of the Convention, together with a date when the convention came into force in those countries.

Major difficulties produced by recent U.K. legislation

A secondary question as to determining which rules apply arises as a result of the 1997 and 1998 Orders referred to above.

As will be seen in your study of the Conventions below, the central factor determining which Convention applies is the reciprocity of (say) France and the U.K. agreeing which version applies. In the case of Warsaw/Hague amended by Montreal Protocol No. 2 there is no difficulty, because we know that both France and the U.K. have signed the No. 2 Protocol.

However, on some routeings it will be apparent that the origin country has not signed Montreal 2, and thus one would suppose the "original" version of Warsaw/Hague should apply. The only problem here is that, so far as can be seen, the recent U.K. legislation (the 1997 Order) has deleted the "original" version of Warsaw/Hague from the statute books. It is very unclear how this problem will be resolved.

Turning to the unamended Convention, the situation would appear to be clearer. Dealing with a more likely and commonplace situation, let us take carriage between the U.K. and the U.S.A. Both are signatories to the unamended Warsaw Convention: the U.S.A. is not a signatory to Montreal No. 1, but the U.K. is. Thus, we have the situation that the U.K. has legislated for Montreal No. 1 in the 1998 Order, but has left the unamended Warsaw Convention on the statute books, and thus we can see that the version of the Convention which applies must be the unamended Warsaw Convention without the "benefit" of Montreal 1.

The central issue which arises concerns which level of limitation applies. As set down in detail below, the two bases for limitation in cargo claims are first, 250 gold francs per kilo, and secondly, 17 Special Drawing Rights per kilo. (There are other issues, of course, but these are not developed here.)

Accordingly, in the study below, these points will be brought out where applicable, but there will be times when it becomes extremely difficult to determine which regime actually applies. Since at the time of writing it appears that the U.K. Foreign Office themselves do not have complete information on which country has signed up to which version of which convention, where claimants and respondents cannot agree or simply do not know which regime to apply, then, for the time being anyway, perhaps they should simply seek to compromise on matters.

However, it should be possible to make a "stab" at determining which regime applies, by reference to the IATA publication "Principal Instruments of the Warsaw System", which carries a listing of signatories to the various Protocols, but, unfortunately, does not seem to have been re-printed since 1991; however, for more up to date information, if it is necessary, one could apply directly to IATA. Finally, one can resort to Shawcross & Beaumont, *Air Law*, published by Butterworths. The latter publication is a highly respected and learned work, but one would need to commit significant funds to its purchase, and its application for an industry claims handler would be difficult to justify.

The prospect for early resolution of these difficulties is gloomy indeed—it may be some years before matters are clarified.

Unamended Warsaw

Chapter I—scope and definitions

The Convention applies to all international transportation, which it defines; it provides that it covers a single carriage performed by carriers one after the other, and is divided as follows:

Article 1

1. The Convention applies to all international transportation of persons, baggage, or goods either free or for reward.

2. For the purpose of the Convention international transportation is defined as carriage between two countries, both of which have signed the Convention and made it their law. This infers that if, for instance, goods are carried from the U.K. to Thailand, which is not a signatory to the Convention, then this is not international transportation for the purposes of Warsaw. However, if when the shipper booked the goods, and accepted and understood that his cargo would be transhipped in Dubai—which is a signatory to the Convention—then it becomes international transportation, and thus falls under the Warsaw system.

3. If a cargo is carried from one place to another by first one carrier and then another, which is quite common, then the complete carriage is regarded as one movement under these rules.

Article 2

This provides that Warsaw applies to carriage undertaken by governments or state entities, provided the carriage falls within the definition in Article 1. It also provides that carriage of mail is not subject to the convention.

Chapter II

Section I—passenger ticket and Section II—baggage check

Articles 3 and 4 are not relevant to cargo liability handlers, and will not be commented upon.

Section III—air waybill

While the provisions concerning passenger tickets and baggage checks are short, the provisions concerning air waybills are lengthy and detailed. The term air waybill will be designated "AWB" from hereon.

Article 5—need for and absence of AWB

This Article tends to have little or no relevance to everyday claims handling, because the use of standard AWBs is industry-wide and it is almost inconceivable that cargo moves without one. Its relevance was probably in the early days, when an AWB, or "air consignment note" as it was originally called, was not always used. One might, however, be concerned with this provision where a charter aircraft is loaded and thought is not given to the completion of an AWB. If, however, cargo is carried without an air waybill having been issued, then limitation cannot be applied to any claims by the carrier.

Article 6—number of copies, and signatures

1. Here the Convention sets out that the consignor must make out certain copies of the AWB. Again, the regular claims handler is unlikely to be concerned with the effect of this sub-clause, because the carriers themselves provide printed stocks of AWB sets which include the appropriate statutory copies. The purpose behind this provision is to ensure that the correct party to the contract has notice of the conditions which apply to it.

2. This provides for how the statutory copies shall be marked, and who shall sign which one. Again the same situation as in sub-clause 1 applies because of the use of standard AWB sets.

3. The carrier must sign the AWB on accepting the goods.

4. The carrier can use a stamp for its signature, and the consignor can print or stamp its signature.

5. There are times when the carrier, instead of the consignor, makes out the AWB and, in such cases, the carrier is considered to be the consignor's agent for this purpose. This is important where an inaccuracy appears in the AWB, and means that the carrier may be able to avoid liability for a problem arising because of that error—always depending on the nature of the problem, of course.

Article 7—one AWB per package?

This probably never happens, but the carrier could insist on a separate AWB for each package of a multi-piece consignment, if it so desired.

Article 8—AWB particulars

In 17 sub-articles, the mandatory details to be shown on the AWB are set down.

Article 9—Effect of absence of particulars

In tandem with Article 8, omission of some items from the AWB can have the most serious effects for a carrier.

Articles 8 and 9 have been subject to considerable legal activity in the U.S.A., where liability limitation has been lost by carriers on several occasions owing to various items having been omitted or deemed to have been omitted.

The law in the U.S.A. was in a state of considerable activity in late 1997 and it may not be settled for some time yet.

Traditionally, air waybill documents are checked cursorily, and, with the number of consignments routinely being accepted, the necessary vigilance cannot be maintained easily without considerable extra staffing costs or significant alterations to acceptance procedures. Doubtless, sooner or later, a case will be considered before the courts, where an airline claims redress from a forwarder or consolidator whose incorrect completion of the air waybill has led to loss of limitation for a carrier. Perhaps such a case will concern a claim by the airline against the forwarder or consolidator for the difference between limitation and the amount of claim which has had to be paid.

Article 10—consignor's responsibility

In two sub-articles, the consignor is charged with responsibility for all the information which he inserts into the AWB; he must also effectively indemnify the carrier and all others who suffer damage if he inserts incorrect or incomplete information.

Article 11—AWB particulars as evidence

1. This makes it clear that the AWB is not the contract, but only evidence for it, for the receipt of the goods and of the conditions. That evidence is *prima facie* only and, accordingly, if the AWB states one thing, but one of the parties involved in a dispute can adduce appropriate evidence, it can succeed in showing that part or parts of the AWB are not correct, and the other party cannot rely on it or them.

2. Specifically, weight, dimensions, packing and the number of packages are also *prima facie* evidence only. If any comments about volume, quantity and condition appear in the AWB, then they can be actual evidence only if the carrier has checked them in the presence of the consignor and they are stated on the AWB to have been so checked.

Article 12—right of stoppage in transit

This deals with the consignor's rights while the cargo is in the possession of the carrier.

1. This confirms the consignor's right of stoppage in transit. He can redirect the cargo, and so on, but must act reasonably at all times, and reimburse any expenses incurred by his doing this.

2. Although one would suppose that this appears to relate directly to sub-article 1, the wording does appear to cover all instructions of a consignor, including—it is suggested—his original instructions for delivery to the consignee named on the AWB. Consequently, it appears that a carrier is obliged immediately to notify a consignor if he is unable to deliver the consignment, whether to the original consignee or to a new one arising from the consignor's right under sub-article 1.

3. This sub-article provides a measure of security to avoid fraudulent instructions being accepted by the carrier for redelivery to other than the originally named consignee. The carrier must comply with fresh instructions only if the consignor's copy of the AWB is produced to him: if he complies without production of that copy, then the carrier may well be liable for the adverse consequences of such altered delivery.

4. This limits the consignor's right of stoppage in transit, such that it ends

when the consignee's rights commence, as defined in the next article. The consignor's right re-activates if the consignee refuses delivery.

Article 13—acquisition of contract rights by consignee

This deals with the consignee's rights on arrival of the cargo

1. On arrival, the consignee is entitled to have the carrier give him the AWB, and deliver the goods on payment of the charges due.

2. The carrier must give notice of arrival to the consignee, unless agreed otherwise.

3. If the carrier admits loss of cargo, or if it does not arrive within seven days of when it should have arrived, then the consignee is entitled to exercise his rights under the contract of carriage. Effectively, this means that he can make his claim against the carrier and expect it to be processed. In practice, it would be exceptional for a carrier to settle a claim so quickly.

Article 14—consignor's and consignee's respective rights

This confirms that the consignor and the consignee can enforce the rights in Articles 12 and 13, whether they act for themselves or for another, providing any obligations imposed by the AWB contract are discharged by them.

Article 15—limiting the effect of Articles 12, 13 and 14

In two sub-articles, it is confirmed that Articles 12, 13 and 14 have no other effect on relations between the consignor, consignee and any party who derives rights from either of them, and that the provisions of those Articles can be varied only by express wording inserted in the AWB. In practice, such variation is seldom, if ever, seen.

Article 16—consignor's responsibility for documents attached to AWB

This is related to Article 10, where the consignor is responsible for information inserted in the AWB. It enlarges the responsibility to include the provision of such information and attachments to the AWB as to allow legal and other formalities to be met in order to allow delivery of the goods. It also sets up an additional indemnity against the consignor for errors therein. Finally, it states that a carrier is not obliged to inquire into the adequacy of the information and documents provided. Occasionally, it is seen that the claimant holds the carrier to account, maintaining that he should not have accepted the cargo if the documents were incorrect. A claim cannot succeed on such grounds.

Chapter III—liability of the carrier

Liability provisions are detailed and comprehensive, but have not avoided varying interpretations between one country and another.

Article 17—passenger liability

This concerns passenger liability and is not commented upon.

Article 18—damage and loss liability

This Article deals with damages arising out of anything that happens directly to the cargo. For a carrier to be liable, the event giving rise to the claim must have occurred during air transportation, as defined.

The sub-articles are as follows:

1. The carrier is liable for damage (financial damages is meant) arising from destruction, loss of or damage to the cargo, provided the event giving rise to it took place during air transportation.

2. Air transportation is defined as the period for which the cargo is in the carrier's possession, whether in an airport or on board an aircraft, or, in the case of a landing outside an airport, in any place. The latter provision seems to cover a crash situation, where the carrier's duty of care continues.

3. The period of air transportation cannot extend to any transportation by land or other mode outside an airport, unless—pursuant to a contract for carriage by air—for the purpose of loading, delivery or transhipment. In the latter situation, if a claim arises, then it is presumed to have been the result of an event which took place during air transportation.

This sub-article gives rise to some difficult situations, because much trucking is carried out, especially in Europe. Indeed it is not unknown for an air carrier to discharge a contract for air carriage by using a truck exclusively.

Thus, we need to give some thought to the meaning of air transportation in this context. It seems likely that, as air carriers continue to use and develop their trucking routes, particularly in Europe, there will be evolution in either the relevant law or the customary manner in which carriers approach claims arising in trucking.

Article 18(3) of the Warsaw Convention refers to transportation by land, by sea or by river, but trucking, of course, is the alternative means of transportation during which difficulties concerning liability can theoretically arise. While there are regular sea movements followed or preceded by air carriage (but not part of the contract agreed for carriage by air), there seems no example of an air carrier itself operating a sea leg where the question would arise whether that sea leg should be considered for liability purposes as air transportation: one supposes that, because sea carriage introduces a much slower and longer sector, this is clearly known of and understood by all parties including the sender and receiver.

On the other hand, air carriers routinely operate trucking legs as principals, and the shipper and consignee will not necessarily know or need to know (for operational purposes) of the fact of road carriage.

Under Article 30(2), it can be seen that the parties to the contract of carriage can agree to apply other conditions to other modes of transportation. Air carriers will occasionally bring trucking sectors to the attention of shippers, but it is seriously doubted that they ever give thought to incorporation of alternative conditions to those sectors. It should be noted that in clause 2(b)(iii) of the air waybill conditions, there is a general reference to "conditions of carriage", from which it may be possible for a carrier to hold that CMR[1] rules could have been incorporated, but it is reasonable to assume, in the absence of any other evidence, that those parties making such contracts would have in mind only the Warsaw Convention or non-Warsaw air carriage rules, plus air waybill contract conditions.

When something goes wrong in road carriage, what are the implications? If other rules can be applied to the road carriage, is the carrier entitled to use defences arising therefrom, and are there any advantages to be gained by the claiming shipper or consignee proceeding under those alternative rules?

It appears to be germane to consider airlines apart from forwarders acting as contracting carriers. For an airline, if the shipper made a contract contemplating the Warsaw Convention or other air carriage rules, within the context of the conditions on the reverse of a standard IATA air waybill contract, then it is difficult to see how an air carrier responding to a claim could apply any other conditions which are more restrictive than these, although an attempt might be made *via* Clause 2(b)(iii) of the air waybill conditions, as mentioned above, if the stakes were high enough.

This would still be the case, it seems, even if the shipper were used to international road carriage, and could be shown to be aware of the CMR rules. After all, the CMR rules do not prevent the parties to an international contract of road carriage from agreeing higher liability limits or more generous time limits, which can be said to have been done when agreeing an AWB contract.

Thus, if the shipper knew of the road carriage sector, and thus that it might not qualify as air transportation, then the air carrier could probably deal with a claim under its AWB conditions, which (presuming the standard IATA set of AWB contract forms had been used) provide for U.S.$ 20.00 per kilo in their clause 4. The other possible advantage to the carrier would be the application of the time limit in the AWB conditions clause 12(a)(iv), which provides for a time limit for the purposes of notice-giving of 120 days in the case of loss. This would not be allowed in the Warsaw context within Europe.

The disadvantage to the claimant would be that for some time the rate of exchange has ensured that U.S.$ 20.00 is less than the statutory U.K. limitation, whether £15.89 or 17 SDRs per kilo. Additionally, the 120-day notice rule could be applied, ruling out a claim where notice had not been properly given.

For a forwarder issuing a house air waybill contract with BIFA conditions on the reverse, and in its capacity as a contracting carrier, the rules could be different.

The standard IATA AWB contemplates Warsaw, non-Warsaw or AWB conditions in the absence of the two former regimes (by clause 2(b)(iii) general

1. The internationally agreed rules on how international carriage by road is regulated as regards liability. Broadly speaking these rules encompass Europe only.

conditions are incorporated, but not all airlines issue a separate set of general conditions). The BIFA conditions do not restrict the applications of any particular rules, but provide for the application of statutory overriding rules. In such a case, one would have to ascertain what was understood within the contract of carriage.

The shipper may have been led to understand that only air carriage was involved. If it was not so led, then it would be possible for the forwarder/contracting carrier to apply other disciplines. In crossing international boundaries, it might be able to apply CMR rules (with its attendant restrictions as compared to Warsaw, or non-Warsaw, rules); in domestic carriage, it should be able to apply BIFA rules.

Categories of road carriage It is useful to analyse the different categories of trucking in which air carriers are involved.

The first category is transfers between airports for the purposes of transhipment, *viz.* arriving in the U.K. on one aircraft and departing on another from a different airport. Transfers between Gatwick Airport and Heathrow would be an example. To a much lesser extent, there are transfers between Heathrow or Gatwick and Manchester, although in the latter case, much would depend on what the shipper understood to be the routeing. In most cases, however, this would appear to be air transportation within the meaning of the Convention.

The second category is carriage within the U.K. from one airport to another for delivery purposes. If an airline AWB provided for delivery at Manchester, but its flight came into Heathrow, then the shipper might well not have known about a transfer by road, in which case it would be difficult for an airline to avoid the application of Warsaw or non-Warsaw air carriage rules.

The third category is occasionally encountered. A carrier operating its flight out of, for instance, Manchester, might well be marketing in the South of England, and will tell its customer in that area that its delivery point is an agent at Heathrow. If it trucks its cargo to Manchester, then that carriage would appear to be for the purpose of loading, and thus be an air transportation for Warsaw purposes. This precise situation arose, and the routeing on the AWB showed the origin as Manchester, but the cargo was delivered to the carrier's agent at Heathrow from where the agent trucked it to Manchester. The conclusion was that the carrier had accepted liability through its agent for the carriage from Heathrow, but no conditions could be identified to cover the Heathrow/Manchester sector, because the AWB contract distinctly showed a contract only for carriage between Manchester and the destination. The carrier was exposed to unlimited liability for the loss and duly paid up.

The final category set down here is carriage from one airport outside the U.K. to another airport in the U.K. If a carrier trucks its cargo from Paris or Frankfurt to Heathrow as its final destination, then it cannot be air transportation in the Article 18(3) sense.

However, it seems that a carrier may well not publicise its trucking schedules, and in such cases it could not apply rules other than Warsaw. Since the shipper had no reason to suppose that other than air carriage was involved, the carrier could not in equity seek to apply claim settlement criteria of lesser benefit than the claimant was entitled to expect. Again, a carrier's general conditions may have been incorporated by reference to them in its AWB contract, but if the shipper had reason to suppose that only air carriage was involved, and not trucking, that purported incorporation could not extend to a set of rules other than those applying under Warsaw.

Carriers at present appear not to seek to apply other than Warsaw rules, but their views may well evolve as trucking continues to be a significant part of their activities.

Where a shipper is made aware of trucking schedules, then the carrier is entitled, probably, to apply its AWB conditions, with U.S.$20.00 per kilo limitation, and the 120-day rule.

Overall, in this area of their activities, it may well be to the benefit of an air carrier to seek to incorporate CMR and other rules, but, of course, an air carrier may feel that it is not necessarily in its interest to profile itself as an international trucker. Notwithstanding all this, it is conceded that other views are probable, and that not all commentators would agree with the above commentary.

Article 19—delay liability

This clearly provides that a carrier is liable for the consequences of delay. The English wording is slightly unfortunate, since it often causes confusion for some claims handlers where perishables are concerned. The word "damage" is intended to cover financial damage, not physical damage that delay can cause to perishables: such latter claims qualify for consideration under Article 18.

It is also quite common for carriers' claims handlers to operate under the impression that they are not responsible for consequential losses. Some major carriers have attempted this line, and one or two major U.S. carriers' claims offices still attempt occasionally to maintain that a CAB rule excludes liability for consequential losses, which—as can be seen below—is contrary (or "repugnant", as is the correct legal term) to the provisions of Article 23, and thus not permitted.

In considering such damages, a carrier needs to be very aware of the methods of judging whether damages claimed for are justified or not, and thus should be familiar with the rule of foreseeability under the general measure of damages principles.

Article 20—carrier's defences

This sets out the defence which a carrier can make to any claim, however founded. If the carrier can prove that it and its agents took all necessary measures to avoid the damage or that it was impossible for it or them to take such measures, then it can avoid having to settle the claim. Again the word "damage" is intended to convey financial damage, which is the result of a claim arising for whatever reason, whether it be in the context of Article 18 or of Article 19.

Some comment is needed on the phrase "all necessary measures". It is generally taken to mean "all *reasonably* necessary measures"; if it did not, then one could suppose a claimant maintaining, by virtue of the damage occurring at all, that it would prove that "*necessary* measures" could not have been taken. The interpretation of "all necessary" as "all reasonably necessary" is well established legally.

A second sub-article provides that if the damage is caused by an error in piloting, then as long as, in all other respects, it and its agents have taken all necessary measures, it can avoid liability. There does not seem to be a record of such a defence being offered.

Article 21—contributory negligence

This also provides a defence in which the carrier is entitled to prove that the claimant contributed to the loss by his act or omission. If the proof exists, then the carrier is entitled to be exonerated in whole or in part from the claim. For example, inadequate packing could be regarded as a contributory factor in damage to cargo—it could enable a carrier to avoid completely having to pay the claim. If perishables had not been properly prepared for carriage, perhaps not pre-cooled, then the carrier would be entitled to avoid the claim. However, it is clear that in some cases it is extremely difficult to decide what proportion of a claim a carrier should be excused. Thus, because of the uncertainty, it can become a powerful negotiating tool for the respondent.

Article 22—limitation of liability

Basic liability limit In practical terms we are concerned only with sub-clause 2 of this article, which states that cargo liability is set at 17 SDRs per kilo, or 250 gold francs per kilo, depending on which version of unamended Warsaw applies. (Please refer to "Major Difficulties produced by recent U.K. legislation" above.)

Clearly, there is no difficulty in determining the value of the SDR.

With the regard to 250 gold francs, in the U.K. this is set at £15.89 by an occasional statutory instrument known as a Sterling Equivalent Order. Until February 1996, when it was set at this level, it had remained unchanged for several years.

If a claim is submitted to a carrier in a particular country, it seems reasonable for the claimant to receive settlement in his own currency. Some U.S. carriers insist on settling in dollars, ignoring requests for sterling; they are not entitled to do this, although claimants may often accept dollar drafts to bring the claim to a conclusion without further delay.

Raising the liability limit A secondary part of sub-article 2 allows the consignor to make a special declaration of value at delivery, when the cargo is handed over to the carrier: the facility for this is provided in the "declared value for carriage" box on the standard AWB. This effectively allows the limitation to rise to the declared value, but the carrier remains permitted to prove the declared value to be in excess of the true value to the consignor.

If it is normal for the carrier to charge for that valuation, then the charge must be paid, or the declaration should have no effect.

However, recently, there were some cases where a shipper, unusually preparing its own AWB documentation, inserted high Declared Values for Carriage—but paid no supplementary charges. The cargoes were delivered to the carrier, who failed to notice the declarations. Serious losses occurred on the consignments, and claims for the full amounts were made.

With AWB documentation almost exclusively being completed by "IATA Cargo Agents" nowadays, it seems that carriers generally have not maintained their vigilance on AWB completion, and it is easy to see why the declarations were missed.

The carrier maintained that since no supplementary charge had been paid, the raised limitation was not included within the contract of carriage, and thus refused to pay more than basic limitation. The cases concluded on the basis that such a position was not certain, and settlements were negotiated at higher-than-basic limitation but not for the full amounts.

It is suggested therefore, that carriers should increase their vigilance as to Declared Values for Carriage.

Article 23—minimum levels of liability

This confirms that the carrier cannot exclude or limit his liability below that set out in the Convention. This applies not only to the limitation in Article 22, but also to provisions such as those relating to time limits on the giving of notice of claim, as set out below in Article 26.

Such ideas as a U.S. carrier stating it is not liable for deterioration to perishables or that its rules require perishables being packed so as to allow for three days' carriage, seem to go against the Article 23 principle. However, it should be noted that while such rules are most unlikely to succeed in the U.K. courts, they may succeed in the U.S. courts, especially where there is no identifiable cause of the damage during the carriage.

A carrier only agreeing to settle a claim for the invoice cost and freight, and declining to pay loss of profit, goes against Article 23 on the basis that the

Convention does not set out any rules for calculating damages. In the absence of any such rules, in the U.K. we can only fall back on the normal common law rules for the measure of damages, which do permit of loss of profit. Accordingly, to decline to pay loss of profit goes against the Convention, which, due to its silence on the question, does effectively allow payment of such loss of profit. The point is sometimes made that just because the Convention is silent on this question, it does not imply acceptance of the position, but it is hard to fault the argument. It may be more a question of the original framers of the Convention, *viz.* those who originally drafted the wording of the Convention, not having addressed the point specifically, thus unintentionally obliging those considering liability to apply the only available law to such issues.

Article 24—permitted context for claims

The first sub-article concerns us, and shows that any claims covered by Articles 18 and 19 cannot be made except according to the conditions and limits of the Convention. Ingenious lawyers have attempted to find ways to make a claim outside the Convention, if they can see some advantage in this, as has happened on a passenger liability claim which had become time-barred under the Convention; but it remained open to the carrier effectively to show that the claim must be subject to the Convention, and thus time-barred. Clearly, the principle is that the Warsaw system excludes any legal remedies other than those available under that Warsaw system.

Article 25—deprivation of limitation

In two sub-articles, the carrier is stripped of his limited liability if his employees, servants or agents commit wilful misconduct or such conduct as is considered to be equivalent to wilful misconduct. Such conduct must take place within the context of the "scope of employment". In this context, it is practically unknown for any claim other than one for theft to arise, and this has led to considerable divergence in interpretation between different countries.

At one end of the scale, one can see in the U.S.A. that it is very unlikely that one can achieve a ruling that theft by an employee would amount to wilful misconduct and thus overturn limited liability. In broad terms, an employee stealing during his normal work hours would be regarded as acting outside the scope of his employment. At the other end of the scale—for instance in Germany—it can be very difficult for a respondent to avoid the court concluding that wilful misconduct did take place in connection with the disappearance of cargo. However, some commentators consider this to be incorrect under the Convention, and one may expect that attempts will be made to set things aright. Thus in the case of an air carrier moving cargo between the U.S.A. and Germany, claimants and respondents may meet with diametrically opposed results depending on where the claim is submitted and pursued.

There are other interpretations falling between these extremes, and in general terms a wilful misconduct result in the U.K. is possible, but difficult. In general terms, carriers will strongly resist attempts to overturn limitation, with their liability insurers often being prepared to invest substantial sums in having lawyers defend such positions.

Thus, the only cases which go any distance are those where transit insurers have settled a very substantial sum for loss of cargo; their investigators have produced reasonable evidence that the air carriers' employees or agents have stolen the cargo, and their recovery advisors have recommended an attempt to overturn limitation.

The stage can be set for a vigorous and expensive struggle between opposing camps. The stakes can be high, with both sides spending considerable sums on litigation, each having some level of confidence in not only winning, but in obtaining a costs award which makes the effort worthwhile.

However, at this point, the stage is often set for compromise, with each side not truly wishing to go to court and spend vast sums on such endeavours. In most situations, the case will not make court and the transit insurer will finish up with a significant percentage of his claim settled, and the air carrier's liability insurers will feel they have avoided settling the whole amount.

Few such cases are likely to affect the everyday claims handler in the U.K. However, there are instances in which it can make a difference. What happens if there is substantial evidence of theft in the carrier's care, while the claim is not very high. Let us take as an example a cargo of watches worth £20,000, which is delivered by the carrier with the box slit open and half the contents undoubtedly pilfered. Is the carrier going to accept that the only possible conclusion is that his employees or agents were guilty of such pilferage in the scope of their employment and settle in full rather than adhere to limitation? The experience in such situations is that each carrier is likely to have a different approach. An American carrier whose local staff are obliged to seek the guidance of their U.S.A.-based claims handling superiors, is likely to handle the claim differently from a U.K. based carrier well versed in the U.K. situation. Much will depend on the claims handler's knowledge of this specific subject: the claimant sure of his ground may be able to persuade a competent respondent to compromise. A claimant unsure of his ground will make no progress, and a respondent unsure of his ground may well refer the matter to his headquarters whereupon it will simply stall. The claimant is left in the invidious position of knowing that the only route to success is litigation, which is likely to entail unacceptable expense in lawyers' fees.

Article 26—delivery and notices of claim

These centrally important points are dealt with in four sub-articles in which it is determined how delivery signatures shall be viewed, how long a claimant has to complain, how he must complain and what happens if no complaint is made as set down.

1. With a little thought, the wording of this is quite clear, but claimants and

respondents still have difficulty with it from time to time. The signature does not determine fully whether a claim is valid or excluded, because the evidence is *prima facie* evidence only. The point can be illustrated by two contrasting examples where, first, the carrier would have to give way and, secondly, a claimant would probably have to concede.

Take as an example a consignment of flowers, with cartons externally sound and no delay having taken place. The collecting driver can do nothing other than give a "clean" signature. Suppose he now trucks them to a depot a mile away, where the boxes are opened about 20 minutes later. The flowers are found dead or otherwise badly deteriorated. Some airlines will stubbornly insist that the signature ends all possibility of a claim, but, providing the claimant can adduce the necessary evidence to show that the damage occurred during carriage by air, the airline is likely to accept liability, albeit after a struggle, perhaps. Notwithstanding this, it is necessary to point out that a "clean signature" having been given, it becomes necessary for a claimant to move well beyond establishing simple reasonable doubt. A professional survey or other qualified testimony will be needed to establish that the damage had to have existed prior to delivery out by the airline.

Conversely, if there is a clean signature and the consignee alleges that there was major damage, which by its nature would probably have been apparent at the time of delivery, a carrier would be entitled to maintain that such extensive damage surely did not exist at the time of delivery. The claimant would have difficulty proving his case.

2. Time limits allowed for the giving of notice are set down here. After discovery of the damage the "person entitled to delivery" of the cargo—who is not necessarily the consignee, of course—must complain to the carrier within seven days. If a delay is the problem, then he has 14 days from the date on which the cargo should have been placed at his disposal in which to complain. It is worth noting at this point that any carrier using a standard IATA AWB is providing 14 days for giving notice for damage, and 21 days for notice of delay. Nothing stops a carrier being more generous than the Convention, of course.

It is most important to note that there is no provision for complaint due to loss, and we will return to this when discussing AWB conditions as they affect liability.

3. The complainant has a choice: either to annotate the "document of transportation"—presumably the delivery copy of the AWB set—to take account of the complaint or to complain in writing dispatched within the times set down in sub-article 2.

Use of the AWB for complaint is seen in the U.S.A., South America and one or two other places, but generally separate notices in writing are the norm. There is some uncertainty about what constitutes a notice, and care must be taken. For instance, where, on a document other than the air waybill, *viz.* the delivery signature book or register, a driver writes "Damaged" against his signature, this would not seem to be sufficient to be classed as a notice of claim.

On the other hand, if the driver writes against his signature "damaged. A claim will be made", then this seems to fulfil the necessary criteria. Counter-signing the damage report made out by the airline may not be regarded as notice of claim.

Certainly, separate notices have become the norm in the U.K. Thus, it is submitted that, for prudence, all claim notices should be given in the form of completely separate notices in writing, by letter or facsimile. It is also submitted that it is imprudent to use a computer-generated message to the airline—as many forwarding agents do—because the file print-out does not show a clear addressee or sender information, and is not properly dated: there is also a slight risk that respondents will try to maintain that such a message is not a "complaint in writing" as specified in the Convention, on the grounds that the framers of the Convention could not have had such a style of message in mind, because such forms were not available at the time.

A word about the term "dispatch": it is quite clear that the notice does not have to be *received* by the carrier. The claimant has only to dispatch it. He may have to prove that he dispatched it within the specified times, but it can be an important point.

4. If no complaint is made within the specified times, it is quite clear that the carrier has no case to answer.

Article 27—"death" of carrier

This Article seems to have little obvious application for the industry claims handler nowadays. Clearly, there are light aircraft operators receiving reward for carrying small items of cargo and, in a fatal crash, the application seems very clear.

Article 28—jurisdiction and legal proceedings

This covers the question of where an unsatisfied claimant can initiate legal proceedings. Generally, he is entitled to submit it in the country of origin, which is usually the country where the contract of carriage was made, the country of destination or the country in which the carrier has his principal place of business. (If the contract were made in country other than of destination, or origin, or the "home" country of the carrier, then if the carrier maintains an office there, the claimant can bring his claim there. It seems that such a situation is not common, and may not in fact be to the advantage of the claimant anyway by virtue of the particular laws existing there.)

The second sub-article shows that the court to which the case is submitted shall proceed with the case according to its own law. One or two strange decisions have been made in the past in Canada and the U.S.A. on this point, but in general it does not give rise to misunderstandings.

Article 29—time bar

Two years are allowed from the date of arrival, the date when the carrying aircraft should have arrived or the date on which transportation stopped. If the claim is not agreed within that time, then *all claim rights are extinguished*: of course, if an agreement to settle has been made prior to the two year time bar but not implemented, then that appears to be a separate "contract", falling outside the Convention—in that sense, of course, the claimant does not lose his rights, becoming entitled to enforce that "'contract" according to common law precedent.

The extinguishing of claim rights seems absolutely clear and, technically, the carrier has no power to extend that period, as is regularly done with sea carriage cases and occasionally in civil contract contexts such as BIFA. This is all well and good if a carrier purports to extend beyond the period for (say) three months, and the claim is settled in that time.

However, if, a few weeks into the purportedly extended period, the carrier finally and positively rejects the claim, the claimant can no longer commence proceedings. His rights are extinguished. A court might consider the respondent's behaviour reprehensible, but would have no choice but to confirm the position. (There have even been a few cases where a claims handler has "extended" the period and cynically repudiated the claim a little way into the "extended" period.)

Article 30—successive carriers

Three sub-articles deal with a cargo movement involving two or more carriers performing successive sectors of the carriage, and what rights the consignor and consignee have against them.

1. The first sub-article confirms that where one carrier performs the first part of a carriage, and then a second performs the next part, and so on, each of those carriers is subject to the Convention. It seldom gives rise to difficulties.

2. The second sub-article is not commented upon, as it concerns passenger liability.

3. The final sub-article shows that the consignor has a right of action against the first carrier, and the consignee a right of action against the final carrier, and that each has a right against the carrier in whose possession the events giving rise to the claim occurred.

Chapter IV—provisions relating to combined transportation—Article 31

It is probable that this provision will become more important as airlines continue to expand their use of trucking, and reference should be made to earlier comments on Article 18(3).

Generally, trucking appears to be carried out by airlines without their ever requesting specific agreement from the cargo owners' representatives, and little thought is given to liability in the event of a loss occurring during trucking. This makes for difficulty in such claims, the airline generally being unable to avoid settling in accordance with Warsaw Convention. Perhaps they could avoid it, but in practical terms avoidance does not appear to have been sought.

This provision allows the airline to incorporate terms other than Warsaw in order to cover trucking. When international borders are crossed, the CMR Convention could be applied to all but personal effects, household goods and funeral consignments; for domestic trucking terms comparable to those of RHA and BIFA might be incorporated. The advantage to the carrier is clear, with smaller limitations and different time limits for notice available. However, there seem to be no moves by airlines to take advantage of this option. Should they seek to do so in future, then they would be prudent to consider "Unfair Contracts" legislation first.

Chapter V—general and final provisions

Practically all the remaining eight Articles are of no relevance to the everyday claims handler, with the exception of Articles 32 and 34.

Article 32 does not permit a carrier and shipper to agree rules different from the Convention on which law or jurisdiction to apply. Some years ago, an East African carrier was seen to stamp AWBs executed in its home country, purporting to require any claims to be settled by the law of that country: this was null and void, and a case brought against that carrier in the U.K. could not be resisted.

Article 34 makes clear that the word "days" in the Convention means current days, and not working days. Thus, seven days allowed for notice cannot be said not to include a weekend.

Warsaw/Hague

The original Warsaw Convention allows any "high contracting party"—which perhaps we would term a "state" in everyday parlance—to call upon the French government to convene a fresh international conference to review the Convention. Such conferences have occurred several times, and a series of revisions has been made to the Convention. However, for many reasons only three have so far been brought into effect. The Warsaw Convention 1929 amended by the Hague Protocol in 1955 found favour in the majority of countries, but the denunciation of it by the U.S.A. some years later ensured that world-wide acceptance was not to be achieved.

The central issues addressed at the 1955 conference were, in fact, the increase of passenger liability limitations and the relaxing of time limits for the giving of notice of claim for both baggage and cargo. Other issues dealt with were a minor change in the definition of international carriage, a declaration that AWBs could be negotiable and modification of provisions dealing with wilful misconduct.

Despite the later denunciation by the U.S.A. of the Protocol, the Americans had urged that liability limits were exclusive of the costs and expenses of litigation. That remains the case today.

The Carriage by Air Act 1961 became U.K. law and subsequently further international conferences were held, at which amendments of Warsaw/Hague were drafted and put forward. Montreal Additional Protocol No. 2 was promulgated in the Carriage by Air and Road Act 1979, from which two important changes were enforced; and this latter Act provides for the later activation of Montreal Protocol Nos. 3 and 4, of which more later.

We will now look at the amendments which distinguish this version of the Convention from the original, in so far as it affects regular claims handling. In general terms we will not cover the minor changes which seldom affect our regular work.

Relevant amended articles

Article 8—AWB particulars

The requirement for AWB particulars is fundamentally simplified, in that the places of departure and destination must be shown; if the places of departure and destination are within the territory of one state (High Contracting Party) adhering to the amended Convention, and there is one agreed stopping place or more, then at least one of the stopping places must be shown; and, finally, there must be a notice on the AWB drawing the attention of the consignor (shipper) to the possible applicability of the Warsaw Convention.

Article 9—effect of absence of AWB particulars

If the carrier agrees[2] to the cargo being loaded on an aircraft without an air waybill or the notice drawing the shipper's attention to the possibility of the Warsaw Convention applying to the carriage having been made out, the carrier is deprived of this limitation of liability.

In practice, due to the general procedures operated by most airlines, the likelihood of loading cargo without AWBs seems remote. This provision appears to be of more relevance to airlines chartering their aircraft to perhaps one shipper, where the requirement for an air waybill may just be overlooked when considering the charter agreement.

Article 15—negotiable AWBs

It appears that there was some expectation that AWBs could become negotiable (analogous to ocean carriage bills of lading). However, this appears unlikely,

2. Note that agreement can be signified by the carrier simply not objecting to loading without an air waybill.

and standard AWB forms generally carry a notice to the effect that they are not negotiable.

On rare occasions, shippers and consignors more accustomed to maritime carriage make assumptions of negotiability, and, in the event of an innocent but mistaken delivery by a carrier, such shippers and consignors may cite the non-production of a particular original copy of the AWB at the time of delivery as grounds for holding the carrier liable. This is, of course, not a valid ground, although other grounds may be.

Article 22—limitation of liability

This provision underwent some change in form, but only three important differences affect us today as far as cargo is concerned.

Limitation amounts As mentioned above, a few months before writing, a fundamental change took place with the promulgation of the Carriage by Air and Road Act 1979 (Commencement No. 2) Order 1997. This Order has provided that limitation is to be expressed in terms of 17 SDRs per kilo, which, of course, is simple to calculate.

However, it should be noted—and at this point again refer to the section entitled "Major Difficulties produced by recent U.K. legislation" above—there may be some difficulty. There is a question as to how far 17 SDRs can be properly applied. Returning to the theme of reciprocity as to which regime applies, it must be noted that with the above legislation, the original version of Warsaw/Hague was effectively "removed" from the statute books. This may leave a vacuum where in a particular claim the origin or destination country is not a signatory to the Montreal 2 version of Warsaw/Hague: it may be that there is no correct law with regard to the limitation to apply to such a claim.

Where such a situation exists, and claimant and respondent cannot agree on the applicable limitation, then it may be better to negotiate a settlement, because the alternative of seeking a judicial decision would seem exceptionally unattractive.

Package weight Sub-article 2(b) provides that the weight to be taken into account in determining the limitation is the total weight of the package or packages concerned. Thus, under the unamended Convention, if 1 kilo were missing from a 10 kilo package, liability would arise on 1 kilo; under Warsaw/Hague, if 1 kilo were missing from a 10 kilo package, then liability would arise on 10 kilos. Clearly, this is of considerable importance, as it represents an improvement for claimants.

Litigation expenses Sub-article 4 makes clear that a court can make costs and expense of litigation awards in excess of liability limits. That is not dealt with under the unamended Convention. It is important to note that if a carrier has made an offer of settlement within six months of the occurrence of the events giving rise to the claim, and a subsequent court case results in a damages award which does not exceed the amount then offered, an award of costs will not be made.

Thus, it is probably prudent for a carrier, where relevant and appropriate, to express a limitation offer in SDRs, rather than in a currency such as dollars or sterling. The point is that if the SDR value changes by the time of the court case, then the actual court award based on SDRs could exceed an original offer expressed in dollars or sterling, even if the carrier had originally based its offer on the then-current value of the SDR. In such a situation, by the literal wording of Article 22(4) an award of costs would be likely to follow.

Expressing a limitation offer in SDRs appears to eliminate the possibility of an award of costs in such cases. But it seems open to the carrier offering such an SDR settlement to indicate to the claimant the value of the SDR at the time of the making of the offer without compromising itself in this respect.

Article 23—minimum levels of liability

An addition was made here to allow provisions for "inherent defect, quality or vice of the cargo" to be applied to the AWB contract without being ruled out by the overall effect of this Article.

When one examines the defence allowed under Article 20 of the unamended Convention, this addition seems almost unnecessary, and it seems seldom to come up in claims considerations. However, it can lead to some difficulties, where a respondent carrier attempts to maintain that an inherent "quality" is involved. Clearly, the use of the words, "defect" and "vice" is easy enough to comprehend, but it is not unknown for a defending carrier to hold that it should not be held to account for a cargo which has an inherent quality of deterioration. It is submitted that by virtue of the term "inherent quality" a respondent is entitled to put a claimant to proof of sound quality prior to tender of the cargo to the respondent. It is difficult to see how any further conclusion could be drawn from the wording.

There is an echo here of occasions on which U.S. carriers mistakenly attempt to use CAB rules (which actually do not apply to international carriage where they conflict with Warsaw rules) to defend themselves against claims for perishables. If the perishables are damaged during delayed transit, carriers have been known to quote a particular CAB tariff rule providing that perishables must be packed to enable them to withstand three days' transit.

There may be an inherent quality of deterioration, but, of course, the carrier cannot abandon or deny his duty of care during the period for which the goods are in its or its agents' care.

Thus, if a delay is unavoidable, perhaps because the aircraft has a mechanical problem, and it is not possible for the carrier to re-accommodate the cargo on another flight to its destination, spring onions (as an example) can be expected to deteriorate inexorably, unless they are cold-stored. The carrier is obliged to cold-store them if that is at all possible, and, if appropriate, invite this shipper to retrieve the goods.

Article 25—intentional or reckless conduct

The wording was changed from "wilful misconduct" to an "act or omission ... done with intent to cause damage or recklessly and with knowledge that damage would probably result".

However, it seems that the regular industry claims handler is unlikely to be involved in strenuous arguments about the meanings involved and, for our purposes, the comments on Article 25 of the unamended Convention should be considered to apply equally.

Article 26—delivery and notices of claim

Two changes are important here: the first is directly within the redrafted wording and the second has been enacted subsequently in U.K. law.

The first change concerned the relaxation of the time limits with regard to notices of claim from seven to 14 days' notice for damage to cargo, reckoned from delivery, and from 14 to 21 for delay to cargo, reckoned from the day the cargo should have been placed at the disposal of the person entitled to delivery. This difference is in line with the provisions shown on the standard IATA 600b AWB contract conditions.

The second change is set down in section 2 of the Carriage by Air and Road Act 1979, which provides that references to "damage" shall include loss of part of the cargo. Thus, it appears that a carrier is entitled to decline a claim for loss of one piece of a multi-piece consignment if no notice of claim has been presented within the time limit specified in the Convention for the giving of notice of claim for damage, *viz.* 14 days.

Future developments—Montreal Protocols Nos. 3 and 4

Of the various attempts made over the years to *fundamentally* amend the original Convention, the only one to get as far as becoming U.K. law is "The Warsaw Convention as amended at the Hague, 1955, and by Montreal Additional Protocol No. 3 and 4, 1975". This version presents very significant changes, whereas Protocols No. 1 and 2 might be termed "tinkering" in comparison.

It was enacted within the Carriage by Air and Road Act 1979 (the full text appearing in schedule I thereto): it has not been brought into effect yet, although it is reported that sufficient nations have signed up to it to enable it to come into force. It remains to be seen how soon the U.K. government will activate it.

At the time of writing, it was reported that the U.S.A. had not signed. Global commercial pressure may bring this about, and there is a feeling amongst champions of these latest amendments that when they come into effect, there will be a subsequent evolution of trading practices, and the U.S.A. will be forced to "conform": considering other areas in which the U.S.A. has taken its own line, this seems uncertain at best, and the level of air cargo between the U.S.A. and the rest of the world—unaffected by this latest revision— will keep many claims handlers working on the original unamended Warsaw Convention for a while yet.

Its coming will change the law of air carriage considerably, and paradoxically will complete the move towards complexity in application of overall law, and simultaneously simplify the liability and mode of operation by carriers.

Thankfully, there seems no further comparable measure in prospect, and one could suppose the next step, if any, will be to resile towards simplification. How that will be dealt with, if at all, is anyone's guess at present. Perhaps we may be set for many years of difficulty.

Simplicity

The air waybill Articles 5 to 16 of Warsaw/Hague are replaced by a new set of provisions. In particular, the AWB is no longer necessary, and can be replaced by "other means which would preserve a record of the carriage to be performed". This appears to open up the way to electronic "AWBs" or "paperless trading". One can envisage no documentation travelling with cargo, which may reduce carriers' costs markedly, enabling a reduction in paper-processing staff, and so on. However, will it be that simple? Will the lack of paperwork give rise to other difficulties? What about harmonising customs procedures around the world with the new scheme? These and many other questions will doubtless be answered.

Liability of the carrier Subject to the question of contributory negligence, and to the event giving rise to the claim having occurred during air transportation, the carrier will be liable for damages sustained due to loss and (physical) damage.

Specific defences are also available: inherent defect, quality or vice; defective packing, provided the carrier has not packed the cargo; an act of war or conflict; and an act of public authority concerning the transit, exit or entry of the cargo in question.

The carrier remains liable for damages caused by delay, subject to the contributory negligence question and to his being able to prove that all necessary measures to avoid the damage were taken, or that it was impossible to do so.

Limit of carrier's liability Limitation is set at 17 SDRs per kilo.

Loss of limitation There will be an unbreakable limitation. A claimant's ability to prove intentional or reckless conduct, thereby depriving the carrier of limitation, will no longer exist. This, of course, will set such air carriage apart from other major international types of carriage in being the only one where claimants have no means of overcoming limits. Doubtless, when this imposes itself on the consciousness of the industry and of transit and liability insurers, it will make a considerable difference to the carriage of high-value goods—bullion and computers and their components shipped in notable bulk come to mind immediately. Doubtless, readers will think of a good number of other cargoes with values well above limitation.

Whilst this appears to be the correct conclusion to be drawn from articles 25 and 25A, there seems to be an absurdity within 25A.1: a reading of this infers strongly that it is anticipated that an action can be brought against a servant or agent of the carrier, and that unless he proves he acted within the scope of his employment, he is not entitled to use limits of liability under the Convention. However, in 25 and 25A.2, there seems an absolute bar to liability falling outside of that laid down in the Convention. So what does it mean? We shall have to wait and see if plaintiffs and their lawyers can be ingenious enough to exploit this apparent absurdity.

Complication

Activation of the Carriage by Air and Road Act 1979 in full will complete a set of six separate schemes of liability for air cargo carriage:

1. Unamended Warsaw Convention carriage, since some nations including the U.S.A. have not signed either Montreal Protocol No. 1, or Montreal Protocols Nos. 3 and 4;
2. Warsaw/Hague carriage, since, again, some nations have not signed Montreal Protocol No. 2. This actually could become an extremely difficult area, since—as noted above—the U.K. government appears to have—in effect—removed the original Warsaw/Hague Convention from the statute books, possibly leaving a legal vacuum. One of the possible routes out of the difficulty may be to accept that any reciprocal treaty which previously governed such carriage no longer exists, and in such cases, "Non-Warsaw" rules may fill that vacuum;
3. Non-Warsaw carriage, which should remain unchanged, where nations have signed none of the Conventions or Protocols;
4. Unamended Warsaw Montreal Protocol No. 1 carriage, activated in 1998 by the U.K. government;
5. Warsaw/Hague Protocol No. 2 carriage, activated in 1997 by the U.K. government; and
6. Warsaw/Hague Montreal Protocols Nos. 3 and 4 carriage, which will presumably activate in the near future.

At the very least, claims handlers' working lives could become very interesting, and where the stakes are high in particular claims, it seems possible that litigation will be ignited by these uncertainties.

GUADALAJARA CONVENTION

The Guadalajara Convention was enacted into U.K. law by the Carriage by Air (Supplementary Provisions) Act 1962. There seem to be few occasions when this Convention is considered actively, so for practical claims-handling purposes it is probably as well simply to describe how it affects the industry more obviously.

Thankfully, there are hardly any reported court cases with regard to the Guadalajara Convention. If the question of its applicability arises, one can note the following. In the U.K., it is almost certainly applicable to all categories of air carriage; the government have ensured so within the various acts and orders referred to above. Presumably, the same will be done for carriage under Montreal Protocols Nos. 3 and 4 as well. Sometimes it is asked if the origin and destination countries both have to be signatories to this Convention. Whilst in a German court case it was found applicable only if both countries are signatories, and in a Belgian case if either country is a signatory, the 1962 U.K. Act appears to contain no such limitations, and thus the Convention is to be applied to any and all Warsaw Convention carriage.

Any forwarder is free to issue its own air waybill contract for the carriage. The motive is to profit by the difference between the amount it charges for freight and the amount it pays the airline for the space. It is probable that the vast majority of air cargo moves in this fashion within consolidations. It is also not unusual for a forwarder issuing its own air waybill to approach another forwarder who in turn issues *its* own air waybill before approaching the consolidator. Such air waybills are known as house air waybills, as opposed to the airline air waybill covering the consolidation, which is then known as the master air waybill.

The forwarder/contracting carrier's liabilities

In such cases, forwarders become principals instead of agents—they are not simply "arranging" the carriage but undertaking themselves to carry, albeit by sub-contracting. The Guadalajara Convention deals directly with this situation, and shows that such a principal's liability must be considered with full adherence to the Warsaw Convention: it classes such a forwarder as a "contracting carrier", and for clarity we will refer to the party as the "forwarder/contracting carrier".

Thus, taking the simplest case of the one forwarder/contracting carrier with his house air waybill, what are his liabilities? In order to comprehend this, we must consider the complete transit from the customer's premises onwards. The first part of the journey is unlikely to be air transportation, since it will probably consist of collection by road from his customer, probably to his own warehouse, where the cargo is prepared for air carriage, *viz.* labelled and marked, and properly weighed, followed by carriage to the consolidator whom he chooses. If anything goes wrong during this period, he is fully entitled to apply his standard trading conditions—BIFA or some variation thereof—because air transportation has clearly not commenced.

Once he has delivered to the consolidator, what are the forwarder/contracting carrier's liabilities up to the time of delivery into the care of the airline? Again, there is no air transportation, and he can still apply his standard trading conditions. There is an added dimension—he can attempt to recover any claim he is called upon to pay out from the consolidator who caused the problem. (It is to be noted that the consolidator is also defined as a contracting carrier, and is in precisely the same position as the forwarder/contracting carrier with whom we started.)

After delivery to the airline by the consolidator, what are his liabilities? They are undeniably Warsaw Convention, with the supplementary facet that he can attempt to take recourse against the consolidator, who must answer the claim in a Warsaw context. The consolidator, in his turn, may attempt recourse against the actual airline.

In practical terms, there is no difficulty where, of course, the actual carrying airline acknowledges the loss and processes the claim. However, an airline refusing to accept the claim poses a serious problem. Can the forwarder/contracting carrier rid himself of the claim by paying on the basis of his standard trading conditions? In a good number of cases, the claimant will accept an offer based on standard trading conditions, whether through ignorance of his entitlements or other reason.

However, the Guadalajara Convention makes it clear that the forwarder/contracting carrier in this position is a carrier falling fully under the Warsaw Convention and its liability provisions.

Taking a slightly different situation, a forwarder/contracting carrier sometimes sub-contracts one airline to a transhipment point and then sub-contracts a second airline—usually operating wholly outside the U.K.—to get the cargo to its final destination. What then is the forwarder/contracting carrier's position? If the first airline is responsible for the loss, the claim can usually proceed more or less. However, it is common in these situations for the second carrier, if responsible for the loss, simply to fail to respond to the forwarder/contracting carrier's entreaties to settle. It is of course unlikely that the forwarder/contracting carrier can get the first carrier to assist, since the forwarder/contracting carrier will have employed separate carriers in an unconnected way.

Simply put, if the forwarder/contracting carrier cannot get the second carrier to settle, then he is going to be responsible for settling the claim. A court would probably order settlement against the forwarder/contracting carrier, leaving him to his own devices concerning recourse.

Delivery out by the final carrying airline usually marks the point at which the house air waybill contract of carriage has run its course, and the forwarder/contracting carrier's liability normally ends fully at that point.

Notices of claim

Another provision of this Convention is that notice of claim against a forwarder/contracting carrier is effectively notice against the actual carrier. The converse is also true. This can theoretically lead to a situation where the actual carrier never learns about a claim situation until the process is perhaps well under way. Yet he can be held liable for a claim which would have normally failed against him due to late notice, had there been no house air waybill involved.

An airline appears unable to defend a claim where the forwarder/contracting carrier did not pass on a notice of claim. However, it is possible that the carrier would have some kind of recourse outside air carriage rules against a forwarder/contracting carrier who failed to pass on such a notice.

CHAPTER 10

NON-WARSAW

Here we are contemplating cargo routeings where origin or destination is in a country which is a non-signatory to any of the versions of the Warsaw Convention currently in force, and the corresponding origin or destination is in the U.K. Claims handlers with more wide-ranging duties may have to deal with the odd exotic routeing which does not involve the Warsaw Convention: such routeings do not constitute the bulk of air cargo, but a typical example would be carriage between Thailand and the U.K.

Under U.K. law, non-Warsaw carriage is termed "non-international carriage"—for some this is confusing because, until recently, carriage between the U.K. and Hong Kong was properly "non-international", which feels slightly odd. However, of course, for most nations which do not have possessions abroad, the term is not confusing. We will stick to the term "non-Warsaw".

The law is contained in Schedule 1 of the Carriage by Air Acts (Application of Provisions) Order 1967. The scheme of the rules follows the Warsaw/Hague version of the Convention, but has no provision for documentation. So far as we are concerned, no air waybill need be issued, although doubtless one is routinely made out. Liability limitation is set at 17 SDRs per kilo by virtue of the Carriage by Air Acts (Application of Provisions) Order 1967, as amended in 1979 and 1981. Few specific issues are known to have arisen under this set of rules.

CHAPTER 11

AIR WAYBILL CONDITIONS

The majority of airlines use the standard IATA resolution 600b set of air waybill conditions. Those who drafted these conditions would appear to have been primarily familiar with passenger conditions, since there are definite echoes of conditions peculiar to passengers.

The conditions are essentially restatements of parts of the Warsaw Convention, contain a few inconsistencies with the Convention and have a small but definite effect on liability. We will run through them, drawing out points of interest.

Notice

This concerns the requirement in Article 8 of the Convention to give notice of the application of Warsaw, and without it the carrier is probably liable for damages without an upper limit.

Paragraph 1—definitions

This sets out a couple of definitions which have no practical effect on everyday claims handling.

Paragraph 2—applicability of rules

Part (a) simply restates the applicability of Warsaw and non-Warsaw rules. However, part (b)(iii) has some important implications for claims arising out of delay. The carrier's schedules are incorporated into the contract of carriage, save for the actual times of departure and arrival. Clearly, this is very important for the consideration of alleged delay.

Paragraph 3—name and address on AWB

In general terms this reflects existing provisions under Warsaw rules.

Paragraph 4—limitation of liability

This paragraph purports to deal with carriage which is not subject to the Warsaw Convention, seeking to apply a limitation of U.S.$ 20 per kilogram in the context of carriage which is not Warsaw.

However, as is readily apparent, it seems redundant where non-Warsaw carriage is concerned, because in the U.K. there are statutory rules on non-Warsaw carriage. In particular, the limitation is 17 SDRs per kilogram. Thus, by virtue of paragraph 23 of the relevant rules, this paragraph becomes null and void. However, in jurisdictions where there are, perhaps, no specific rules on non-Warsaw carriage, it is almost certainly applicable.

Finally, if an airline is trucking cargo between airports, and this is known and agreed to by the shipper, and there is no reason to categorise this sector of the carriage as air transportation, then it would appear that the U.S.$ 20 limitation applies. (It seems that this point seldom occurs to an airline claims handler, and thus he does not seek to apply it.)

Paragraph 5—special declaration of value

This echoes the provisions of paragraph 22 of both the Warsaw and non-Warsaw rules concerning a special declaration of value. Its effect is simply to raise the limitation of liability to the specified level and it changes nothing concerning the question of liability itself. However, experience is that this facility is seldom used.

Paragraph 6—package weight limitation

While the meaning of this clause seems clear, it is null and void in certain contexts of Warsaw/Hague. First, the conditions seek to apply the Warsaw/Hague rule of package weight for determining limitation to the whole of the carriage. This is all well and good with respect to unamended Warsaw, since it is more generous than Warsaw Article 22. However, the AWB condition is null and void in relation to Article 22(2)(b) of Warsaw/Hague where it is provided that if loss of part of the consignment affects the value of the remainder, then liability arises on the whole: Article 22 ensures this.

Finally, for carriage involving the U.S.A. as origin or destination, an additional clause provides that the weight used for calculating the freight will be the one used for calculating the limitation. Thus, claimants in relation to a very light-weight cargo subject to a "volumetric" charge for freight, will be entitled to limitation based on the "volumetric" weight.

Paragraph 7—protection of agents, and others

This condition seeks to extend limitation rules and other ancillary benefits to agents, servants and representatives of the actual carrier and of the contracting carrier.

In practice, there is seldom any benefit in pursuing such parties direct, and in recent years this has been almost unheard of. Some lawyers have sought this route to compensation for their clients, but there seems little benefit, and in some cases such actions are ill-founded. (Those familiar with ocean carriers' bills of lading will be aware of "Himalaya" clauses.)

Paragraph 8—reasonable dispatch (avoidance of delay)

This is of considerable importance in claims.

In both parts of this paragraph, the carrier undertakes to complete the carriage with reasonable dispatch, and this is relevant to assessing claims for delay. The term "reasonable dispatch" may be different where perishables are concerned, as compared to dry goods, machinery and so on.

The carrier's knowledge of the needs of the commodity will be relevant to consideration of a claim. After all, for example, the carrier knows that delay to fish must be avoided, and there are few excuses for delay in such circumstances. On the other hand, a consolidation where the consolidator is buying at a cheap rate because the carrier does not guarantee immediate dispatch to its destination must be judged differently: if the delay becomes more than a couple of days, then this may constitute a delay, but not otherwise.

The carrier is authorised to substitute other air carriers and other means of transportation. This is seldom a problem under U.K. law, but in some jurisdictions this would be tantamount to a "deviation" from the agreed carriage, bringing with it penalties of loss of limitation and so on. This provision makes it clear that the shipper agrees that deviation from the routeing indicated on the face of the air waybill is allowed.

Paragraph 9—period of responsibility

This is a straight statement of liability wholly in line with paragraph 18 of the Warsaw and non-Warsaw rules.

Paragraph 10—shipper's guarantee and payment of freight

Part (a) of this paragraph sets up a guarantee that the shipper will pay the charges for carriage. The practical effect of this seems to be that if a consignment reaches its destination with a "charges collect" arrangement and the consignee fails to pay the charges, the carrier is entitled to demand the freight from the shipper. The carrier is likely to succeed if it can show that it was unable to obtain payment from the consignee.

There seem to be no cases known involving this principle, although from time to time it has been possible to succeed with this. It is supposed that few cases of this sort involve large sums of money and, accordingly, would be most unlikely to reach court and thus be reported as a precedent.

Part (b) is a little odd, because a carrier cannot refuse to settle a claim when freight charges have not been paid: such an attempt appears to be ruled out by virtue of paragraph 23 of the Warsaw and non-Warsaw rules, since the body of those rules says nothing about such a principle.

Action for payment of freight is a separate issue subject to its own very strong rules. As seen above, there are few defences against a claim by a carrier for its freight.

Occasionally, a carrier takes a position and refuses to deal with a claim for loss until the freight is paid: the carrier may technically be entitled to do this, but to do so may be quite absurd in terms of both customer relations and practicality.

Paragraph 11—notice of arrival

This merely restates the statutory provisions concerning the giving of notice of arrival at destinations and has no practical effect different from existing rules.

Paragraph 12—notice periods

Parts (a)(i), (ii), and (iii) effectively standardise notice periods as related to the unamended Warsaw and Warsaw/Hague Conventions: it will be recalled that Warsaw/Hague is more generous on notice periods than the unamended version.

All notice periods are generally brought into line with Warsaw/Hague provisions. While one would suppose that the shorter notice periods under the unamended Warsaw Convention would be favoured by American carriers, nearly all of them have nonetheless adopted the IATA standard conditions.

Parts (a)(i) and (ii) seem to be unnecessarily separated, since the term "damage" is not further defined either by the Convention or by non-Warsaw rules. There seems to be a slight echo of the CMR rules here, since they set out different rules for damage visible at time of delivery and concealed damage.

Part (a)(iv) is redundant under U.K. law, since it is not permitted by virtue of Article 23 of the Convention and the non-Warsaw rules.

Defences to claims have been made in Europe on this basis, but have failed. It seems that no carrier would attempt a defence on this ground again. However—surprisingly—it will succeed in the U.S.A., as some cases have shown.

It should be noted in particular that no notice is required for loss—except that under Warsaw/Hague carriage, U.K. law equates partial loss to damage, and thus a notice of claim is required.

Paragraph 13—shippers' obligations

Again, this is a restatement of the shipper's obligations.

Paragraph 14—authority to vary air waybill conditions

This is interesting, because if a senior cargo sales manager or director of an airline makes some special agreement with a shipper—perhaps a valued consolidator producing a lot of business—then can the airline in a claims situation maintain that the manager or director acted outside his authority? No examples of this are known, but some readers may know of some relevant situations.

Paragraph 15—transit insurance

This sets out the general provisions of transit insurance which may be available from some carriers. Such insurance tends seldom to be used, since it can be expensive in relation to other transit insurance available from the more traditional insurance world. The tendency is for most parties requiring transit insurance to purchase cover for individual consignments through insurance brokers or to have a standing transit insurance policy for their cargo movements. Occasionally, personal effects shippers and people moving their household goods by air arrange air waybill insurance, but it is the exception rather than the rule.

Finally, a number of carriers in fact offer no such transit insurance facility, despite using an air waybill form with a box for insurance valuation on the front, and conditions referring to it on the reverse.

CHAPTER 12

AIRLINE HANDLING AGREEMENTS

The principle that it is cheaper for airlines to "farm out" both cargo handling and cargo sales has long been a part of the airline industry. A number of larger consolidators (forwarder/contracting carriers) have also adopted this principle. This tendency continues to grow, and most airline executives would probably agree that this is a better option, although it is not without its difficulties. It seems likely that "self-handling" of cargo by airlines will continue to dwindle to only main airports in the carrier's home country, and will be retained there for other than essentially commercial reasons.

As for consolidators, many remain "self-handling", and it seems unlikely that many more will wish to move towards "farming out" in the near future.

General sales agents (GSAs) do not have a great effect on liability apart from, occasionally, booking cargo on their customers' route systems and purporting to set up a transit which for one reason or another turns out to be impossible to perform without delay or to perform at all.

Of course, general handling agents (GHAs) are far more often the source of claims than GSAs. Loss, damage and mis-routeings leading to delay occur in their warehouses in the familiar manner. Accordingly, we will concentrate on GHAs.

The liability issue between airlines and consolidators and their GHAs is controlled by a more or less standard IATA form of contract. It has been undergoing some evolution in recent years, but the basic principles have remained unchanged from the early days. The bulk of the contract deals with duties to be undertaken and accounting practices between the parties, but there is always a clause—usually number 8 and generally known as the "hold harmless" agreement—in which both parties agree not to hold each other liable if one party causes the other to sustain a claim. The effect is heavily loaded in favour of the agent, since the frequency of claims against the agent—of which the airlines or consolidators may be the cause—is low indeed, as compared to claims against the airlines of which the agent is the cause.

The one exception to this rule is when wilful misconduct is involved. Wilful misconduct in this context can surely only mean theft by agents' staff—a Warsaw Convention Article 25 issue—and this leads to loss by agents of the "hold harmless" boon. They must indemnify their customers. (On very rare occasions, there is malicious damage or vandalism by an employee. However, it is common for agents to avoid having to indemnify their customers where pilferage is concerned. Sometimes such pilferage is blatant, but few airlines' or consolidators' executives will press the issue and obtain the indemnity to which they are entitled where petty theft is involved.)

It has been reported that in some handling agreements recently negotiated, or renewed, the "hold harmless" clause has been substituted with a simple negligence clause, wherein the handling agent is required to answer for claims arising from his act of omission. In most Warsaw carriage contexts the agent will remain eligible to use Warsaw limited liability; it will now be effectively exposed to situations where limited liability may be overturned.

There appears to be strong competition among potential GHAs for the business of handling airlines' and consolidators' cargo, and understandably this drives down the prices paid to GHAs by their customers. While the "hold harmless" agreement seems too heavily weighted in favour of the GHAs, there is a reasonable argument for limiting or substantially reducing the agents' exposure to claims in return for keeping down handling charges. This argument appears to have gone too far in some people's view, with a general acceptance that an agent may be responsible for the most serious losses, but, because they occur through the agent's employees' simple but otherwise innocent negligence, the agent cannot be held liable to pay the claim or reimburse the settlement which his client must pay.

While the keen rates paid for the service are to the benefit of the airlines and consolidators, there are grounds for maintaining that they cannot expect too much from the agents. They should not expect claims to be freely reimbursed nor—as many industry members will corroborate—should they expect the service levels to be very high.

In practice, there may be ways and means for airlines and consolidators to persuade the agent to pay up, but much depends on the client's standing with the agent. It is not difficult, if the agent is so minded, to dismiss its client's pressure to contribute to a loss on which a claim has had to be paid. The importance of the client to the agent and the client's ability or resolve to move to another agent may be tested to the extreme—otherwise, the client will have to put up with bad service and regular claims, about which he can effectively do nothing.

There is little more to be said about the "hold harmless" wording, except to note that there have been some attempts to reinterpret it.

Apart from the handling agreement contract terms, the agent will often be trading under standard conditions in other contexts, and may use BIFA or perhaps even RHA terms. Some lawyers have attempted to show that even if the wilful misconduct rider is invoked, liability remains limited to the standard liability under the agents' other standard BIFA or RHA trading conditions. In almost every case the handling agreement will have been negotiated between the agent and the airline or consolidator without any reference to BIFA or RHA conditions, and as such it cannot or should not have been incorporated into the handling agreement.

Perhaps a single reading of the "hold harmless" clause seems to show that it stands by itself, and does not require the addition of other conditions in order to operate properly. Let us examine the situation where the consolidator or airline is threatened with loss of limited liability due to the GHA's staff having been responsible for theft of cargo. If such a situation becomes a serious matter, it is almost certain to be because the subject cargo was of high value. In such cases, the airline or consolidator must involve its insurers at the earliest possible stage, and they are almost certain to take over the conduct of the claim from that point. However, the alternatives are actually fairly straightforward and number two only.

When the loss has been investigated, it will be more—or less—clear whether the GHA's staff are responsible. If it is not certain that they are, then the airline's or consolidator's insurers may elect to allow litigation to proceed, knowing that if the case is found for the claimants, then the likelihood is that the GHA will have no choice but to indemnify the airline or consolidator for the claim which must be paid, and for all the legal costs involved. It is almost certain that the airline's or consolidator's insurers will have ensured that the GHA is "joined" to the legal action at an early stage if the claimants have not already made sure of that.

However, by the time such a case reaches its conclusion all parties will have incurred significant legal costs with lawyers. So is there an alternative? If it seems likely that limitation cannot be defended, or that the defence is not certain, claimants may be induced on a "without prejudice"[1] basis to enter into negotiations fairly early on. Prior to such negotiations, discussions between the airline's or consolidator's insurers' representatives and the GHA's similar representatives should take place. The case for potential loss of limitation should be recognised in the discussions and an understanding and acceptance of that position by the GHA's representatives should be sought, along with a recognition of the potentially high costs of defence. If this is achieved, then tripartite negotiation should be attempted between claimants, airline or consolidator, and the GHA, in which a settlement agreement is sought. Claimants will normally recognise that they face similar high costs and an uncertain time-scale, and may be prepared to concede a proportion of the claim to permit an early result.

Common-sense results have been obtained where the claimant has conceded

1. The term "without prejudice" denotes that in such negotiations much can be said by one party which cannot later be quoted or relied upon by the other. That is the theory, but, in fact, often facts are revealed in "without prejudice" discussions, and if those discussions come to nought, then the other party has learned something which cannot fail to influence its future conduct of the matter. Accordingly, "without prejudice" negotiations should be handled only by the most skilful of negotiators.

a third of the claim; the airline or consolidator and the agent have each contributed a third in payment to the claimant; and high claims handling costs have been avoided. Depending on the circumstances of each case, variations on these proportions, are, of course, possible.

CHAPTER 13

CLAIMS DECISIONS

Claims decisions concern a good deal more than whether the claim is going to be paid or not. They concern the decisions the claimant has to make concerning against whom to make the claim, how to calculate the losses and what the expectation for settlement should be, having regard to the contract context in which the claimant finds itself and the quality of the respondent against whom it is acting.

Of course, the claimant's actions must be based on the same factors which the respondent claims handler must consider, and these are now set out in substantial detail.

WHICH LIABILITY CONTEXT?

Clearly, different parts of the transit are subject to different rules and—of fundamental importance to both claimant and respondent—different liability regimes and limitations of settlement. If air transportation has commenced, air cargo rules will apply, but are they unamended Warsaw, Warsaw/Hague or non-Warsaw?

If air transportation has not legally commenced—and remember it *normally probably* commences on delivery into the airline's shed—then the forwarder is moving your goods under his contract conditions, which are likely to be BIFA.

On occasions, you may find that RHA is the contract context in which goods were being moved at the time the claim arose, but generally RHA conditions will be mainly of interest to airlines and forwarders trying to obtain compensation after having settled a claim for goods being moved between, for instance, Heathrow and Manchester. (In some carriers cases will have arranged with their regular sub-contracted road carriers that the carrier shall increase its limitation to the level of Warsaw.)

Further, there is always the possibility that an airline, moving goods across international frontiers by road, may have to consider pursuing reimbursement from its sub-contracted haulier within the terms of the CMR. This is not dealt with here, mainly because it is understood that some, if not most, hauliers regularly moving cargo from airlines will have agreed to increase their limitation to match Warsaw, like the RHA carriers in the last paragraph.

Trucking of air cargo

A great deal of trucking of air cargo goes on, and is certain to continue. As an example of how it affects liability let us suppose cargo is routed from Manchester to Heathrow to New York. The cargo is lost or destroyed between Manchester and Heathrow. A HAWB had been prepared which showed Manchester as the origin, with the cargo connecting to a flight departing from Heathrow. The airline MAWB covers only the carriage from Heathrow to New York.

The likelihood is that on the reverse of the HAWB are written conditions consistent with or similar to BIFA's. If the cargo is trucked from Manchester to Heathrow, then it is self-evident that air transportation has not commenced, and it is fairly clear that BIFA terms and liabilities will apply if the cargo is lost during that sector. Two SDRs per kilo is the maximum compensation available.

However, had there been no HAWB and had the cargo moved subject only to an airline AWB being prepared for the same routeing, what would be the effect of the dissimilar set of conditions on the Bill's reverse? The same general question arises if the HAWB existed, but was part of a consolidation already subject to a MAWB showing its origin as Manchester.

It would be most unusual for the set of conditions on the reverse of the MAWB or AWB not to be in the "IATA Resolution 600(b)" format—the standard conditions used by almost every airline, which provide for $20 per kilo, which is the standard liability applicable in the U.S.A. and a few other countries, but not in the U.K. It is difficult not to read the AWB conditions as indicating that U.S.$ 20 per kilo is the applicable compensation when an airline's AWB applies in a non-air transportation context.

At the time of writing, settlement limitation at $20 per kilo is about seven-and-a-half times as much as settlement at two SDRs per kilo. Accordingly, it is vital to know whether the cargo travelled from Manchester to Heathrow subject to a HAWB only and carried by the forwarder's trucker; if the HAWB was already covered by a MAWB from Manchester; or if there was an airline AWB only covering the consignment for the whole journey.

Air transportation or not?

For similar reasons, it may be necessary to be alert to whether an airline is trucking cargo or not. If the airline does not publicise that it trucks cargo on certain routes between the U.K. and European airports, from which it is possible to truck cargo without unacceptable delay to Heathrow, then—in the case of unamended Warsaw carriage—a claimant is entitled to expect normal air cargo liability limitation to apply at £15.89 or 17 SDRs per kilo (equivalent to approximately U.S.$26.22 or 22.44 respectively at the time of writing). However, if an airline openly advertises that it has truck connections to such airports, then no-one may assume that air transportation is involved either in reality or by technically legal definition, and the standard airline AWB liability in the absence of air transportation is U.S.$20 (approximately £12.12 at the time of writing). The difference of as much as £1.65 per kilo could be of enormous importance where a consignment weighing perhaps 1,500 kilos is lost or destroyed. That few airlines would attempt to apply other than Warsaw limits in this situation must be noted. However, it appears to be open to them to apply the U.S.$20 per kilo.

WORTHY CLAIMANTS AND RESPONDENTS AND "BAD ATTITUDE"

The claimant will need to be alert to the potential worth of a respondent. Conversely, the respondent must be wary of questionable or even fraudulent claims.

Clearly, commercial organisations vary greatly in their levels of efficiency, and some forwarders and airlines are very inefficient in claims handling. There are a number of shippers and importers who will not act honourably in claims situations, and there are documented records of claimants—fortunately few—submitting wholly fraudulent claims.

It seems most unlikely that any sizeable forwarder is uninsured, but a number of small or medium-sized companies actually do not have liability cover. Thus, when a claim arrives with them, they are bemused about what to do: the more usual result is for the claim to languish with no progress being made. Doubtless, on some rare occasions, a cynical executive will consciously seek to obfuscate matters, or simply delay and delay in the hope that the matter goes away. In such cases, claimants must be prepared to "grasp the nettle" of litigation if they are unable to bring enough pressure to bear on the respondent to make progress. If the case is sound, then a respondent delaying deliberately is most unlikely to have an arguable defence.

There are also a small number of claims handlers in airlines and larger forwarders who appear to have a serious problem with their attitude to claimants and claims handling and whose conduct appears to go unchecked by their superiors. Certainly some U.S. airlines will unyieldingly resist dealing with a claimant direct if the claimant's cargo was subject to a forwarder's HAWB, demanding that the claimant obtain settlement from the forwarder, and the forwarder make his own claim against them. Continual advice to the airline that under U.K. law an airline cannot ultimately insist on this seems to fall on deaf ears. If the airline's fault in the claim is proven, then the forwarder rightly recognises that the claimant has a direct right of claim against it, and there is no justification for the forwarder funding the claim.

Those same airlines, plus one or two others, will insist as unyieldingly on obscure and complex claims forms being completed, despite claimants having already supplied full and sufficient documentation. Following on from that, those same companies will demand an occasional obscure or irrelevant document to support the claim. The U.K. offices of some Middle East-based airlines routinely redirect claims to their headquarters, and that often appears to be the last one hears of them. No answers come forth, and claimants have to become very angry or litigate to make any progress. There is little difference in claims handling terms between these airlines and West-African and some East-African airlines. Accordingly, the claimant must be prepared sometimes for serious difficulty and unacceptable delay, and also be ready to use county court small claims procedures or to instruct lawyers in order to make any progress.

Having dealt with some of the less efficient airline claims handling, it is fair and proper to recall that some airlines have been the targets of fraudulent claimants, which have made them very wary and understandably suspicious. There are plenty of stories of claimants who have refused to accept that an airline has a sound and reasonable defence and, finding that they are unable to succeed legally, resort to threats to report cases to the more sensational newspapers in order to damage the airline's image. It is not then surprising that claimants of the highest integrity are occasionally astonished to find that their claims are treated with suspicion and non-co-operation.

For airlines—as for larger forwarders and consolidators in this position—there must at some stage be a readiness to state unequivocally to a claimant that his claim will not be settled. A stated refusal to communicate on the matter any further may also be necessary and may often be effective, because only the most "hard-nosed" honest claimants or the most brazen of fraudulent ones attempt to further their claims by litigation, exposing themselves to serious risk if their claims are rejected by the court.

Anger and aggression from claimants

Some anger from claimants is understandable and must be regarded as a normal hazard of the job. An importer whose deal has been ruined by transit problems, a forwarder whose customer is intolerably pressuring him, or a personal effects claimant whose treasured possessions have disappeared or been destroyed will obviously be distressed. In such situations, traditional sympathy and a stated willingness to do all that is possible to make amends as quickly as possible are the only measures which have any chance of defusing the situation.

Respondents must also recognise that sooner or later they will encounter a situation where the claimant simply will not be mollified, in which case the matter must be dealt with in the best way possible.

However, if anger escalates to aggression and perhaps personal abuse—which is not unknown—it may be difficult to determine the best course of action. Respondent claims handlers must understand that the aggression and abuse are not directed at them personally, since it is unlikely that the claimant has ever met the claims handler. If the situation cannot be defused, then ultimately there simply may be no alternative but to tell the claimant firmly that he will not be dealt with unless his attitude is moderated.

SETTLEMENT CRITERIA

There are three broad questions to be answered: entitlement to claim, correct quantification of and evidential support for the claim amount, and proof that the respondent is liable and has no defence. Sometimes each of these questions can be only partially answered, and respondent claims handlers may be tempted to deal with the points sequentially. Although a competent claimant would hope to have "pre-answered" all the points when submitting the formal claim, there are often outstanding points which come to light. It is recommended that respondent claims handlers deal with all points as far as possible at the same time; in other words, that they take the entitlement question as far as possible, noting any unanswered point, and do the same with the quantum, and so on. Then they should put all unanswered points to the claimant at the same time. To ask the claimant to deal with an entitlement point, and when he has done that write to him again with a quantum question, surely irritates a claimant who may be a good client.

Entitlement to claim

There are a number of factors which must be examined by respondents in order to assure themselves that the claimant has a right to make the claim. For instance, if the respondent agrees to pay the claimant, and then another claimant comes into view and shows that the respondent was imprudent to settle with the earlier claimant, the respondent may find himself unable to resist the second claim. Also, has the claimant fulfilled certain legal obligations which should have preserved his right to claim under the applicable law, and so on?

Freight

The terms "freight" and "cargo" are interchangeable within the freight industry, but claims handlers should be very clear about the real distinction between them: freight is the transportation charge. While it does not bear directly on the claimant's entitlement to claim, the payment of freight can be regarded as a prerequisite to a claimant pursuing a claim, and thus in some respects appears to "entitle" a claimant to pursue his claim. Legal precedent is very strong concerning the payment of freight, and in practically every case a claimant is not entitled to withhold freight as a "set-off" against his claim for damages: this is not to say that a respondent may not agree to this if it considers it in its interests, perhaps for customer relations. Indeed, the standard IATA 600b type AWB conditions allow for the non-payment of freight in the event of loss of the complete consignment.

It is not unknown for a claimant to use a minor claim problem as grounds for withholding a disproportionate amount of freight, or even for an unscrupulous claimant submitting a dubious or even fraudulent claim in order to avoid paying freight. Therefore, depending on the situation, respondents may be able protect themselves from such claimants by insisting on the claimant paying the freight prior to consideration of the claim.

Title to goods

Whereas a forwarder (acting purely as an agent) considering a claim against him will not have a problem being certain—or reasonably so—that the claimant is the person entitled to make the claim, the question can be more difficult for airlines and forwarders acting as contracting carriers. For some years now under U.K. law, airlines and forwarders acting as contracting carriers have been unable to insist on dealing only with the shipper or consignee named on the (M)AWB or HAWB.[1] This is not necessarily so in other countries. Accordingly, they must take reasonable precautions to ensure that the claimant has an entitlement in the matter.

The two central factors in judging entitlement to claim is a right to claim flowing from the contract of carriage and ownership of the affected goods. First, is there a clear tie-in between the shipper or consignee named in the waybill and the party making the claim? If not, then the connection must be clarified to your satisfaction, for it is not unknown for claimants without entitlement to inveigle respondents into settling with them. Secondly, a reasonable question is: if the claimant is the consignee, did he own the goods at the time of the loss or has he paid for them under the terms of his purchase contract? The answer is normally yes, but from time to time—especially in the perishables shipping world—a consignee will not pay the shipping invoice if the goods have lost all or most of their value during transit. In this situation, you should consider questions such as: did the consignee actually take delivery of the goods? Thus, is it reasonable to assume that under the contract of sale (represented in the shipping invoice) he was bound to pay for the goods? It is important to keep in mind that risk normally passes from shipper to consignee on shipment at the airport of origin, and once that has occurred the payment terms of the contract of sale between supplier and buyer can normally be enforced by the supplier.

Now, essentially, this becomes a dispute between the supplier and the buyer, where the supplier's claim is against the buyer for failure to pay for the goods, but that technically correct position will not necessarily mean that respondents will escape becoming embroiled in what is essentially a dispute not directly relevant to the cargo claim.

The corollary is that, if the shipper remains unpaid, he has a better claim right, and perhaps the consignee is not entitled to make the claim.

In most cases, you will be able to deal confidently with the claimant confronting you, but if you have the slightest doubt it is prudent to request the claimant to ask the other party to the carriage contract to confirm in writing that

1. See *Gatewhite Ltd* v. *Iberia Lineas Aereas de España SA* (1988) 1 S & B Av. R V11/305, [1990] QB 326, [1989] 1 All ER 944, [1989] Lloyd's Rep 150. However, it should be noted that this decision was unpopular at the time of judgment, and that there have been some indications in recent years that it may be challenged.

the claimant with whom you are dealing is entitled to pursue the claim. (Bear in mind also that the "other" party may have no obvious connection with the carriage contract, so you may need to assure yourself of its right to give such clearance to deal with the claimant.)

These points having been made, it should be noted that the majority of claims will not involve the need to be so analytical: it is mainly claims of high value, and perhaps of some obscurity, which need careful thought.

Subrogation

From time to time respondents receive claims from transit insurers, who have settled transit claims: such claims are referred to in the insurance industry as "recoveries": the same term is applied to claims direct from shippers and consignees, but is seldom used.

When the insured has received his settlement he should sign a subrogation receipt, evidencing receipt of the settlement and his assignment of claim rights to the insurer concerned. The insured is said to have "subrogated" his claim rights. Such rights are limited and, unlike in some other countries where insurers may acquire a very solid claim right, the insurer—if he needs to initiate legal action to force a settlement—must pursue the claim in the name of the original claimant, with, if necessary, the original claimant appearing as a witness in the court action. The subrogation form or receipt usually provides for this.

Respondents are entitled to see this form, and should insist on it or some satisfactory alternative document, because—although thankfully rarely—fraudulent claims have been brought by persons representing themselves as subrogated parties entitled to pursue when they were not.

Notice of claim

A claim situation, especially for airlines and forwarders acting as contracting air carriers, usually requires a written claim notice. This applies to all contractual systems referred to herein: Warsaw and non-Warsaw air carriage, RHA and BIFA.

In air carriage if the claimant has not sent a written notice of claim in the form and within the period specified in BIFA and RHA conditions, the relevant Article 26 of the Warsaw Convention, or applicable non-Warsaw air carriage rules, he has lost his claim rights. This seems absolute with regard to air carriage, but in BIFA and RHA the claimant can show that it was not possible for him to submit the notice of claim within the specified periods.

Airline or forwarder/contracting carriers need not further consider the claim, and it can be rejected outright without fear of the claimant succeeding against them, however much fuss he makes. (Beware, however, that outside the U.K.—especially in the U.S.A.—one may not have confidence that such a defence will succeed in the context of air carriage.)

With regard to the issuing of such claim notice, it is important to note that, bizarre as it may seem, a respondent does not have to *receive* the claim notice. The relevant provisions in Article 26 of Warsaw and parallel non-Warsaw rules state only that the notice has to be "dispatched", so, if a claimant can produce reasonable evidence of having dispatched the notice, the airline or forwarder/contracting carrier is not entitled to reject on the ground of lack of notice.

Notice to contracting carrier only

Another important point which is seldom realised is that, by virtue of the Guadalajara Supplementary Convention, a claimant can give notice of claim to a forwarder/contracting carrier, and if the forwarder/contracting carrier fails to give (or redirect) a claim notice to the airline responsible for the claim arising, the airline is not entitled to reject on the grounds of lack of notice. This Convention provides that notice to the one is to be equivalent to notice to the other. (If the airline perceives that its position has been prejudiced or unnecessarily damaged by the forwarder/contracting carrier's failure to redirect the notice, it seems likely that the airline will have recourse against the forwarder/contracting carrier in some way. No such recourse is provided within the air carriage legislation, but that does not rule out the possibility.)

Jurisdiction

An important question is: has the claimant submitted his claim in the correct jurisdiction, which we can define for our purposes as a territory over which a state's legal system presides. BIFA and RHA rules probably only apply in the U.K., because it seems unlikely that a foreign court would ever have reason or authority to determine cases brought under these contracts. If such were to happen, the situation would fall outside the scope of this present work. Air Carriage rules provide that a claimant may bring his claim in the country of origin, the country of destination or the country in which the carrier has its main office or headquarters.

There is an occasional debate about whether a consignee is entitled to bring a claim in the country of origin, if it is to his advantage to do so, or whether conversely, the shipper may bring a case in the country of destination. Sometimes, legal rules directly connected with air carriage in such countries illustrate such advantages and disadvantages. The air carriage rules appears to have nothing to say about this, so there is no obvious reason for not doing so.

The nearest the rules appear to come to this point is in Article 30 of the Convention, providing that the shipper has a right of action against the first carrier and the consignee has a right against the final carrier, and each has a right against the carrier in whose care the claim arose.

However, where the case is substantial, a claimant may be faced with some form of objection by the respondent.

Time bars

Time bar deals with the setting of an overall time limit, after which the respondent does not have to consider the claim.

RHA conditions show no time bar but, of course, are subject to the normal limitation of six years applicable to most claims for compensation not otherwise regulated as to time bar or time limit for actions.

BIFA conditions allow a period of nine months. To avoid the claim "dying" the claimant must have commenced legal action and to have given written notice to the respondent of this—both actions must be carried out prior to operation of the time bar.

If the claimant does not attend to these two points, his claim rights have simply ceased to exist, but, as the conditions are regulated only by civil contract, the respondent—if requested—is free to agree an extension for the claim to continue to be investigated or negotiated. This is obviously a sensible move for both sides, since both parties will be spared the possible expense of instructing solicitors and each will avoid the risk of having to pick up the other's legal costs in the event of losing the case. The same applies to air carriage rules, but a two-year period is allowed before a time bar operates: if you get close to the end of the period, be sure to understand the provisions of Article 29 of the Warsaw Convention and parallel non-Warsaw rules.

A fundamental difference in air carriage concerns the ability to extend the period. The words of Article 29 are that "claim rights are extinguished, unless an action is brought". From time to time, claimants request extensions and carriers purport to agree them, but since the relevant words are part of U.K. statute law, it is evident that carriers have no power to extend the period beyond two years.

The "action" to be brought is clearly a legal action, which requires the issue of a writ. Thus, a carrier has no power to extend the period, and it is a claimant's obligation to protect his claim rights by commencing a legal action. There has been at least one instance where a carrier purported to agree an extension for six months, and some few weeks into the "extension" period gave a "final" denial, noting that the time bar had in fact operated. The claimant now found all avenues blocked, and his naïveté was to blame; however, the carrier's conduct was dishonourable in the extreme.

If the two-year time bar approaches, claimants should not fail to issue a writ: it needs to be served before four months have passed,[2] but to try to persuade the carrier to continue to negotiate you will need to send him a copy of the writ—but not by way of official service. It will cost a certain amount for solicitors to arrange for issue—much less if you are prepared to do it yourself in the county court—but it will not be outrageously expensive.

Finally, there may be a reasonable chance of recovering the cost of issue from the respondent eventually.

2. Six months if outside U.K. jurisdiction.

Delays in pursuit of claims

Respondents sometimes are very puzzled about why a claim which is obviously payable is not pursued for a very long time: it is usually because a transit insurer takes a significant amount of time to agree his insured's claim, to pay it, to obtain a subrogation receipt and pass instructions out to either a recovery agent or solicitor. It is also a fact that a number of transit insurers are either not efficient or, amazingly, not apparently bothered about routinely effecting recoveries against respondents. This explains why some claims, eminently payable, are never pursued. (However, respondents should be alert to claims pursued after a long delay by uninsured claimants. It is sometimes worth inquiring into the circumstances of that delay, because there may be something irregular involved.)

Proving liability

Since claimants must provide evidence for the points which respondent claims handlers have to consider in making decisions about claim settlements, we need to consider the standards of proof which must be achieved.

Each party to a dispute has a duty to establish the facts. If a claimant asserts that a certain thing happened which caused the claim, in general terms it is he who must prove it by showing that, on a "balance of probabilities", the thing which he asserts was true. Conversely, a party defending a claim must prove that on a balance of probabilities that which he asserts in his defence is true. If either party cannot show the balance in favour of his position, then his cause will fail.

If the case reaches court, the judge must be in a position to say that "he thinks it more probable than not". If he cannot, then the cause is lost. Accordingly, in RHA and BIFA cases, the claimant must produce his balance of probabilities for his claim, and the respondent can produce his, and the two parties can allow their positions to be judged, failing a settlement of some sort being agreed between them.

With air cargo liability claims, the position is slightly but importantly modified by statute law. The claimant has merely to show that the loss occurred during air transportation. It is not incumbent upon him to show how it occurred and why. The respondent carrier is now in the position where it is bound to produce a defence, but, of course, that defence must still be based on a balance of probabilities. (Once such a defence has been put, the claimant is, of course, entitled to try to show that it is not valid, and, of course, his rebuttal is itself to be based on a balance of probabilities.)

Air carriage

The following points appear to represent recurring criteria to be considered when attempting to confirm or establish liability against an actual air carrier or forwarder acting as a carrier.

Transhipments and successive or preceding carriers

On a minority of occasions, it may be that the respondent being presented with the claim has no real knowledge of the circumstances of how it arose, because the claim was caused by a carrier to whom he delivered the cargo for onward carriage or from whom he took delivery for the next sector. The shipper has an established right of action under the air cargo rules to submit the claim to the first carrier, and the consignee submits it against the final carrier. Each may submit its claim to the carrier who was in possession of the goods when the event giving rise to the claim occurred. In practice this means that while the respondent must attempt to deal with the claim, it is open to him to invite the claimant to re-submit the claim against the carrier who caused the problem and deal with him direct: this is not unreasonable, but the claimant may well shy away from this if the carrier concerned is located in another country and is difficult or impossible for him to deal with. It is suggested that if this is the case, the original respondent's correct course is himself to re-submit the claim to the defaulting carrier and seek instructions for settlement and the funds for it.

Since this process can be very long drawn out, with the second carrier not responding properly, it is not unknown for the claimant to initiate legal action against the original respondent, as is his right. In such cases, the respondent must, of course, deal with the action. He may be in a position to force the second carrier into the action by having his lawyer issue a "third party notice".

In extreme circumstances, the original respondent may have to initiate proceedings in a foreign jurisdiction in order to obtain reimbursement of any settlement the court may order him to pay.

Force majeure

The general principle is that if an event occurs which is unpredictable and beyond the carrier's control, and causes loss, damage or delay which the carrier cannot avoid, despite efforts to retrieve the position, the carrier is absolved from the subsequent claim. Naturally, there is a tendency for carriers to claim that certain things are out of their control, but the carrier may not be able to maintain the position if the claimant gives some thought to it.

Perceived force majeure Carriers sometimes announce that an unpredictably reduced cargo capacity has forced them to offload cargo from a flight. This is very important to perishables exporters and importers and to other cargo owners to whom getting the cargo to destination on time is vital. If such a defence is offered, claimants are entitled to question it. Such specific questions as "why did you offload my cargo, which was perishable, when you left dry goods on board?" are difficult for a carrier to answer.

Of course, the extent to which you can push such questions depends much on your determination to succeed with your claim. If you have reached as far as putting such questions, you may well be into litigation anyway, with funds committed to solicitors in order for them to force the relevant information out of the respondent, in the hope that it cannot ultimately maintain the offered defence.

Strikes at airports and cancelled flights are sometimes cited as unpredictable causes of delay. If the carrier actually knew in advance, or should have known, that such a strike was to take place, then it can hardly be *force majeure*. After all one does not walk knowingly into a bad situation if one can avoid it, and such situations are nearly always avoidable or capable of resolution in one way or another. In the case of a strike known to be going to happen, the carrier should not have accepted the cargo without warning the shipper of the likely delays. If he does, the shipper is entitled to assume that the carrier has a means to avoid the effects of the strike.

The message to be conveyed here is that a claimant is not obliged to accept the respondents' defence of *force majeure* if it seems clear that the situation was avoidable.

Undoubted force majeure A claim that loading machinery broke down unexpectedly causing delay or damage to your cargo is a defence which will nearly always succeed. Naturally, you are entitled to be provided with evidence of this, and if the stakes are high enough and legal action follows, documents like maintenance records will have to be produced to prove ultimately that everything had been done to avoid such a breakdown.

The same principles apply in theory to an aircraft which suffers a mechanical failure which delays or cancels a flight, but, in practice of course, the standards of aircraft maintenance tend to be so high that such a position is probably not worth attacking.

Naturally, if your cargo is lost in an air crash, with the cause truly outside the carrier's control, there can be no successful claim. A crash without proof of cause will enable a claim to succeed, because the carrier is unable to substantiate *force majeure*.

Continuing duty of care Even if the carrier has encountered circumstances truly beyond his control, he cannot abandon his duty of care towards the cargo, since he continues to be a bailee with positive duties in that regard. He cannot simply leave flowers and fruit on an aircraft delayed overnight without proving that he made a positive attempt to safeguard their condition but could truly do nothing to ameliorate the problem of inevitable deterioration.

If cargo was damaged for reasons outside his control while in his possession, he cannot simply abandon it. It must still do its best to look after it, and either get it to its destination or send it back to the shippers (depending on their instructions).

Contributory negligence

From time to time, shippers or their forwarders or packers make mistakes which lead to a claim. The respondent is entitled to repudiate the claim or to be exonerated to some degree from complete blame. If the respondent cannot wholly exonerate himself, the sensible thing to do is to negotiate a settlement acceptable to both sides.

Errors in documentation or handling instructions The shipper, through his forwarder, is responsible for the correctness of shipping documentation, and if there is any error which leads to a problem in transit—even a confiscation by Customs either at a transhipment point, or at destination—the carrier cannot be held responsible. Perhaps incorrect handling instructions were given or the consignee was entered wrongly on the air waybill.

Inadequate packing It is not unusual to see packing crates break open and cartons burst because their contents are too heavy. The carrier cannot agree to settle a claim in this event. However, it remains open to the claimant to show that the packing was adequate and that the damage might have been caused perhaps by over-stowage of heavy pieces.

Machines with projecting fragile or breakable parts are sometimes shipped strapped to pallets without crating to protect them. Heavy gearboxes and machine parts have been shipped "naked", and cargo owners have been surprised when their claims were rightly rejected.

There are many other examples which readers will no doubt call to mind.

Imprudent loading In recent years, with the advent of ever-more-sophisticated computers and mobile telephones, consignments of exceptionally high value have been regularly included within consolidations.

While carriers' employees or agents can never be excused from stealing cargo of any description, airlines have rightly felt resentful that such high-value consignments are not shipped under their own airline air waybill as a single consignment—known as an "IATA shipment"—with special or valuables handling requested and paid for.

There is a degree of imprudence in shippers moving such consignments in this manner. It is a reality that cargo handlers are often able to identify commodities and are occasionally tempted into theft. It may be only they who recognise the potential value of the goods. Airline cargo operational managers and supervisors do not necessarily actually see the cargo close up, and since a proper and accurate description does not necessarily appear on any of the papers with which they are dealing they have no chance of ensuring that protective measures are brought into operation.

Some airlines have taken to specific examination of consolidation manifests to see if any such cargo is included, but this is not necessarily effective, since computer components can be described simply as "electrical parts".

It is understandable that shippers of such commodities wish to keep freight charges as low as possible, but, in consolidating, they deprive airline staff responsible for cargo security of the opportunity to protect cargo from theft.

How far this argument can be advanced in order to combat the overturning of limitation remains to be seen.

Delivery signatures

There is much myth and misunderstanding about delivery signatures. Attitudes range from a "clean" signature being a complete and sound defence to a claim for damage, to remarks such as "it's not worth the paper it's written on". The reality is that both are true depending on the circumstances.

You must not lose sight of Article 26(1) of the Warsaw Convention, which provides in so many words that a clean signature is *prima facie* evidence only, but the situation can only be judged from the individual circumstances involved.

For instance, suppose a driver signs for two pieces, and on arrival back at his depot asserts he was given only one piece: he will have difficulty denying the accuracy of the signature in such circumstances, where it was simple to ensure the presence of two pieces. However, if he were signing for 200, and reported only 199 on his arrival at his depot, it would be reasonable to accept that the delivery signature may not have been accurate: of course, the driver's company would have to produce additional reasonable evidence to support its position.

A clean signature will be a probable defence to wet damage, which should have been visible externally at the time of the delivery.

If a signature for damage is given, and there is a written record of a split seam or box flap open, with the contents having been checked and found correct, a claim cannot be raised for shortage. Similarly, a signature for damage is not *carte blanche* for a claimant to raise a claim for just anything.

Thus, delivery signatures must be treated with care and common sense by both parties, but the experience is that much difficulty is caused by inaccurate and incomplete "clausing". Concealed damage, *viz.* unexpected damage noticed on opening up a box or crate, is always difficult because it is seldom that it can be shown how the damage occurred. Inadequate packing may be to blame, but an unrecorded heavy impact of the carton during transit may have occurred. In such situations, the only way out may be a negotiated and compromised settlement.

ULDs and delivery circumstances With the increased use of ULDs, the liability issues can become blurred, but it is quite easy to be clear about matters most of the time. There appear to be three distinct situations:

1. The forwarder offers a pre-loaded ULD for carriage which is designated as one piece. A claim for loss from the ULD is usually avoidable by the carrier, unless there is evidence to show that interference has taken place prior to delivery at the destination, in which case the carrier must answer the claim;
2. A pre-loaded ULD is delivered for carriage, and at its destination is unloaded by the carrier for delivery of individual HAWB lots. This is quite common. If there is a shortage on delivery, unless the carrier can show that the shortage was noted when it unloaded the ULD, the carrier must answer the claim; and
3. A loose piece consolidation or multi-piece single consignment is delivered to the carrier who loads it into a ULD. At destination, the loaded ULD is delivered out—which is a regular feature of perishables delivered at Heathrow. Shortage shows up when the ULD is tallied, and the carrier must answer for this. (It is difficult to understand why carriers would agree to this method of delivery, when they expose themselves to claims without a proper chance of a defence.)

Perishables—damaged by delay

The problems which arise concerning perishables are generally more difficult than most others to resolve. For instance, there is sometimes no proper proof of sound export condition at origin, but most fruits, vegetables and flowers do not prosper from being cooped up in a container for excessive periods, and delay is thus a direct cause of damage.

It has also to be accepted that practically no-one would send a consignment of perishables which could not withstand normal transit—there is no reason to do so, and shippers would knowingly incur certain losses. At the same time, some shippers ship unwisely, sending less than good quality produce which may just not survive a normal transit in good shape.

Perishables shippers and importers are often regarded by carriers with suspicion, since there have been a number of claims submitted for what was demonstrably not the carriers' fault. One or two well-known importers have also been seen to alter Ministry of Agriculture certificates of condition in order to support their otherwise weak claims.

Carriers' claims handlers are right to be wary, but there are plenty of sound and honest perishables exporters and importers. They will submit the claim simply on the ground that they handed the goods to the carrier in sound condition and the carrier delivered them damaged at destination: this is a very reasonable ground for a claim. The carrier must discharge his normal duties and, if he cannot show that the cause of damage pre-existed at the time of delivery at origin or that the damage happened outside the carriers' control, a settlement must be made.

Inherent vice

A discussion of perishables leads on to this point.

It is very unusual nowadays, but perishables can carry pathogens which are sparked into life during transit, multiply at an unacceptable rate and manifest themselves as an obvious problem on delivery at the destination. The fact that there was no obvious sign on delivery at origin is not a ground for holding the carrier responsible.

On the other hand, adverse or unexpected transit conditions may spark into life an otherwise harmless but omni-present and normally dormant pathogen, such as botrytis. It may cause major damage to the perishables, and for this the carrier may well be responsible.

Other examples of inherent vice are a live animal which carried some pre-existing infection which caused its death in transit, for which the carrier could not be held responsible; clothing packed in a very humid atmosphere, coming into a much colder one, has been known to suffer rots and mould due to sweating and re-condensation, when the moisture sparked ever-present mould spores—normally not a problem—into life.

Claims handlers should be on the look-out for causes of damage attributable to inherent vice.

Claim amount (quantum)

The industry almost exclusively uses the term "claim amount" and not "quantum". Quantum is the term used at all times by both the insurance and legal worlds. We will use the term "quantum" hereafter.

There are a number of important points which must be considered when looking at quantum, since respondents are entitled to seek ways of reducing the amounts they have to pay out if they can.

The measure of damages

Both RHA and BIFA conditions set out clear rules concerning how much a claimant is allowed to claim, and in general terms it is seen to be the value at the time of shipment. While some interpretation of this is possible, it is generally not found to be difficult to work with.

However, things are notably different with regard to air carriage. Air carriage rules are silent about how damages should be calculated, but the relevant Article 23 of Warsaw and parallel non-Warsaw rule prevents respondents from reducing further the levels of liability set within the Convention. So how do we tackle this point?

In view of the silence of Warsaw and non-Warsaw rules, it appears that the measure of damages allowed generally by legal precedent in the U.K. must be those applicable, since Article 23 seems to indicate that carriers could not set down any rules for damages calculation below that which is allowed by Warsaw and non-Warsaw.

In practice the point is not one that is open to argument, but from time to time respondents do seek to impose certain restrictions. Thus, it is not unknown, for instance, for a carrier to hold that the claimant is entitled only to receive the cost of the goods and the freight involved. Ultimately, this argument must fail, but in some cases, unless proceedings are commenced, those few respondents will not abandon this incorrect position.

Foreign currencies

In general terms, it seems reasonable for a claimant to quantify his claim in the currency in which he has sustained his loss. Since access to most foreign currencies is easy in the U.K., it seems unreasonable for a respondent to object.

Sound-arrived-value

It is well established by precedent that, in general terms, the carrier is liable for sound-arrived-value: in other words, the carrier is liable to compensate the claimant, such that the claimant is placed in the position he would have been in had nothing gone wrong.

There may be good reasons why a claimant would be satisfied with being paid only the cost of buying the goods from the shipper, plus the freight he has incurred, but if he insists that he is entitled to the value he could expect to sell the goods for after delivery by the airline, the airline has no right to deny this to him. It is equally valid for the claimant to calculate his damages by adding together all his costs and adding a reasonable profit too: the courts will endorse this unless it can be shown that the claimant could not reasonably have expected to sell the goods for a profit, in which case the settlement should not include one.

Added value

It is fair to say that the carrier is liable for the value of the goods only up to the point at which he would have delivered them.

As will be readily understood, the importer would normally incur costs additional to that of transport up to the point of delivery by the carrier. Such costs would be reflected in his eventual selling price, and are thus regarded as added value. Such costs should not be borne in claims settlements by the respondent.

Subrogated claims

Transit insurers' settlements are mainly based on a formula arrived at by adding the cost of the goods, plus the freight, plus an uplift, which may range from 10 per cent upwards. When insurers have paid such a claim and obtained the subrogation receipt they submit a claim to the carrier. The experience is that when respondents settle such claims, they almost invariably deduct the uplift, maintaining that they cannot be held responsible for it. This seems wrong, and if insurers were to decide it was worthwhile, they could probably succeed in obtaining payment of it. It is likely that the settlement would have been below the insured party's sound-arrived-value, with the uplift going some way to cover expenses additional to cost and freight and some of the profit.

It seems that a respondent can produce no argument to rule out the uplift, in fact, since it must inevitably fall within the sound-arrived-value.

Interest

On the basis of the principle of compensating a claimant to the extent of placing him in the position he would have been in had nothing gone wrong, it seems to follow that the claimant is entitled to receive interest on his claim, considering that the original loss caused him additional financial hardship in being out of pocket for a significant time.

Interest is certainly payable, and will be ordered by any court finding for the claimant/plaintiff. But the reality is that respondents generally refuse to pay interest, knowing that only a court order can force them to pay up. The amount of interest applicable tends in the majority of cases to be small in relation to the quantum, and the claimant is usually relieved to be paid at all, so he seldom makes an issue of it. If, however, claimants feel strongly enough about it they should make an issue of it, if their circumstances permit it.

A word of warning about interest, however, which will be repeated below in the section on limitation of liability: if the respondent is permitted to limit the amount of settlement to your quantum or below, interest cannot be added to the settlement.

Consequential losses

These concern solely claims arising owing to delayed delivery.

This can be an area of considerable difficulty for both sides: for instance, in the case of exhibition goods, the claimant may assert he could have sold "millions" if the respondent had not delayed his cargo, and prevented him from exhibiting.

There should be no difficulty in re-claiming consequential expenses which can be proven to have been incurred unavoidably and reasonably; but what of the other elements of the claim?

Proof The loss of a contract worth an enormous amount or frustrated sales at an exhibition may be involved, but can the claimant prove it? In the case of a lost contract, it is conceivable, if possibly a little unlikely, that the claimant could obtain the co-operation of the party who refused to award the contract owing to the cargo turning up late to confirm that in writing. More than once, there have been pilot consignments of fresh fruit and vegetables going to supermarkets, which, owing to delay, refused to award a regular contract to the shipper or importer, on the ground of non-reliability. The weight of such a consignment can be considerable and when the limitation is calculated can give the claimant hope of a considerable settlement.

Claims have been brought against respondents where a frustrated exhibitor was able to produce a series of letters from frustrated buyers who confirmed that they would definitely have bought the produce had it appeared at the exhibition.

Lost contracts owing to delayed papers and bids are subject to very low limitation due to the weight, and nowadays such documents are generally not carried as traditional cargo, there being many courier companies. Note, however, that "courier material" is still cargo within the meaning of the Warsaw Convention system.

Foreseeability A further criterion is one of foreseeability: was it reasonable for the carrier to be aware that special damages would be incurred if the consignment were delayed? The point may be illustrated by exhibition goods consigned on an AWB, prominently marked "exhibition goods—do not delay under any circumstances". The carrier may not be aware of the precise type of injury which may be incurred, but the general idea is conveyed, and it may not be able to resist a claim for consequential loss. If the exhibitor has dealt with the carrier's salesman in setting up the transit, and perhaps even put it in writing to him or to the carrier in general how urgent it is to get the consignment to the exhibition, he is in an even stronger position.

Similar points arise when the shipper has made the carrier aware that the consignment contains spares for the repair of broken-down factory plant or a ship stuck in harbour. "AOGs" (aircraft on ground) are relevant. Also, there seems to be a fairly regular traffic of supplies to cruise and cargo ships timed to be in a particular harbour on a certain date: these cargoes, if delayed, give rise to consequential losses which are eligible for consideration as claims.

Mitigation

A claimant must act prudently in keeping the losses suffered as a result of a claim to the absolute minimum, and the respondent is entitled to expect him to have done this. Various examples are quoted to illustrate the principles involved. It is for respondents to identify areas within claims where mitigation should have taken place but may not have been attended to: if such omissions are found, respondents are entitled to object to the claim if the situation warrants it or to negotiate an allowance against settlement to reflect the lack of mitigation.

Delayed perishables

The importer who abandons a perishables consignment because it is a day late, when he should have attempted to sell it for best possible prices, is risking the respondent taking the view that his failure to mitigate caused the complete loss of the consignment. If he does, the respondent will be unable to escape liability completely, but will be in a strong position to negotiate the claim settlement downwards. Such mitigation may well be irksome to the importer, but he is obliged to do it. The importer's correct course would have been to take the consignment under protest, instruct a surveyor so that independent evidence of deteriorated condition could be adduced, sell the perishables for best possible prices and submit a claim based on the depreciation suffered plus the surveyors' fee. He would be entitled to receive compensation at that level, although respondents often incorrectly deduct the survey fee.

Consequential losses

In a delay situation where the shipper can demonstrate that he had no choice but to fly out to the destination to deal with the resultant problems, he cannot fly first-class and automatically expect the fare to form part of the claim: the respondent will probably be entitled to reimburse the claimant only for an economy fare.

Damage

If a valuable machine is damaged, the importer cannot simply abandon it if it is repairable. He is obliged to repair, and if the costs are considerable the respondent is entitled to expect the importer to organise competitive repair bids, if practical, to ensure minimum repair costs. In such a situation, the respondent is entitled to expect that the importer will invite the respondent to survey the damaged goods and perhaps involve himself in the repair situation, so that both parties can agree on how to handle the problem. It goes almost without saying that if this can happen, most of the pitfalls and problems in obtaining settlements will be avoided.

Reasonableness of mitigation

Claimants are not expected to gamble on the outcome of attempting to mitigate their losses. Respondents cannot expect them to incur expenses in no more than the hope that they can repair the goods or find some other way to market them. If, however, such expenses are incurred with the encouragement or tacit agreement of the respondent, then the respondent will probably be liable for them.

Accurate calculation and supporting documents

Although this seems obvious, respondents must check that the quantum is mathematically correct and fully supported by documents. Considerable care is needed where calculations are complex, and respondents are entitled to receive documents supporting and proving each element of the quantum. (One of the more usual legal terms for such supporting documents is "vouchers".)

Personal effects and household goods

However, in the case of claims for personal effects and household effects, it is generally unlikely that claimants can produce vouchers for everything lost or damaged. Few people retain till and sales receipts for clothes and personal possessions. Respondents must be reasonable and fair in these circumstances.

Settlement amount and limitation

Currencies

While a respondent can have no valid objection to settling in foreign exchange, a valid question is "how should we match a potential settlement in foreign exchange to a limitation expressed in sterling?" Let us take the example of a claim settlement to be made in U.S. dollars which must equate to a limitation of £100. It is submitted that the practical solution is to settle sufficient U.S. dollars so that, if the recipient were to convert them to £s, he would receive the correct sum. Accordingly, it seems clear that the U.K. bank "buying rate" for U.S. dollars should be used to convert limitation to U.S. dollars, since the recipient will hypothetically have to sell the dollars to the bank to convert them into £s.

Having examined the claim in light of all the foregoing points and having decided what is the correct quantum, the respondent is entitled to apply limitation. We know that limitation is based on weight, and we must first deal with that point.

Weight basis

If a complete consignment has been lost or destroyed, there is no problem with the weight to be used for limitation purposes. However, where only part of a consignment is involved, the respondent is entitled to be provided with evidence of the weight. It is accepted that in some circumstances this can be very difficult, but there are methods of dealing with the problem. In such circumstances, one can attempt to revert to the shipping documents in general, checking for what weight information there may be. From such information, it is normally possible to estimate or apportion weight to the affected part and usually for such weight to be agreed between the parties.

In cases of severe difficulty, a compromise between the parties must be aimed at.

RHA

In the case of RHA the limit of compensation is quite straightforwardly £1,300 per tonne (subject to any volumetric basis for calculating limitation). This will not change until the Road Haulage Association decides that it is time to change and its members agree.

It should be noted, however, that at the time of writing the RHA is changing the volumetric calculation which can be applied to limitation calculation.

BIFA

Two special drawing rights per kilo is the compensation limit. The SDR is an artificial currency used in some specialised ways for international accounting, but those who framed the BIFA conditions presumably saw it as a means of keeping liability limits under this discipline abreast of inflation. It seems to have proved successful in this, and, accordingly, it looks as if no revision of the basic liability need be considered for the foreseeable future. However, the SDR also strongly reflects the comparative value of sterling and, thus, when sterling rides high against other currencies claimants actually receive smaller settlements where the limitation operates.

Since the value of the SDR varies over a period of time, it is important to know which value to apply. The BIFA conditions provide that the SDR value applicable on the day of the incident is the correct value.

Air carriage

With recent changes in the law, the following liability limitations are in force:

1. Unamended Warsaw Convention carriage—remains expressed in terms of 250 gold francs per kilo, which until the 1996 Sterling Equivalent Order is revised, stands at £15.89;
2. Warsaw/Hague carriage—this is subject to previous comments about the uncertainty of its application due to the U.K. government appearing to have—in effect—removed the original Warsaw/Hague Convention from the statute books, possibly leaving a legal vacuum. However, if it is found applicable, or agreed between claimant and respondent to be applicable, then it remains expressed in terms of 250 gold francs per kilo, which until the 1996 Sterling Equivalent Order is revised, stands at £15.89;
3. Non-Warsaw carriage—17 SDRs per kilo;
4. Unamended Warsaw Montreal Protocol No. 1 carriage—17 SDRs per kilo;
5. Warsaw/Hague Protocol No. 2 carriage—17 SDRs per kilo; and

6. Warsaw/Hague Montreal Protocols Nos. 3 and 4 carriage when introduced—17 SDRs per kilo.

Package limit under Warsaw/Hague and non-Warsaw

Warsaw/Hague and non-Warsaw limitation is further modified by reference to package weights. Article 22(2)(a) provides that the weight of the package affected is to be used as the weight applied to limitation. Thus, if one small item, perhaps weighing a few grammes, is missing from one package with a weight of 10 kilos, the liability limit will be based on the 10 kilos. Also, Article 22(2)(b) provides that the weight to be taken into account for limitation purposes, where loss, damage or delay to one of the packages affects the value of the other packages in the consignment, shall be the total weight of such packages. For example, a machine dismantled for carriage, and thus broken down into several packages, would probably be useless if one of the packages was lost or damaged: in such a case, the weight of the complete consignment is the relevant weight for limitation purposes.

Volumetric variance under unamended Warsaw

IATA airlines have agreed to vary their liability limits in relation to carriage between the U.S.A. and elsewhere, and this is reflected on the reverse of IATA standard 600b AWBs. If the weight of the consignment was such that an "artificial" weight was used to calculate the freight, the artificial weight should be used for calculating limitation.

This applies only to routeings involving the U.S.A. as an origin or destination.

Declared value for carriage

If the shipper considers that the compensation limit is not high enough for the value of his cargo, it is open to him by virtue of Article 22 of the Convention and its amendments to raise that limit. Each AWB carries a box marked "declared value for carriage" and the shipper is entitled to insert a value there, and the carrier to make a supplementary charge based on that value. The only effect of this facility is to raise the limitation to the value shown in the box, but it changes no other considerations: the claim must be judged in accordance with all normal liability provisions, just as all other claims.

This facility is now largely disused, but respondents should remain alert to it—the problem, of course, is that it is seldom used, so carriers' claims handlers are not accustomed to it, will overlook it and can get caught out when they offer settlement in accordance with normal limitation.

There is also a problem where shippers insert into the box whatever value they feel is correct, and offer cargo and AWB to the carrier without bringing the matter specifically to the carrier's attention. Owing to its unfamiliarity, airline cargo staff do not notice the entry and the carrier is faced with a considerably raised limit on which no extra charge has been made. There are arguments to be made that it was not a term incorporated into the contract because the shipper did not bring it specifically to the carrier's attention, but the carrier is directly responsible for the contract document he offers and cannot really deny his exposure to the raised limit.

Limitation breaking

There is no means of breaking the compensation limits set in RHA and BIFA conditions, but in air carriage there is: it is familiarly known as an "Article 25" situation. Fortunately for carriers and forwarders it is not a regular feature of their work, but when such problems arise they are fundamentally difficult. Such issues will usually involve high-value claims, and a respondent in this position should normally have involved his insurer in the problem early on. In such situations, it is not unusual to see major law firms brought in by insurers, and in such cases a fairly hard struggle between opposing parties can arise.

It is understandable that carriers will want as strongly as possible to resist settling for more than limitation, and their insurers agree with them, although few parties are prepared to allow such cases to go to actual trial. The majority are settled by compromise but, from time to time, cases do go to "judgment", and become cases of particular interest, both to the legal profession from an academic point of view and, more importantly, to the airlines and their insurers as they try to assess the likely impact on future claim settlements.

However, there is a simple answer to the difficulties here for cargo owners: Article 22 of the Warsaw Convention permits a special declaration of value which allows the limitation to be increased to the true value of the goods. The charges applicable are often notably more than the premium payable under regular insurance cover. Consequently, it is often the case that such special declaration of value is not considered at all, and thus difficult disputes arise between cargo owners and airlines—such disputes are, of course, actually driven by the transit insurers settling the claims and the airlines' insurers.

Another answer is for the cargo owner to effect air waybill insurance, since some airlines offer this facility, and indeed the standard air waybill contract form has a specific box for this purpose. Again, the cost involved tends to be in excess of regular transit insurance and the cover under such air waybill insurance is not usually as wide as that under a regular policy.

Interest

In the majority of cases in which settlement is agreed without too much difficulty, interest is never raised as an aspect of settlement. However, the principle is that interest is payable on the claimed amount if the respondent can be persuaded—short of litigation—to add it to the settlement. One finds that if negotiations proceed some distance, and if the party representing the claimant has some skill in his task, with the respondent or his representative also having some understanding of the issues involved, an interest element is achievable.

It has been established in court that interest is not payable in addition to limitation settlement under Warsaw rules. If interest is paid, the settlement plus the interest cannot exceed the applicable limitation applied.

Undesirable settlement practices

Some carriers with headquarters in the U.S.A. have for some time been guilty of several practices which can be highly irritating to U.K. claimants and which are certainly incorrect. These carriers' claims-handling procedure in the U.K. is usually to refer most claims back to their U.S. headquarters for processing. Their headquarters may take the following lines:

1. A consolidator having received a claim from a co-loader (*viz.* a forwarder issuing his own house air waybill) who is presenting his client's claim, will be told to settle the claim before the carrier will consider it;
2. The carrier will apply a limitation of U.S.$ 20 per kilo to any settlement, and perhaps issue and send a cheque for limitation (incorrect at U.S.$ 20 per kilo) in dollars to the claimant without discussion or negotiation, and will appear to continue to refuse to discuss issues; and
3. The carrier will refuse to accept that a claimant is entitled to receive the proper measure of damages, usually sound-arrived-value, even though U.S. law generally endorses this principle.

Taking each of these points in order:

1. Under U.K. law by virtue of the rule in *Gatewhite* v. *Iberia* (referred to above), the actual cargo owner, irrespective of the name appearing on the air waybill (house and/or master) is entitled to make a claim in his own name.

   If a co-loader presents such a claim to a consolidator who refers it to the airline then both co-loader and consolidator can be said to be acting as agents for the actual claimant.

   Both co-loader and consolidator have no beneficial interest in the claim, and the respondent is not entitled to object to such a claim and insist on it being settled first by the consolidator as a prerequisite.
2. This is, of course, clearly invalid under U.K. law. Compensation limitation is expressed in the U.K. in sterling, whether in actual sterling or SDRs for which the sterling value is immediately accessible, and not in dollars. In recent years the value of the dollar has been such that 20 of them are worth less than the statutory limitation for a kilogramme under U.K. law.

   There is also the question of bank charges for conversion to sterling, which further reduce the final sum available: it cannot be right for the claimant to have his entitlement eroded further by such charges.

Ennui will undoubtedly often set in with smallish claims and in most cases the claimant will accept the dollar cheque, but usually feel aggrieved.

Claimants always find this high-handed and irritating. In the face of refusal to respond to arguments, the only way forward may be to commence proceedings, but, as always, common sense must prevail. The difference between the sterling residue from conversion of the dollar draft and the U.K. limitation may make the option of legal proceedings a folly.

3. The final point is a matter of U.K. law, but a carrier's U.S. office claims handler may be unmoved by any arguments put even in a formal and proper way.

   Again, commencing proceedings may be the only way forward, and to litigate even successfully will probably result in some of the legal costs having to be borne by the claimant himself, although any U.S. carrier faced with such a case will have to instruct U.K. lawyers, who would be unlikely to advise a client to defend so erroneous a point.

Negotiation

Negotiation in the classic sense does not really have a place in claims handling except in isolated instances where lawyers become involved, or where the most skilled of industry claims handlers are responsible for concluding sizeable claims with their liability insurers' endorsement, or where large excesses are involved.

The most a negotiation is likely to consist of is a meeting between opposing sides and a rehearsal of points of claim and points of defence. If there is unwillingness to test issues in court, one side will probably suggest a percentage of the settlement claimed, and the two sides will work towards an agreed settlement.

However, it is evident that such scenarios arise only when either or both sides are not totally certain of their position and reluctant to go to court.

Settlement

Once a settlement has been agreed, the party settling is generally entitled to require the party it is settling with to complete a formal document stating that the amount to be paid is a final payment in the matter and that the claimant will cease pursuing the matter.

Effectively, the claimant releases the respondent from liability—accordingly, the document is known as "release of liability" or a "discharge of liability". Such release or discharge is given in "escrow": this means the document is signed before actual payment of the settlement and becomes effective only when the settlement is paid over. There is no set or standard wording, and some respondents will be comfortable with a short letter from the claimant releasing the respondent. Alternatively, some releases are framed in archaic legal wording and require witnesses to the claimant's signature, which seems somewhat out of place in today's tendency toward simplicity in legal documents.

Some respondents force such releases on all claimants when they are patently unnecessary. For instance, if a limitation properly applies, the claimant cannot possibly continue his claim, because there is no way in which he can force the respondent to pay more. Releases are even seen in small claims settled in full, when it is completely evident to the respondent that no further claim could possibly be made. Nevertheless, of course, it is better to sign such a document to obtain the settlement than to argue with the respondent about it!

Lawyers and litigation

Generally, a claimant who aspires to be a plaintiff faces greater problems to begin with than a respondent. The respondent is required only to maintain his position, knowing that the claimant must metaphorically take a "very deep breath" and steel himself for legal expenses and the commitment of time to solicitors. While panic often sets in in a respondent's office when a writ arrives, it usually finds its way quickly to liability insurers and is passed to solicitors, and matters settle down.

The claimant will have had to consult a lawyer and—if the lawyer is looking out for his client's true interests—will have had to convince the lawyers to agree with his desire for action. Prudence requires that proper evidence is taken and considered at this point, before the writ is issued.

If the plaintiff and his solicitor have done the job properly, it is now the respondent's turn to work hard to marshall his defence: evidence is examined in detail and perhaps difficult decisions are made concerning future conduct of the case.

At this stage, each side is probably as aware of the strengths and weaknesses of its case as it is likely to be.

If neither side will withdraw, litigation processes follow steadily with both sides incurring fees and disbursements, sometimes at a horrifying rate. However, neither side should ever forget that it can call a halt to the process at any time and seek an agreed result. In the U.K., a "defeated" side will almost always pay half to two-thirds of the other side's costs to enable it to withdraw: the "winner" will still bear half to one third of its own costs, which can produce a pyrrhic victory on occasion. The costs the winner has to bear are termed "irrecoverable" costs. The side withdrawing prior to trial will probably be forced to pay some or all of the other side's costs to date in order to withdraw. Failing that, the other side can probably obtain a costs order against the side withdrawing.

It remains a simple fact that only the isolated case goes the whole way to trial and judgment, and that litigation almost invariably extends claims into a long and uncertain future.

Few hard rules can be drawn from all this, but there are "rules of thumb" which are traditionally applied. There is a feeling in some quarters that when a claimant with a large claim feels strong he may be willing to accept an 80 to 85 per cent settlement simply to avoid the case dragging on, with uncertainty about both when the case will conclude and how much the bill for "irrecoverable" costs will be. In other situations, a respondent may assess the situation, examine the evidence and suggest to the other side that a settlement is worth only (say) 60 per cent of the claim. What does this mean? Perhaps it is supposed to mean that there is a 60 per cent chance of success in court. Who can really assess such a chance in this manner? It is a true imponderable and represents merely a desire to conclude matters for as little as possible, since the party to whom such an offer is put will probably have no real idea why such a figure has been chosen and may not ask for an explanation, but will simply put a counter-offer of (say) 80 per cent. Once this process is under way it usually leads to an agreed conclusion.

APPENDIX 1

ROAD HAULAGE ASSOCIATION LIMITED CONDITIONS OF CARRIAGE 1991

EFFECTIVE FROM 1 JUNE 1991

All readers must note that the use of the RHA Conditions of Carriage is open only to members of the Road Haulage Association.

SPECIMEN

(hereinafter referred to as "the Carrier") is not a common carrier and accepts goods for carriage only upon that condition and the Conditions set out below. No servant or agent of the Carrier is permitted to alter or vary these Conditions in any way unless expressly authorised in writing to do so.

1. Definitions

In these Conditions:
"Customer" means the person or company who contracts for the services of the Carrier including any other carrier who gives a Consignment to the Carrier for carriage.
"Contract" means the contract of carriage between the Customer and the Carrier.
"Consignee" means the person or company to whom the Carrier contracts to deliver the goods.
"Consignment" means goods in bulk or contained in one parcel, package or container, as the case may be, or any number of separate parcels, packages or containers sent at one time in one load by or for the Customer from one address to one address.
"Dangerous Goods" means dangerous substances listed by the Health and Safety Commission in Part I of the Authorised and Approved List of Dangerous Substances, explosives, radioactive substances and any other substance presenting a similar hazard.

2. Parties and Sub-Contracting

(1) The Customer warrants that he is either the owner of the goods in any Consignment or is authorised by such owner to accept these Conditions on such owner's behalf.

(2) The Carrier and any other carrier employed by the Carrier may employ the services

of any other carrier for the purpose of fulfilling the Contract in whole or in part and the name of every other such carrier shall be provided to the Customer upon request.

(3) The Carrier contracts for itself and as agent of and trustee for its servants and agents and all other carriers referred to in (2) above and such other carrier's servants and agents and every reference in Conditions 3–19 inclusive hereof "the Carrier" shall be deemed to include every other such carrier, servant and agent with the intention that they shall have the benefit of the Contract and collectively and together with the Carrier be under no greater liability to the Customer or any other party than is the Carrier hereunder.

(4) Notwithstanding Condition 2(3) the carriage of goods in any Consignment by rail, sea, inland waterway or air is arranged by the Carrier as agent of the Customer and shall be subject to the Conditions of the rail, shipping, inland waterway or air carrier contracted to carry the goods. The Carrier shall be under no liability whatever to whomsoever and however arising in respect of such carriage. Provided that where goods are carried partly by road and partly by such other means of transport any loss, damage or delay shall be deemed to have occurred while the goods were being carried by road unless the contrary is proved by the Carrier.

3. Dangerous Goods

Dangerous Goods must be disclosed by the Customer and if the Carrier agrees to accept them for carriage they must be classified, packed and labelled in accordance with the statutory regulations for the carriage by road of the substance declared. Transport Emergency Cards (Tremcards) or information in writing in the manner required by the relevant statutory provisions must be provided by the Customer in respect of each substance and must accompany the Consignment.

4. Loading and Unloading

(1) Unless the Carrier has agreed in writing to the contrary with the Customer:

- (a) The Carrier shall not be under any obligation to provide any plant, power or labour, other than that carried by the vehicle, required for loading or unloading the Consignment.
- (b) The Customer warrants that any special appliances required for loading or unloading the Consignment which are not carried by the vehicle will be provided by the Customer or on the Customer's behalf.
- (c) The Carrier shall be under no liability whatever to the Customer for any damage whatever, however caused, if the Carrier is instructed to load or unload goods requiring special appliances which, in breach of the warranty in (b) above, have not been provided by the Customer or on the Customer's behalf.
- (d) The Carrier shall not be required to provide service beyond the usual place of collection or delivery but if any such service is given by the Carrier it shall be at the sole risk of the Customer.

(2) The Customer shall indemnify the Carrier against all claims and demands whatever which could not have been made if such instructions as are referred to in (1)(c) of this Condition and such service as is referred to in (1)(d) of this Condition had not been given.

5. Consignment Notes

The Carrier shall, if so required, sign a document prepared by the sender acknowledging the receipt of the Consignment but no such document shall be evidence of the condition or of the correctness of the declared nature, quantity, or weight of the Consignment at the time it is received by the Carrier.

6. Transit

(1) Transit shall commence when the Carrier takes possession of the Consignment whether at the point of collection or at the Carrier's premises.

(2) Transit shall (unless otherwise previously determined) end when the Consignment is tendered at the usual place of delivery at the Consignee's address within the customary cartage hours of the district.

Provided that:

(a) if no safe and adequate access or no adequate unloading facilities there exist then transit shall be deemed to end at the expiry of one clear day after notice in writing (or by telephone if so previously agreed in writing) of the arrival of the Consignment at the Carrier's premises has been sent to the Consignee; and

(b) when for any other reason whatever a Consignment cannot be delivered or when a Consignment is held by the Carrier "to await order" or "to be kept till called for" or upon any like instructions and such instructions are not given or the Consignment is not called for and removed, within a reasonable time, then transit shall be deemed to end.

7. Undelivered or Unclaimed Goods

Where the Carrier is unable for any reason to deliver a Consignment to the Consignee or as he may order, or where by virtue of the proviso to Condition 6(2) hereof transit is deemed to be at end, the Carrier may sell the goods and payment or tender of the proceeds after deduction of all proper charges and expenses in relation thereto and of all outstanding charges in relation to the carriage and storage of the goods shall (without prejudice to any claim or right which the Customer may have against the Carrier otherwise arising under these Conditions) discharge the Carrier from all liability in respect of such goods, their carriage and storage.

Provided that:

(1) the Carrier shall do what is reasonable to obtain the value of the Consignment and

(2) the power of sale shall not be exercised where the name and address of the sender or of the Consignee is known unless the Carrier shall have done what is reasonable in the circumstances to give notice to the sender or, if the name and address of the sender is not known, to the Consignee that the goods will be sold unless within the time specified in such notice, being a reasonable time in the circumstances from the giving of such notice, the goods are taken away or instructions are given for their disposal.

8. Carrier's Charges

(1) The Carrier's charges shall be payable by the Customer without prejudice to the Carrier's rights against the Consignee or any other person. Provided that when goods are consigned "carriage forward" the Customer shall not be required to pay such charges unless the consignee fails to pay after a reasonable demand has been made by the Carrier for payment thereof.

(2) Except where a quotation states otherwise all quotations based on a tonnage rate shall apply to the gross weight unless:

(a) the goods exceed 2.25 cubic metres in measurement per tonne, in which case the tonnage rate shall be computed upon and apply to each measurement of 2.25 cubic metres or any part thereof, or

(b) the size or shape of a Consignment necessitates the use of a vehicle of greater carrying capacity than the weight of the Consignment would otherwise require, in which case the tonnage rate shall be computed upon and apply to the carrying capacity of such vehicle as is reasonably required.

(3) Charges shall be payable on the expiry of any time limit previously stipulated and the Carrier shall be entitled to interest at 5 per cent above the Clearing Bank Base Rate current at this time, calculated on a daily basis on all amounts overdue to the Carrier.

9. Liability for Loss and Damage

(1) The Customer shall be deemed to have elected to accept the terms set out in (2) of this Condition unless, before the transit commences, the Customer has agreed in writing that the Carrier shall not be liable for any loss or mis-delivery of or damage to goods however or whenever caused and whether or not caused or contributed to directly or indirectly by any act, omission, neglect, default or other wrongdoing on the part of the Carrier.

(2) Subject to these Conditions the Carrier shall be liable for:

(a) loss or mis-delivery of or damage to livestock, bullion, money, securities, stamps, precious metals or precious stones only if:
- (i) the Carrier has specifically agreed in writing to carry any such items and
- (ii) the Customer has agreed in writing to reimburse the Carrier in respect of all additional costs which result from the carrying of the said items and
- (iii) the loss, mis-delivery or damage is occasioned during transit and results from negligent act or omission by the Carrier;

(b) any loss or mis-delivery of or damage to any other goods occasioned during transit unless the same had arisen from, and the Carrier has used reasonable care to minimise the effects of:
- (i) Act of God;
- (ii) any consequences of war, invasion, act of foreign enemy, hostilities (whether war or not), civil war, rebellion, insurrection, military or usurped power or confiscation, requisition, or destruction of or damage to property by or under the order of any government or public or local authority;
- (iii) seizure or forfeiture under legal process;
- (iv) error, act, omission, mis-statement or mis-representation by the Customer or other owner of the goods or by servants or agents of either of them;
- (v) inherent liability to wastage in bulk or weight, latent defect or inherent defect, vice or natural deterioration of the goods;
- (vi) insufficient or improper packing;
- (vii) insufficient or improper labelling or addressing;
- (viii) riot, civil commotion, strike, lockout, general or partial stoppage or restraint of labour from whatever cause;
- (ix) Consignee not taking or accepting delivery within a reasonable time after the Consignment has been tendered.

(3) The Carrier shall not in any circumstances be liable for loss of or damage to goods after transit of such goods is deemed to have ended within the meaning of Condition 6(2) hereof, whether or not caused or contributed to directly or indirectly by any act, omission, neglect, default or other wrongdoing on the part of the Carrier.

10. Fraud

The Carrier shall not in any circumstances be liable in respect of a Consignment where there has been fraud on the part of the Customer or the owner of the goods or the servants or agents of either in respect of that Consignment, unless the fraud has been contributed by the complicity of the Carrier or of any servant of the Carrier acting in the course of his employment.

11. Limitation of Liability

(1) Except as otherwise provided in these Conditions, the liability of the Carrier in respect of loss or mis-delivery of or damage to goods, however sustained, shall in all circumstances be limited as follows:

(a) To the value of the Consignment where, at any time prior to the commencement of transit, the Customer has given seven days' written notice to the Carrier requiring that the limit of the Carrier's liability be set at the value of the Consignment where this value exceeds £1,300 per tonne or, if no such notice has been given;

(b) To £1,300 per tonne on either the gross weight of the Consignment or, where applicable, the tonnage computed in accordance with Condition 8(2)(a) or (b) hereof; or

(c) To the proportion of the sum, ascertained in accordance with (1)(a) or (b) of this Condition, which the actual value of part of the Consignment bears to the actual value of the whole of the Consignment where loss, mis-delivery or damage, however sustained, is in respect of that part of the Consignment.

Provided that:

(i) nothing in this Condition shall limit the liability of the Carrier to less than the sum of £10;

(ii) the Carrier shall be entitled to require proof of the value of the whole of the Consignment and of any part thereof lost, mis-delivered or damaged;

(iii) the Customer shall be required to agree with the Carrier the carriage charges appropriate to the value of the Consignment where the limit of liability is increased above £1,300 per tonne in accordance with (1)(a) of this Condition.

(2) Notwithstanding Condition 11(1), the liability of the Carrier in respect of the indirect or consequential loss or damage, however arising and including loss of market, shall not exceed the amount of the carriage charges in respect of the Consignment or the amount of the claimant's proved loss, whichever is the smaller, unless,

(a) at the time of entering into the Contract with the Carrier the Customer declares to the Carrier a special interest in delivery in the case of loss or damage or of an agreed time limit being exceeded and agrees to pay a surcharge calculated on the amount of that interest, and

(b) prior to the commencement of transit the Customer has delivered to the Carrier written confirmation of the special interest, agreed time limit and amount of the interest.

12. Insurance

The Carrier shall insure his liabilities arising out of the carriage of goods under these Conditions.

13. Indemnity to the Carrier

The Customer shall indemnify the Carrier against:

(1) all consequences suffered by the Carrier (including but not limited to claims, demands, proceedings, fines, penalties, damages, costs, expenses and loss of or

damage to the carrying vehicle and to other goods carried) of any error, omission, mis-statement or mis-representation by the Customer or other owner of the goods or by any servant or agent of either of them, insufficient or improper packing, labelling or addressing of the goods or fraud as in Condition 10;

(2) all claims and demands whatever by whomsoever made in excess of the liability of the Carrier under these Conditions;

(3) all losses suffered by and claims made against the Carrier resulting from loss of or damage to property caused by or arising out of the carriage by the Carrier of Dangerous Goods whether or not declared by the Customer as such;

(4) all claims made upon the Carrier by H.M. Customs and Excise in respect of dutiable goods consigned in bond whether or not transit has ended or been suspended.

14. Time Limits for Claims

The Carrier shall not be liable for:

(1) loss from a parcel, package or container or from an unpacked Consignment or for damage to a Consignment or any part of a Consignment unless he is advised thereof in writing otherwise than upon a consignment note or delivery document within three days, and the claim is made in writing within seven days, after the termination of transit;

(2) loss, mis-delivery or non-delivery of the whole of a Consignment or of any separate parcel, package or container forming part of a Consignment unless he is advised of the loss, mis-delivery or non-delivery in writing otherwise than upon a consignment note or delivery document within twenty-eight days, and the claim is made in writing within forty-two days, after the commencement of transit.

Provided that if the Customer proves that,

(a) it was not reasonably possible for the Customer to advise the Carrier or make a claim in writing within the time limit applicable and

(b) such advice or claim was given or made within a reasonable time,

the Carrier shall not have the benefit of the exclusion of liability afforded by this Condition.

15. Lien

The Carrier shall have a general lien against the Customer, where the Customer is the owner of the goods, for any monies whatever due from the Customer to the Carrier. If such a lien is not satisfied within a reasonable time, the Carrier may, at his absolute discretion sell the goods, or part thereof, as agent for the Customer and apply the proceeds towards the monies due and the expenses of the retention, insurance and sale of the goods and shall, upon accounting to the Customer for any balance remaining, be discharged from all liability whatever in respect of the goods. Where the Customer is not the owner of the goods, the Carrier shall have a particular lien against said owner, allowing him to retain possession, but not dispose of, the goods against monies due from the Customer in respect of the Consignment.

16. Unreasonable Detention

The Customer shall be liable for the cost of unreasonable detention of any vehicle, trailer, container or sheet but the rights of the Carrier against any other person in respect thereof shall remain unaffected.

17. Computation of Time

In the computation of time where any period provided by these Conditions is seven days or less, Saturdays, Sundays and all statutory public holidays shall be excluded.

18. Loss Adjustment

The value of a Consignment or part Consignment shall be taken as its invoice value if the goods have been sold. Otherwise it shall be taken as the cost thereof to the owner.

19. Impossibility of Performance

The Carrier shall be relieved of its obligation to perform the Contract to the extent that the performance is prevented by failure of the Customer, fire, weather conditions, industrial dispute, labour disturbance or cause beyond the reasonable control of the Carrier.

APPENDIX 2

BIFA STANDARD TRADING CONDITIONS 1989*

All readers must note that the use of BIFA Standard Trading Conditions is open only to members of the British International Freight Association.

The Customer's attention is drawn to the Clauses hereof which exclude or limit the Company's liability and those which require the Customer to indemnify the Company in certain circumstances.

Definitions and application

1 In these Conditions:

"Company"	Is the BIFA Member trading under these Conditions.
"Person"	Includes persons or any Body or Bodies Corporate.
"The Owner"	Means the Owner of the goods (including any packaging, containers or equipment) to which any business concluded under these Conditions relates and any other person who is or may become interested in them.
"Customer"	Means any person at whose request or on whose behalf the Company undertakes any business or provides advice, information or services.

2(A) Subject to Sub-Paragraph (B) below, all and any activities of the Company in the course of business whether gratuitous or not are undertaken subject to these Conditions.

(B) If any legislation is compulsorily applicable to any business undertaken, these Conditions shall, as regards such business, be read as subject to such legislation and nothing in these Conditions shall be construed as a surrender by the Company of any of its rights or immunities or as an increase of any of its responsibilities or liabilities under such legislation and if any part of these Conditions be repugnant to such legislation to any extent such part shall as regards such business be overridden to that extent and no further.

3 The Customer warrants that he is either the Owner or the authorised Agent of the Owner and also that he is accepting these Conditions not only for himself but also as Agent for and on behalf of the Owner.

4 In authorising the Customer to enter into any Contract with the Company and/or in accepting any document issued by the Company in connection with such Contract, the Owner and Consignee accept these Conditions for themselves and their Agents and for any parties on whose behalf they or their Agents may act, and in particular, but without prejudice to the generality of this Clause, they accept that the Company shall have the right to enforce against them jointly and severally any liability of the Customer under these Conditions or to recover from them any sums to be paid by the Customer which upon proper demand have not been paid.

* Reproduced by kind permission of BIFA, tel: 0181 844 2266, fax: 0181 890 5546.

The company

5(A) Subject to Clauses 13 and 14 below, the Company shall be entitled to procure any or all of its services as an Agent or to provide those services as a Principal.

(B) The offer and acceptance of an inclusive price for the accomplishment of any service or services shall not itself determine whether any such service is or services are to be arranged by the Company acting as Agent or to be provided by the Company acting as a Contracting Principal.

(C) When acting as an Agent the Company does not make or purport to make any Contract with the Customer for the carriage, storage, packing or handling of any goods nor for any other physical service in relation to them and acts solely on behalf of the Customer in securing services by establishing Contracts with Third Parties so that direct contractual relationships are established between the customer and such Third Parties.

(D) The Company shall on demand by the Customer provide evidence of any Contract entered into as Agent for the Customer. Insofar as the Company may be in default of this obligation, it shall be deemed to have contracted with the Customer as a Principal for the performance of the Customer's instructions.

6 When and to the extent that the Company has contracted as Principal for the performance of any of its services, it undertakes to perform and/or in its own name to procure the performance of those services, and subject always to the totality of these Conditions and in particular to Clauses 26–29 hereof accepts liability for loss of or damage to goods taken into its charge occurring between the time when it takes the goods into its charge and the time when the Company is entitled to call upon the Customer, Consignee or Owner to take delivery of the goods.

7 When and to the extent that the Company in accordance with these Conditions is acting as an Agent on behalf of the Customer, the Company shall be entitled and the Customer hereby expressly authorises the Company to enter into Contracts on behalf of the Customer—

(A) for the carriage of goods by any route or means or person;

(B) for the storage, packing, trans-shipment, loading, unloading or handling of the goods by any person at any place and for any length of time;

(C) for the carriage or storage of goods in or on transport units as defined in Clause 19 and with other goods of whatever nature; and

(D) to do such acts as may in the opinion of the Company be reasonably necessary in the performance of its obligations in the interests of the Customer.

8 The Company reserves to itself a reasonable liberty as to the means, route and procedure to be followed in the handling, storage and transportation of goods.

9 The Company shall be entitled to perform any of its obligations herein by itself or by its parent, subsidiary or associated Companies.

In the absence of agreement to the contrary any Contract to which these Conditions apply is made by the Company on its own behalf and also as Agent for and on behalf of any such parent, subsidiary or associated Company, and any such Company shall be entitled to the benefit of these Conditions.

10(A) Subject to Sub-Clause (B) hereof, the Company shall have a general lien on all goods and documents relating to goods in its possession, custody or control for all sums due at any time from the Customer or Owner and shall be entitled to sell or dispose of such goods or documents as Agent for and at the expense of the Customer and apply the proceeds in or towards the payment of such sums on 28 days notice in writing to the Customer. Upon accounting to the Customer for any balance remaining after payment of any sum due to the Company and the costs of sale or disposal the Company shall be discharged of any liability whatsoever in respect of the goods or documents.

(B) When the goods are liable to perish or deteriorate, the Company's right to sell or dispose of the goods shall arise immediately upon any sum becoming due to the Company subject only to the Company taking reasonable steps to bring to the Customer's attention its intention of selling or disposing of the goods before doing so.

11 The Company shall be entitled to retain and be paid all brokerages, commissions allowances and other remunerations customarily retained by or paid to Freight Forwarders.

12(A) If delivery of the goods or any part thereof is not taken by the Customer, Consignee or Owner, at the time and place when and where the Company is entitled to call upon such person to take delivery thereof, the Company shall be entitled to store the goods or any part thereof at the sole risk of the Customer, whereupon the liability of the Company in respect of the goods or that part thereof stored as aforesaid shall wholly cease and the cost of such storage if paid for or payable by the Company or any Agent or Sub-Contractor of the Company shall forthwith upon demand be paid by the Customer to the Company.

(B) The Company shall be entitled at the expense of the Customer to dispose of (by sale or otherwise as may be reasonable in all the circumstances):-

(i) on 28 days notice in writing to the Customer, or where the Customer cannot be traced and reasonable efforts have been made to contact any parties who may reasonably be supposed by the Company to have any interest in the goods, any goods which have been held by the Company for 90 days and which cannot be delivered as instructed; and

(ii) without prior notice, goods which have perished, deteriorated or altered or are in immediate prospect of doing so in a manner which has caused or may reasonably be expected to cause loss or damage to Third Parties or to contravene any applicable laws or regulations.

13(A) No Insurance will be effected except upon express instructions given in writing by the Customer and all Insurances effected by the Company are subject to the usual exceptions and conditions of the Policies of the Insurance Company or Underwriters taking the risk. Unless otherwise agreed in writing the Company shall not be under any obligation to effect a separate Insurance on each consignment but may declare it on any open or general Policy held by the Company.

(B) Insofar as the Company agrees to arrange Insurance, the Company acts solely as Agent for the Customer using its best endeavours to arrange such Insurance and does so subject to the limits of liability contained in Clause 29 hereof.

14(A) Except under special arrangements previously made in writing or under the terms of a printed document signed by the Company, any instructions relating to the delivery or release of goods in specified circumstances only, such as (but without prejudice to the generality of this Clause) against payment or against surrender of a particular document, are accepted by the Company only as Agents for the Customer where Third Parties are engaged to effect compliance with the instructions.

(B) The Company shall not be under any liability in respect of such arrangements as are referred to under Sub-Clause (A) hercof save where such arrangements are made in writing.

(C) In any event, the Company's liability in respect of the performance or arranging the performance of such instructions shall not exceed that provided for in these Conditions in respect of loss of or damage to goods.

15 Advice and information, in whatever form it may be given, is provided by the Company for the Customer only and the Customer shall indemnify the Company against any liability, claims, loss, damage, costs or expenses arising out of any other persons relying upon such advice or information. Except under special arrangements previously made in writing, advice and information which is not related to specific instructions accepted by the Company is provided gratuitously and without liability.

16(A) Except under special arrangement previously made in writing the Company will not accept or deal with bullion, coin, precious stones, jewellery, valuables, antiques, pictures, human remains, livestock or plants. Should any Customer nevertheless deliver any such goods to the Company or cause the Company to handle or deal with any such goods otherwise than under special arrangements previously made in writing the Company shall be under no liability whatsoever for or in connection with such goods howsoever arising.

(B) The Company may at any time waive its rights and exemptions from liability under Sub-Clause (A) above in respect of any one or more of the categories of goods mentioned herein or of any part of any category. If such waiver is not in writing, the onus of proving such waiver shall be on the Customer.

17 Except following instructions previously received in writing and accepted by the Company, the Company will not accept or deal with goods of a dangerous or damaging nature, nor with goods likely to harbour or encourage vermin or other pests, nor with goods liable to taint or affect other goods. If such goods are accepted pursuant to a special arrangement and then in the opinion of the Company they constitute a risk to other goods, property, life or health, the Company shall where reasonably practicable contact the Customer, but reserves the right at the expense of the Customer to remove or otherwise deal with the goods.

18 Where there is a choice of rates according to the extent or degree of the liability assumed by carriers, warehousemen or others, no declaration of value where optional will be made except under special arrangements previously made in writing.

The customer

19 The Customer warrants:

(A) that the description and particulars of any goods furnished by or on behalf of the Customer are full and accurate.

(B) that all goods have been properly and sufficiently prepared, packed, stowed, labelled and/or marked, and that the preparation, packing, stowage, labelling and marking are appropriate to any operations or transactions affecting the goods and the characteristics of the goods.

(C) that where the Company receives the goods from the Customer already stowed in or on a container, trailer, tanker, or any other device specifically constructed for the carriage of goods by land, sea or air (each hereafter individually referred to as "the transport unit"), the transport unit is in good condition, and is suitable for the carriage to the intended destination of the goods loaded therein or thereon.

20 Should the Customer otherwise than under special arrangements previously made in writing as set out in Clause 17 above deliver to the Company or cause the Company to deal with or handle goods of a dangerous or damaging nature, or goods likely to harbour or encourage vermin or other pests, or goods liable to taint or affect other goods, he shall be liable for all loss or damage arising in connection with such goods and shall indemnify the Company against all penalties, claims, damages, costs and expenses whatsoever arising in connection therewith, and the goods may be dealt with in such manner as the Company or any other person in whose custody they may be at any relevant time shall think fit.

21 The Customer undertakes that no claim shall be made against any Director, Servant, or Employee of the Company which imposes or attempts to impose upon them any liability in connection with any services which are the subject of these Conditions and if any such claim should nevertheless be made, to indemnify the Company against all consequences thereof.

22 The Customer shall save harmless and keep the Company indemnified from and against—

(A) All liability, loss, damage, costs and expenses whatsoever (including without prejudice to the generality of the foregoing, all duties, taxes, imposts, levies, deposits and outlays of whatsoever nature levied by any authority in relation to the goods) arising out of the Company acting in accordance with the Customer's instructions or arising from any breach by the Customer of any Warranty contained in these Conditions or from the negligence of the Customer, and

(B) Without derogation from Sub-Clause (A) above, any liability assumed or incurred by the Company when by reason of carrying out the Customer's instructions the Company has reasonably become liable or may become liable to any other party, and

(C) All claims, costs and demands whatsoever and by whomsoever made or preferred in excess of the liability of the Company under the terms of these Conditions regardless whether such claims, costs and demands arise from or in connection with the negligence or breach of duty of the Company its Servants, Sub-Contractors or Agents, and

(D) Any claims of a General Average nature which may be made on the Company.

23(A) The Customer shall pay to the Company in cash or as otherwise agreed all sums immediately when due without reduction or deferment on account of any claim, counterclaim or set-off.

(B) In respect of all sums which are overdue the Customer shall be liable to pay to the Company interest calculated at 4% above the Base Rate for the time being of Midland Bank Plc.

24 Despite the acceptance by the Company of instructions to collect freight, duties, charges or other expenses from the Consignee or any other person the Customer shall remain responsible for such freight, duties, charges or expenses on receipt of evidence of proper demand and in the absence of evidence of payment (for whatever reason) by such Consignee or other person when due.

25 Where liability for General Average arises in connection with the goods, the Customer shall promptly provide security to the Company or to any other party designated by the Company in a form acceptable to the Company.

Liability and limitation

26 The Company shall perform its duties with a reasonable degree of care, diligence, skill and judgement.

27 The Company shall be relieved of liability for any loss or damage if and to the extent that such loss or damage is caused by—

(A) strike, lock-out, stoppage or restraint of labour, the consequences of which the Company is unable to avoid by the exercise of reasonable diligence;

(B) any cause or event which the Company is unable to avoid and the consequences whereof the Company is unable to prevent by the exercise of reasonable diligence.

28 Except under special arrangements previously made in writing the Company accepts no responsibility for departure or arrival dates of goods.

29(A) Subject to Clause 2(B) above and Sub-Clause (D) below the Company's liability howsoever arising and notwithstanding that the cause of loss or damage be unexplained shall not exceed

(i) in the case of claims for loss or damage to goods

(a) the value of any goods lost or damaged, or
(b) a sum at the rate of two Special Drawing Rights as defined by the International Monetary Fund (hereinafter referred to as SDRs), per kilo of gross weight of any goods lost or damaged

whichever shall be the least

(ii) in the case of all other claims

(a) the value of the goods the subject of the relevant transaction between the Company and its Customer, or
(b) a sum at the rate of two SDRs per kilo of the gross weight of the goods the subject of the said transaction, or
(c) 75,000 SDRs in respect of any one transaction

whichever shall be the least.

For the purposes of Clause 29(A) the value of the goods shall be their value when they were or should have been shipped. The value of SDRs shall be calculated as at the date when the claim is received by the Company in writing.

(B) Subject to Clause 2(B) above, and Sub-Clause (D) below, the Company's liability for loss or damage as a result of failure to deliver or arrange delivery of goods in a reasonable time or (where there is a special arrangement under Clause 28) to adhere to agreed departure or arrival dates shall not in any circumstances whatever exceed a sum equal to twice the amount of the Company's charges in respect of the relevant transaction.

(C) Save in respect of such loss or damage as is referred to at Sub-Clause (B) and subject to Clause 2(B) above and Sub-Clause (D) below, the Company shall not in any circumstances whatsoever be liable for indirect or consequential loss such as (but not limited to) loss of profits, loss of market or the consequences of delay or deviation however caused.

(D) By special arrangement agreed in writing, the Company may accept liability in excess of the limits set out in Sub-Clauses (A) to (C) above upon the Customer agreeing to pay the Company's additional charges for accepting such increased liability. Details of the Company's additional charges will be provided upon request.

30(A) Any claim by the Customer against the Company arising in respect of any service provided for the Customer or which the Company has undertaken to provide shall be made in writing and notified to the Company within 14 days of the date upon which the Customer became or should have become aware of any event or occurrence alleged to give rise to such claim and any claim not made and notified as aforesaid shall be deemed to be waived and absolutely barred except where the Customer can show that it was impossible for him to comply with this Time Limit and that he has made the claim as soon as it was reasonably possible for him to do so.

(B) Notwithstanding the provisions of Sub-Paragraph (A) above the Company shall in any event be discharged of all liability whatsoever howsoever arising in respect of any service provided for the Customer or which the Company has undertaken to provide unless suit be brought and written notice thereof given to the Company within nine months from the date of the event or occurrence alleged to give rise to a cause of action against the Company.

Jurisdiction and law

31 These Conditions and any act or contract to which they apply shall be governed by English Law and any dispute arising out of any act or contract to which these Conditions apply shall be subject to the exclusive jurisdiction of the English Courts.

APPENDIX 3

THE UNAMENDED WARSAW CONVENTION 1929

CONVENTION FOR THE UNIFICATION OF CERTAIN RULES RELATING TO INTERNATIONAL TRANSPORTATION BY AIR*

CHAPTER I

SCOPE — DEFINITIONS

Article 1

1. This convention shall apply to all international transportation of persons, baggage, or goods performed by aircraft for hire. It shall apply equally to gratuitous transportation by aircraft performed by an air transportation enterprise.

2. For the purposes of this convention the expression "international transportation" shall mean any transportation in which, according to the contract made by the parties, the place of departure and the place of destination, whether or not there be a break in the transportation or a transshipment, are situated either within the territories of two High Contracting Parties, or within the territory of a single High Contracting Party, if there is an agreed stopping place within a territory subject to the sovereignty, suzerainty, mandate or authority of another power, even though that power is not a party to this convention. Transportation without such an agreed stopping place between territories subject to the sovereignty, suzerainty, mandate, or authority of the same High Contracting Party shall not be deemed to be international for the purposes of this convention.

3. Transportation to be performed by several successive air carriers shall be deemed, for the purposes of this convention, to be one undivided transportation, if it has been regarded by the parties as a single operation, whether it has been agreed upon under the form of a single contract or of a series of contracts, and it shall not lose its international character merely because one contract or a series of contracts is to be performed entirely within a territory subject to the sovereignty, suzerainty, mandate, or authority of the same High Contracting Party.

Article 2

1. This convention shall apply to transportation performed by the state or by legal entities constituted under public law provided it falls within the conditions laid down in Article 1.

* The French text is the only authoritative text. The translation presented here is that followed by the United States (49 Stat. 3000; T.S. 876).

2. This convention shall not apply to transportation performed under the terms of any international postal convention.

CHAPTER II

SECTION I — PASSENGER TICKET

Article 3

1. For the transportation of passengers the carrier must deliver a passenger ticket which shall contain the following particulars:
   a) the place and date of issue;
   b) the place of departure and of destination;
   c) the agreed stopping places, provided that the carrier may reserve the right to alter the stopping places in case of necessity, and that if he exercises that right, the alteration shall not have the effect of depriving the transportation of its international character;
   d) the name and address of the carrier or carriers;
   e) a statement that the transportation is subject to the rules relating to liability established by this convention.

2. The absence, irregularity, or loss of the passenger ticket shall not affect the existence or the validity of the contract of transportation, which shall none the less be subject to the rules of this convention. Nevertheless, if the carrier accepts a passenger without a passenger ticket having been delivered he shall not be entitled to avail himself of those provisions of this convention which exclude or limit his liability.

SECTION II — BAGGAGE CHECK

Article 4

1. For the transportation of baggage, other than small personal objects of which the passenger takes charge himself, the carrier must deliver a baggage check.

2. The baggage check shall be made out in duplicate, one part for the passenger and the other part for the carrier.

3. The baggage check shall contain the following particulars:
   a) the place and date of issue;
   b) the place of departure and of destination;
   c) the name and address of the carrier or carriers;
   d) the number of the passenger ticket;
   e) a statement that delivery of the baggage will be made to the bearer of the baggage check;
   f) the number and weight of the packages;
   g) the amount of the value declared in accordance with Article 22(2);
   h) a statement that the transportation is subject to the rules relating to liability established by this convention.

4. The absence, irregularity, or loss of the baggage check shall not affect the existence or the validity of the contract of transportation which shall none the less be subject to the rules of this convention. Nevertheless, if the carrier accepts baggage without a baggage check having been delivered, or if the baggage check does not contain the particulars set out at d), f) and h) above, the carrier shall not be entitled to avail himself of those provisions of the convention which exclude or limit his liability.

SECTION III — AIR WAYBILL

Article 5

1. Every carrier of goods has the right to require the consignor to make out and hand over to him a document called an "air waybill"; every consignor has the right to require the carrier to accept this document.

2. The absence, irregularity, or loss of this document shall not affect the existence or the validity of the contract of transportation which shall, subject to the provisions of Article 9, be none the less governed by the rules of this convention.

Article 6

1. The air waybill shall be made out by the consignor in three original parts and be handed over with the goods.

2. The first part shall be marked "for the carrier", and shall be signed by the consignor. The second part shall be marked "for the consignee"; it shall be signed by the consignor and by the carrier and shall accompany the goods. The third part shall be signed by the carrier and handed by him to the consignor after the goods have been accepted.

3. The carrier shall sign on acceptance of the goods.

4. The signature of the carrier may be stamped; that of the consignor may be printed or stamped.

5. If, at the request of the consignor, the carrier makes out the air waybill, he shall be deemed, subject to proof to the contrary, to have done so on behalf of the consignor.

Article 7

The carrier of goods has the right to require the consignor to make out separate waybills when there is more than one package.

Article 8

The air waybill shall contain the following particulars:

a) the place and date of its execution;
b) the place of departure and of destination;
c) the agreed stopping places, provided that the carrier may reserve the right to alter the stopping places in case of necessity, and that if he exercises that right the alteration shall not have the effect of depriving the transportation of its international character;
d) the name and address of the consignor;
e) the name and address of the first carrier;
f) the name and address of the consignee, if the case so requires;
g) the nature of the goods;
h) the number of packages, the method of packing, and the particular marks or numbers upon them;
i) the weight, the quantity, the volume, or dimensions of the goods;
j) the apparent condition of the goods and of the packing;
k) the freight, if it has been agreed upon, the date and place of payment, and the person who is to pay it;
l) if the goods are sent for payment on delivery, the price of the goods, and, if the case so requires, the amount of the expenses incurred;

m) the amount of the value declared in accordance with Article 22(2);
n) the number of parts of the air waybill;
o) the documents handed to the carrier to accompany the air waybill;
p) the time fixed for the completion of the transportation and a brief note of the route to be followed, if these matters have been agreed upon;
q) a statement that the transportation is subject to the rules relating to liability established by this convention.

Article 9

If the carrier accepts goods without an air waybill having been made out, or if the air waybill does not contain all the particulars set out in Article 8 a) to i), inclusive, and q), the carrier shall not be entitled to avail himself of the provisions of this convention which exclude or limit his liability.

Article 10

1. The consignor shall be responsible for the correctness of the particulars and statements relating to the goods which he inserts in the air waybill.
2. The consignor shall be liable for all damages suffered by the carrier or any other person by reason of the irregularity, incorrectness or incompleteness of the said particulars and statements.

Article 11

1. The air waybill shall be *prima facie* evidence of the conclusion of the contract, of the receipt of the goods and of the conditions of transportation.
2. The statements in the air waybill relating to the weight, dimensions, and packing of the goods, as well as those relating to the number of packages, shall be *prima facie* evidence of the facts stated; those relating to the quantity, volume, and condition of the goods shall not constitute evidence against the carrier except so far as they both have been, and are stated in the air waybill to have been, checked by him in the presence of the consignor, or relate to the apparent condition of the goods.

Article 12

1. Subject to his liability to carry out all his obligations under the contract of transportation, the consignor shall have the right to dispose of the goods by withdrawing them at the airport of departure or destination, or by stopping them in the course of the journey on any landing, or by calling for them to be delivered at the place of destination, or in the course of the journey to a person other than the consignee named in the air waybill, or by requiring them to be returned to the airport of departure. He must not exercise this right of disposition in such a way as to prejudice the carrier or other consignors, and he must repay any expenses occasioned by the exercise of this right.
2. If it is impossible to carry out the orders of the consignor the carrier must so inform him forthwith.
3. If the carrier obeys the orders of the consignor for the disposition of the goods without requiring the production of the part of the air waybill delivered to the latter, he will be liable, without prejudice to his right of recovery from the consignor, for any damage which may be caused thereby to any person who is lawfully in possession of that part of the air waybill.

4. The right conferred on the consignor shall cease at the moment when that of the consignee begins in accordance with Article 13, below. Nevertheless, if the consignee declines to accept the waybill or the goods, or if he cannot be communicated with, the consignor shall resume his right of disposition.

Article 13

1. Except in the circumstances set out in the preceding Article, the consignee shall be entitled, on arrival of the goods at the place of destination, to require the carrier to hand over to him the air waybill and to deliver the goods to him, on payment of the charges due and on complying with the conditions of transportation set out in the air waybill.
2. Unless it is otherwise agreed, it shall be the duty of the carrier to give notice to the consignee as soon as the goods arrive.
3. If the carrier admits the loss of the goods, or if the goods have not arrived at the expiration of seven days after the date on which they ought to have arrived, the consignee shall be entitled to put into force against the carrier the rights which flow from the contract of transportation.

Article 14

The consignor and the consignee can respectively enforce all the rights given them by Articles 12 and 13, each in his own name, whether he is acting in his own interest or in the interest of another, provided that he carries out the obligations imposed by the contract.

Article 15

1. Articles 12, 13 and 14 shall not affect either the relations of the consignor and the consignee with each other or the relations of third parties whose rights are derived either from the consignor or from the consignee.
2. The provisions of Articles 12, 13 and 14 can only be varied by express provision in the air waybill.

Article 16

1. The consignor must furnish such information and attach to the air waybill such documents as are necessary to meet the formalities of customs, octroi, or police before the goods can be delivered to the consignee. The consignor shall be liable to the carrier for any damage occasioned by the absence, insufficiency, or irregularity of any such information or documents, unless the damage is due to the fault of the carrier or his agents.
2. The carrier is under no obligation to inquire into the correctness or sufficiency of such information or documents.

CHAPTER III

LIABILITY OF THE CARRIER

Article 17

The carrier shall be liable for damage sustained in the event of the death or wounding of a passenger or any other bodily injury suffered by a passenger, if the accident which caused the damage so sustained took place on board the aircraft or in the course of any of the operations of embarking or disembarking.

Article 18

1. The carrier shall be liable for damage sustained in the event of the destruction or loss of, or of damage to, any checked baggage or any goods, if the occurrence which caused the damage so sustained took place during the transportation by air.

2. The transportation by air within the meaning of the preceding paragraph shall comprise the period during which the baggage or goods are in charge of the carrier, whether in an airport or on board an aircraft, or, in the case of a landing outside an airport, in any place whatsoever.

3. The period of the transportation by air shall not extend to any transportation by land, by sea, or by river performed outside an airport. If, however, such transportation takes place in the performance of a contract for transportation by air, for the purpose of loading, delivery or transshipment, any damage is presumed, subject to proof to the contrary, to have been the result of an event which took place during the transportation by air.

Article 19

The carrier shall be liable for damage occasioned by delay in the transportation by air of passengers, baggage, or goods.

Article 20

1. The carrier shall not be liable if he proves that he and his agents have taken all necessary measures to avoid the damage or that it was impossible for him or them to take such measures.

2. In the transportation of goods and baggage the carrier shall not be liable if he proves that the damage was occasioned by an error in piloting, in the handling of the aircraft, or in navigation and that, in all other respects, he and his agents have taken all necessary measures to avoid the damage.

Article 21

If the carrier proves that the damage was caused by or contributed to by the negligence of the injured person the court may, in accordance with the provisions of its own law, exonerate the carrier wholly or partly from his liability.

Article 22

1. In the transportation of passengers the liability of the carrier for each passenger shall be limited to the sum of 125 000 francs. Where, in accordance with the law of the court to which the case is submitted, damages may be awarded in the form of periodical payments, the equivalent capital value of the said payments shall not exceed 125 000 francs. Nevertheless, by special contract, the carrier and the passenger may agree to a higher limit of liability.

2. In the transportation of checked baggage and of goods, the liability of the carrier shall be limited to a sum of 250 francs per kilogram, unless the consignor has made, at the time when the package was handed over to the carrier, a special declaration of the value at delivery and has paid a supplementary sum if the case so requires. In that case the carrier will be liable to pay a sum not exceeding the declared sum, unless he proves that that sum is greater than the actual value to the consignor at delivery.

3. As regards objects of which the passenger takes charge himself the liability of the carrier shall be limited to 5 000 francs per passenger.

4. The sums mentioned above shall be deemed to refer to the French franc consisting of 65-1/2 milligrams of gold at the standard of fineness of nine hundred thousandths. These sums may be converted into any national currency in round figures.

Article 23

Any provision tending to relieve the carrier of liability or to fix a lower limit than that which is laid down in this convention shall be null and void, but the nullity of any such provision shall not involve the nullity of the whole contract, which shall remain subject to the provisions of this convention.

Article 24

1. In the cases covered by Articles 18 and 19 any action for damages, however founded, can only be brought subject to the conditions and limits set out in this convention.

2. In the cases covered by Article 17 the provisions of the preceding paragraph shall also apply, without prejudice to the questions as to who are the persons who have the right to bring suit and what are their respective rights.

Article 25

1. The carrier shall not be entitled to avail himself of the provisions of this convention which exclude or limit his liability, if the damage is caused by his wilful misconduct or by such default on his part as, in accordance with the law of the court to which the case is submitted, is considered to be equivalent to wilful misconduct.

2. Similarly the carrier shall not be entitled to avail himself of the said provisions, if the damage is caused under the same circumstances by any agent of the carrier acting within the scope of his employment.

Article 26

1. Receipt by the person entitled to the delivery of baggage or goods without complaint shall be *prima facie* evidence that the same have been delivered in good condition and in accordance with the document of transportation.

2. In case of damage, the person entitled to delivery must complain to the carrier forthwith after the discovery of the damage, and, at the latest, within 3 days from the date of receipt in the case of baggage and 7 days from the date of receipt in the case of goods. In case of delay the complaint must be made at the latest within 14 days from the date on which the baggage or goods have been placed at his disposal.

3. Every complaint must be made in writing upon the document of transportation or by separate notice in writing dispatched within the times aforesaid.

4. Failing complaint within the times aforesaid, no action shall lie against the carrier, save in the case of fraud on his part.

Article 27

In the case of the death of the person liable, an action for damages lies in accordance with the terms of this convention against those legally representing his estate.

Article 28

1. An action for damages must be brought, at the option of the plaintiff, in the territory of one of the High Contracting Parties, either before the court of the domicile of the carrier or of his principal place of business, or where he has a place of business through which the contract has been made, or before the court at the place of destination.

2. Questions of procedure shall be governed by the law of the court to which the case is submitted.

Article 29

1. The right to damages shall be extinguished if an action is not brought within 2 years, reckoned from the date of arrival at the destination, or from the date on which the aircraft ought to have arrived, or from the date on which the transportation stopped.

2. The method of calculating the period of limitation shall be determined by the law of the court to which the case is submitted.

Article 30

1. In the case of transportation to be performed by various successive carriers and falling within the definition set out in the third paragraph of Article 1, each carrier who accepts passengers, baggage or goods shall be subject to the rules set out in this convention, and shall be deemed to be one of the contracting parties to the contract of transportation insofar as the contract deals with that part of the transportation which is performed under his supervision.

2. In the case of transportation of this nature, the passenger or his representative can take action only against the carrier who performed the transportation during which the accident or the delay occurred, save in the case where, by express agreement, the first carrier has assumed liability for the whole journey.

3. As regards baggage or goods, the passenger or consignor shall have a right of action against the first carrier, and the passenger or consignee who is entitled to delivery shall have a right of action against the last carrier, and further, each may take action against the carrier who performed the transportation during which the destruction, loss, damage, or delay took place. These carriers shall be jointly and severally liable to the passenger or to the consignor or consignee.

CHAPTER IV

PROVISIONS RELATING TO COMBINED TRANSPORTATION

Article 31

1. In the case of combined transportation performed partly by air and partly by any other mode of transportation, the provisions of this convention shall apply only to the transportation by air, provided that the transportation by air falls within the terms of Article 1.

2. Nothing in this convention shall prevent the parties in the case of combined transportation from inserting in the document of air transportation conditions relating to

other modes of transportation, provided that the provisions of this convention are observed as regards the transportation by air.

CHAPTER V

GENERAL AND FINAL PROVISIONS

Article 32

Any clause contained in the contract and all special agreements entered into before the damage occurred by which the parties purport to infringe the rules laid down by this convention, whether by deciding the law to be applied, or by altering the rules as to jurisdiction, shall be null and void. Nevertheless for the transportation of goods arbitration clauses shall be allowed, subject to this convention, if the arbitration is to take place within one of the jurisdictions referred to in the first paragraph of Article 28.

Article 33

Nothing contained in this convention shall prevent the carrier either from refusing to enter into any contract of transportation or from making regulations which do not conflict with the provisions of this convention.

Article 34

This convention shall not apply to international transportation by air performed by way of experimental trial by air navigation enterprises with the view to the establishment of regular lines of air navigation, nor shall it apply to transportation performed in extraordinary circumstances outside the normal scope of an air carrier's business.

Article 35

The expression "days" when used in this convention means current days, not working days.

Article 36

This convention is drawn up in French in a single copy which shall remain deposited in the archives of the Ministry for Foreign Affairs of Poland and of which one duly certified copy shall be sent by the Polish Government to the Government of each of the High Contracting Parties.

Article 37

1. This convention shall be ratified. The instruments of ratification shall be deposited in the archives of the Ministry for Foreign Affairs of Poland, which shall give notice of the deposit to the Government of each of the High Contracting Parties.
2. As soon as this convention shall have been ratified by five of the High Contracting Parties it shall come into force as between them on the ninetieth day after the deposit of the fifth ratification. Thereafter it shall come into force between the High Contracting Parties which shall have ratified and the High Contracting Party which deposits its instrument of ratification on the ninetieth day after the deposit.
3. It shall be the duty of the Government of the Republic of Poland to notify the Government of each of the High Contracting Parties of the date on which this convention comes into force as well as the date of the deposit of each ratification.

Article 38

1. This convention shall, after it has come into force, remain open for adherence by any state.

2. The adherence shall be effected by a notification addressed to the Government of the Republic of Poland, which shall inform the Government of each of the High Contracting Parties thereof.

3. The adherence shall take effect as from the ninetieth day after the notification made to the Government of the Republic of Poland.

Article 39

1. Any one of the High Contracting Parties may denounce this convention by a notification addressed to the Government of the Republic of Poland, which shall at once inform the Government of each of the High Contracting Parties.

2. Denunciation shall take effect six months after the notification of denunciation, and shall operate only as regards the party which shall have proceeded to denunciation.

Article 40

1. Any High Contracting Party may, at the time of signature or of deposit of ratification or of adherence, declare that the acceptance which it gives to this convention does not apply to all or any of its colonies, protectorates, territories under mandate, or any other territory subject to its sovereignty or its authority, or any other territory under its suzerainty.

2. Accordingly any High Contracting Party may subsequently adhere separately in the name of all or any of its colonies, protectorates, territories under mandate, or any other territory subject to its sovereignty or to its authority or any other territory under its suzerainty which have been thus excluded by its original declaration.

3. Any High Contracting Party may denounce this convention, in accordance with its provisions, separately or for all or any of its colonies, protectorates, territories under mandate, or any other territory subject to its sovereignty or to its authority, or any other territory under its suzerainty.

Article 41

Any High Contracting Party shall be entitled not earlier than two years after the coming into force of this convention to call for the assembling of a new international conference in order to consider any improvements which may be made in this convention. To this end it will communicate with the Government of the French Republic which will take the necessary measures to make preparations for such conference.

This convention, done at Warsaw on October 12, 1929, shall remain open for signature until January 31, 1930.

APPENDIX 4

THE WARSAW CONVENTION AS AMENDED AT THE HAGUE, 1955 AND BY MONTREAL PROTOCOL NO. 2, 1975

(INCORPORATING MONTREAL ADDITIONAL PROTOCOL NO. 2 (1975))

CHAPTER 1

SCOPE—DEFINITIONS

Article 1

(1) This Convention applies to all international carriage of persons, baggage or cargo performed by aircraft for reward. It applies equally to gratuitous carriage by aircraft performed by an air transport undertaking.

(2) For the purposes of this Convention, the expression *international carriage* means any carriage in which, according to the agreement between the parties, the place of departure and the place of destination, whether or not there be a break in the carriage or a transhipment, are situated either within the territories of two High Contracting Parties or within the territory of a single High Contracting Party if there is an agreed stopping place within the territory of another State, even if that State is not a High Contracting Party. Carriage between two points within the territory of a single High Contracting Party without an agreed stopping place within the territory of another State is not international carriage for the purposes of this Convention.

(3) Carriage to be performed by several successive air carriers is deemed, for the purposes of this Convention, to be one undivided carriage if it has been regarded by the parties as a single operation, whether it had been agreed upon under the form of a single contract or of a series of contracts, and it does not lose its international character merely because one contract or a series of contracts is to be performed entirely within the territory of the same State.

Article 2

(1) This Convention applies to carriage performed by the State or by legally constituted public bodies provided it falls within the conditions laid down in Article 1.

(2) This Convention shall not apply to carriage of mail and postal packages.

CHAPTER II: DOCUMENTS OF CARRIAGE

SECTION 1 — PASSENGER TICKET

Article 3

(1) In respect of the carriage of passengers a ticket shall be delivered containing:

(a) an indication of the places of departure and destination;

(b) if the places of departure and destination are within the territory of a single High Contracting Party, one or more agreed stopping places being within the territory of another State, an indication of at least one such stopping place;

(c) a notice to the effect that, if the passenger's journey involves an ultimate destination or stop in a country other than the country of departure, the Warsaw Convention may be applicable and that the Convention governs and in most cases limits the liability of carriers for death or personal injury and in respect of loss of or damage to baggage.

(2) The passenger ticket shall constitute *prima facie* evidence of the conclusion and conditions of the contract of carriage. The absence, irregularity or loss of the passenger ticket does not affect the existence or the validity of the contract of carriage which shall, none the less, be subject to the rules of this Convention. Nevertheless, if, with the consent of the carrier, the passenger embarks without a passenger ticket having been delivered, or if the ticket does not include the notice required by paragraph (1)(c) of this Article, the carrier shall not be entitled to avail himself of the provisions of Article 22.

SECTION 2 — BAGGAGE CHECK

Article 4

(1) In respect of the carriage of registered baggage, a baggage check shall be delivered, which, unless combined with or incorporated in a passenger ticket which complies with the provisions of Article 3, paragraph (1), shall contain:

(a) an indication of the places of departure and destination;

(b) if the places of departure and destination are within the territory of a single High Contracting Party, one or more agreed stopping places being within the territory of another State, an indication of at least one such stopping place;

(c) a notice to the effect that, if the carriage involves an ultimate destination or stop in a country other than the country of departure, the Warsaw Convention may be applicable and that the Convention governs and in most cases limits the liability of carriers in respect of loss of or damage to baggage.

(2) The baggage check shall constitute *prima facie* evidence of the registration of the baggage and of the conditions of the contract of carriage. The absence, irregularity or loss of the baggage check does not affect the existence or the validity of the contract of carriage which shall, none the less, be subject to the rules of this Convention. Nevertheless, if the carrier takes charge of the baggage without a baggage check having been delivered or if the baggage check (unless combined with or incorporated in the passenger ticket which complies with the provisions of Article 3, paragraph (1)(c)) does not include the notice required by paragraph (1)(c) of this Article, he shall not be entitled to avail himself of the provisions of Article 22, paragraph (2).

SECTION 3 — AIR WAYBILL

Article 5

(1) Every carrier of cargo has the right to require the consignor to make out and hand over to him a document called an "air waybill"; every consignor has the right to require the carrier to accept this document.

(2) The absence, irregularity or loss of this document does not affect the existence or the validity of the contract of carriage which shall, subject to the provisions of Article 9, be none the less governed by the rules of this Convention.

Article 6

(1) The air waybill shall be made out by the consignor in three original parts and be handed over with the cargo.

(2) The first part shall be marked "for the carrier", and shall be signed by the consignor. The second part shall be marked "for the consignee"; it shall be signed by the consignor and by the carrier and shall accompany the cargo. The third part shall be signed by the carrier and handed by him to the consignor after the cargo has been accepted.

(3) The carrier shall sign prior to the loading of the cargo on board the aircraft.

(4) The signature of the carrier may be stamped; that of the consignor may be printed or stamped.

(5) If, at the request of the consignor, the carrier makes out the air waybill, he shall be deemed, subject to proof to the contrary, to have done so on behalf of the consignor.

Article 7

The carrier of cargo has the right to require the consignor to make out separate waybills when there is more than one package.

Article 8

The air waybill shall contain:

(a) an indication of the places of departure and destination;

(b) if the places of departure and destination are within the territory of a single High Contracting Party, one or more agreed stopping places being within the territory of another State, an indication of at least one such stopping place;

(c) a notice to the consignor to the effect that, if the carriage involves an ultimate destination or stop in a country other than the country of departure, the Warsaw Convention may be applicable and that the Convention governs and in most cases limits the liability of carriers in respect of loss of or damage to cargo.

Article 9

If, with the consent of the carrier, cargo is loaded on board the aircraft without an air waybill having been made out, or if the air waybill does not include the notice required by Article 8, paragraph (c), the carrier shall not be entitled to avail himself of the provisions of Article 22, paragraph (2).

Article 10

(1) The consignor is responsible for the correctness of the particulars and statements relating to the cargo which he inserts in the air waybill.

(2) The consignor shall indemnify the carrier against all damage suffered by him, or by

any other person to whom the carrier is liable, by reason of the irregularity, incorrectness or incompleteness of the particulars and statements furnished by the consignor.

Article 11

(1) The air waybill is *prima facie* evidence of the conclusion of the contract, of the receipt of the cargo and of the conditions of carriage.

(2) The statements in the air waybill relating to the weight, dimensions and packing of the cargo, as well as those relating to the number of packages, are *prima facie* evidence of the facts stated; those relating to the quantity, volume and condition of the cargo do not constitute evidence against the carrier except so far as they both have been, and are stated in the air waybill to have been, checked by him in the presence of the consignor, or relate to the apparent condition of the cargo.

Article 12

(1) Subject to his liability to carry out all his obligations under the contract of carriage, the consignor has the right to dispose of the cargo by withdrawing it at the aerodrome of departure or destination, or by stopping it in the course of the journey on any landing, or by calling for it to be delivered at the place of destination or in the course of the journey to a person other than the consignee named in the air waybill, or by requiring it to be returned to the aerodrome of departure. He must not exercise this right of disposition in such a way as to prejudice the carrier or other consignors and he must repay any expenses occasioned by the exercise of this right.

(2) If it is impossible to carry out the orders of the consignor the carrier must so inform him forthwith.

(3) If the carrier obeys the orders of the consignor for the disposition of the cargo without requiring the production of the part of the air waybill delivered to the latter, he will be liable, without prejudice to his right of recovery from the consignor, for any damage which may be caused thereby to any person who is lawfully in possession of that part of the air waybill.

(4) The right conferred on the consignor ceases at the moment when that of the consignee begins in accordance with Article 13. Nevertheless, if the consignee declines to accept the waybill or the cargo, or if he cannot be communicated with, the consignor resumes his right of disposition.

Article 13

(1) Except in the circumstances set out in the preceding Article, the consignee is entitled, on arrival of the cargo at the place of destination, to require the carrier to hand over to him the air waybill and to deliver the cargo to him, on payment of the charges due and on complying with the conditions of carriage set out in the air waybill.

(2) Unless it is otherwise agreed, it is the duty of the carrier to give notice to the consignee as soon as the cargo arrives.

(3) If the carrier admits the loss of the cargo, or if the cargo has not arrived at the expiration of seven days after the date on which it ought to have arrived, the consignee is entitled to put into force against the carrier the rights which flow from the contract of carriage.

Article 14

The consignor and the consignee can respectively enforce all the rights given them by Articles 12 and 13, each in his own name, whether he is acting in his own interest or in the interest of another, provided that he carries out the obligations imposed by the contract.

Article 15

(1) Articles 12, 13 and 14 do not affect either the relations of the consignor or the consignee with each other or the mutual relations of third parties whose rights are derived either from the consignor or from the consignee.

(2) The provisions of Articles 12, 13 and 14 can only be varied by express provision in the air waybill.

(3) Nothing in this Convention prevents the issue of a negotiable air waybill.

Article 16

(1) The consignor must furnish such information and attach to the air waybill such documents as are necessary to meet the formalities of customs, octroi or police before the cargo can be delivered to the consignee. The consignor is liable to the carrier for any damage occasioned by the absence, insufficiency or irregularity of any such information or documents, unless the damage is due to the fault of the carrier or his servants or agents.

(2) The carrier is under no obligation to enquire into the correctness or sufficiency of such information or documents.

CHAPTER III: LIABILITY OF THE CARRIER

Article 17

The carrier is liable for damage sustained in the event of the death or wounding of a passenger or any other bodily injury suffered by a passenger, if the accident which caused the damage so sustained took place on board the aircraft or in the course of any of the operations of embarking or disembarking.

Article 18

(1) The carrier is liable for damage sustained in the event of the destruction or loss of, or of damage to, any registered baggage or any cargo, if the occurrence which caused the damage so sustained took place during the carriage by air.

(2) The carriage by air within the meaning of the preceding paragraph comprises the period during which the baggage or cargo is in charge of the carrier, whether in an aerodrome or on board an aircraft, or, in the case of a landing outside an aerodrome, in any place whatsoever.

(3) The period of the carriage by air does not extend to any carriage by land, by sea or by river performed outside an aerodrome. If, however, such a carriage takes place in the performance of a contract for carriage by air, for the purpose of loading, delivery or transshipment, any damage is presumed, subject to proof to the contrary, to have been the result of an event which took place during the carriage by air.

Article 19

The carrier is liable for damage occasioned by delay in the carriage by air of passengers, baggage or cargo.

Article 20

The carrier is not liable if he proves that he and his servants or agents have taken all necessary measures to avoid the damage or that it was impossible for him or them to take such measures.

Article 21

If the carrier proves that the damage was caused by or contributed to by the negligence of the injured person the court may, in accordance with the provisions of its own law, exonerate the carrier wholly or partly from his liability.

Article 22

(1) In the carriage of persons the liability of the carrier for each passenger is limited to the sum of 16,600 Special Drawing Rights.

Where, in accordance with the law of the court seised of the case, damages may be awarded in the form of periodical payments the equivalent capital value of the said payments shall not exceed this limit. Nevertheless, by special contract, the carrier and the passenger may agree to a higher limit of liability.

(2)—(a) In the carriage of registered baggage and of cargo, the liability of the carrier is limited to a sum of 17 Special Drawing Rights per kilogramme, unless the passenger or consignor has made, at the time when the package was handed over to the carrier, a special declaration of interest in delivery at destination and has paid a supplementary sum if the case so requires. In that case the carrier will be liable to pay a sum not exceeding the declared sum, unless he proves that that sum is greater than the passenger's or consignor's actual interest in delivery at destination.

(b) In the case of loss, damage or delay of part of registered baggage or cargo, or of any object contained therein, the weight to be taken into consideration in determining the amount to which the carrier's liability is limited shall be only the total weight of the package or packages concerned. Nevertheless, when the loss, damage or delay of a part of the registered baggage or cargo, or of an object contained therein, affects the value of other packages covered by the same baggage check or the same air waybill, the total weight of such package or packages shall also be taken into consideration in determining the limit of liability.

(3) As regards objects of which the passenger takes charge himself the liability of the carrier is limited to 332 Special Drawing Rights per passenger.

(4) The limits prescribed in this Article shall not prevent the court from awarding, in accordance with its own law, in addition, the whole or part of the court costs and of the other expenses of the litigation incurred by the plaintiff. The foregoing provision shall not apply if the amount of the damages awarded, excluding court costs and other expenses of the litigation, does not exceed the sum which the carrier has offered in writing to the plaintiff within a period of six months from the date of the occurrence causing the damage, or before the commencement of the action, if that is later.

(5) The sums mentioned in terms of the Special Drawing Right in this Article shall be deemed to refer to the Special Drawing Right as defined by the International Monetary Fund. Conversion of the sums into national currencies shall, in case of judicial proceedings, be made according to the value of such currencies in terms of the Special Drawing Right at the date of the judgment. The value of a national currency, in terms of the Special Drawing Right, of a High Contracting Party which is a Member of the International Monetary Fund shall be calculated in accordance with the method of valuation, applied by the International Monetary Fund, in effect at the date of the

judgment, for its operations and transactions. The value of a national currency, in terms of the Special Drawing Right, of a High Contracting Party which is not a member of the International Monetary Fund, shall be calculated in a manner determined by that High Contracting Party.

Nevertheless, those States which are not Members of the International Monetary Fund and whose law does not permit the application of the provisions of paragraphs 1, 2(a) and 3 of Article 22 may at the time of ratification or accession or at any time thereafter, declare that the limit of liability of the carrier in judicial proceedings in their territories is fixed at a sum of 250 000 monetary units per passenger with respect to paragraph 1 of Article 22; 250 monetary units per kilogramme with respect to paragraph 2(a) of Article 22; and 5 000 monetary units per passenger with respect to paragraph 3 of Article 22. This monetary unit corresponds to sixty-five and a half milligrammes of gold of millessimal fineness nine hundred. These sums may be converted into the national currency concerned in round figures. The conversion of these sums into national currency shall be made according to the law of the State concerned.

Article 23

(1) Any provision tending to relieve the carrier of liability or to fix a lower limit than that which is laid down in this Convention shall be null and void, but the nullity of any such provision does not involve the nullity of the whole contract, which shall remain subject to the provisions of this Convention.

(2) Paragraph (1) of this Article shall not apply to provisions governing loss or damage resulting from the inherent defect, quality or vice of the cargo carried.

Article 24

(1) In the cases covered by Articles 18 and 19 any action for damages, however founded, can only be brought subject to the conditions and limits set out in this Convention.

(2) In the cases covered by Article 17 the provisions of the preceding paragraph also apply, without prejudice to the questions as to who are the persons who have the right to bring suit and what are their respective rights.

Article 25

The limits of liability specified in Article 22 shall not apply if it is proved that the damage resulted from an act or omission of the carrier, his servants or agents, done with intent to cause damage or recklessly and with knowledge that damage would probably result; provided that, in the case of such act or omission of a servant or agent, it is also proved that he was acting within the scope of his employment.

Article 25A

(1) If an action is brought against a servant or agent of the carrier arising out of damage to which this Convention relates, such servant or agent, if he proves that he acted within the scope of his employment, shall be entitled to avail himself of the limits of liability which that carrier himself is entitled to invoke under Article 22.

(2) The aggregate of the amounts recoverable from the carrier, his servants and agents, in that case, shall not exceed the said limits.

(3) The provisions of paragraphs (1) and (2) of this Article shall not apply if it is proved

that the damage resulted from an act or omission of the servant or agent done with intent to cause damage or recklessly and with knowledge that damage would probably result.

Article 26

(1) Receipt by the person entitled to delivery of baggage or cargo without complaint is *prima facie* evidence that the same has been delivered in good condition and in accordance with the document of carriage.

(2) In the case of damage, the person entitled to delivery must complain to the carrier forthwith after the discovery of the damage, and, at the latest, within seven days from the date of receipt in the case of baggage and fourteen days from the date of receipt in the case of cargo. In the case of delay the complaint must be made at the latest within twenty-one days from the date on which the baggage or cargo have been placed at his disposal.

(3) Every complaint must be made in writing upon the document of carriage or by separate notice in writing despatched within the times aforesaid.

(4) Failing complaint within the times aforesaid, no action shall lie against the carrier, save in the case of fraud on his part.

Article 27

In the case of the death of the person liable, an action for damages lies in accordance with the terms of this Convention against those legally representing his estate.

Article 28

(1) An action for damages must be brought, at the option of the plaintiff, in the territory of one of the High Contracting Parties, either before the court having jurisdiction where the carrier is ordinarily resident, or has his principal place of business, or has an establishment by which the contract has been made or before the court having jurisdiction at the place of destination.

(2) Questions of procedure shall be governed by the law of the court seised of the case.

Article 29

(1) The right to damages shall be extinguished if an action is not brought within two years, reckoned from the date of arrival at the destination, or from the date on which the aircraft ought to have arrived, or from the date or which the carriage stopped.

(2) The method of calculating the period of limitation shall be determined by the law of the court seised of the case.

Article 30

(1) In the case of carriage to be performed by various successive carriers and falling within the definition set out in the third paragraph of Article 1, each carrier who accepts passengers, baggage or cargo is subjected to the rules set out in this Convention, and is deemed to be one of the contracting parties to the contract of carriage in so far as the contract deals with that part of the carriage which is performed under his supervision.

(2) In the case of carriage of this nature, the passenger or his representative can take action only against the carrier who performed the carriage during which the accident or the delay occurred, save in the case where, by express agreement, the first carrier has assumed liability for the whole journey.

(3) As regards baggage or cargo, the passenger or consignor will have a right of action against the first carrier, and the passenger or consignee who is entitled to delivery will

have a right of action against the last carrier, and further, each may take action against the carrier who performed the carriage during which the destruction, loss, damage or delay took place. These carriers will be jointly and severally liable to the passenger or to the consignor or consignee.

CHAPTER IV: PROVISIONS RELATING TO COMBINED CARRIAGE

Article 31

(1) In the case of combined carriage performed partly by air and partly by any other mode of carriage, the provisions of this Convention apply only to the carriage by air, provided that the carriage by air falls within the terms of Article 1.

(2) Nothing in this Convention shall prevent the parties in the case of combined carriage from inserting in the document of air carriage conditions relating to other modes of carriage, provided that the provisions of this Convention are observed as regards the carriage by air.

CHAPTER V: GENERAL AND FINAL PROVISIONS

Article 32

Any clause contained in the contract and all special agreements entered into before the damage occurred by which the parties purport to infringe the rules laid down by this Convention, whether by deciding the law to be applied, or by altering the rules as to jurisdiction, shall be null and void. Nevertheless for the carriage of cargo arbitration clauses are allowed, subject to this Convention, if the arbitration is to take place within one of the jurisdictions referred to in the first paragraph of Article 28.

Article 33

Nothing contained in this Convention shall prevent the carrier either from refusing to enter into any contract of carriage, or from making regulations which do not conflict with the provisions of this Convention.

Article 34

The provisions of Articles 3 to 9 inclusive relating to documents of carriage shall not apply in the case of carriage performed in extraordinary circumstances outside the normal scope of an air carrier's business.

Article 35

The expression "days" when used in this Convention means current days not working days.

Article 36

The Convention is drawn up in French in a single copy which shall remain desposited in the archives of the Ministry for Foreign Affairs of Poland and of which one duly certified copy shall be sent by the Polish Government to the Government of each of the High Contracting Parties.

Article 40A

(1) [*This paragraph is not reproduced. It defines "High Contracting Party".*]

(2) For the purposes of the Convention the word *territory* means not only the metropolitan territory of a State but also all other territories for the foreign relations of which that State is responsible.

[*Articles 37, 38, 39, 40 and 41 and the concluding words of the Convention are not reproduced. They deal with the coming into force of the Convention.*]

ADDITIONAL PROTOCOL

(With reference to Article 2)

The High Contracting Parties reserve to themselves the right to declare at the time of ratification or of accession that the first paragraph of Article 2 of this Convention shall not apply to international carriage by air performed directly by the State, its colonies, protectorates or mandated territories or by any other territory under its sovereignty, suzerainty or authority.

APPENDIX 5

THE UNAMENDED WARSAW CONVENTION AS AMENDED BY ADDITIONAL PROTOCOL NO. 1 OF MONTREAL 1975

(AS SET OUT IN THE CARRIAGE BY AIR ACT (APPLICATION OF PROVISIONS) (4th AMENDMENT) ORDER 1998

CHAPTER I

SCOPE—DEFINITIONS

Article 1

(1) This Schedule applies to all international carriage of persons, baggage or cargo performed by aircraft for reward. It applies equally to gratuitous carriage by aircraft performed by an air transport undertaking.

(2) "International carriage" means any carriage in which, according to the contract made by the parties, the place of departure and the place of destination, whether or not there be a break in the carriage or a transhipment, are situated either within the territories of two States Parties to the Convention for the Unification of Certain Rules relating to International Carriage by Air signed at Warsaw on behalf of His Majesty on 12th October 1929 as amended by Additional Protocol No. 1 of Montreal 1975, or within the territory of a single such State, if there is an agreed stopping place within the territory subject to the sovereignty, suzerainty, mandate or authority of another State, even though that State is not a party to the said Convention of 1929 as so amended.

(3) A carriage to be performed by several successive air carriers is deemed, for the purposes of this Schedule, to be one undivided carriage, if it has been regarded by the parties as a single operation, whether it had been agreed upon under the form of a single contract or of a series of contracts, and it does not lose its international character merely because one contract or a series of contracts is to be performed entirely within a territory subject to the sovereignty, suzerainty, mandate or authority of the same High Contracting Party.

Article 2

(1) This Schedule applies to carriage performed by the State, not being a State which has availed itself of the Additional Protocol to the Warsaw Convention, or by legally constituted public bodies, provided it falls within the conditions laid down in Article 1.

(2) This Schedule does not apply to carriage performed under the terms of any international postal Convention.

CHAPTER II: DOCUMENTS OF CARRIAGE

SECTION 1 — PASSENGER TICKET

Article 3

(1) For the carriage of passengers the carrier must deliver a passenger ticket which shall contain the following particulars—

(a) the place and date of issue;
(b) the place of departure and of destination;
(c) the agreed stopping places, provided that the carrier may reserve the right to alter the stopping places in case of necessity, and that if he exercises that right, the alteration shall not have the effect of depriving the carriage of its international character;
(d) the name and address of the carrier or carriers;
(e) a statement that the carriage is subject to the rules relating to liability established by the Warsaw Convention.

(2) The absence, irregularity or loss of the passenger ticket does not affect the existence or the validity of the contract of carriage, which shall none the less be subject to the rules of this Schedule. Nevertheless, if the carrier accepts a passenger without a passenger ticket having been delivered he shall not be entitled to avail himself of those provisions of this Schedule which exclude or limit his liability.

SECTION 2 — BAGGAGE CHECK

Article 4

(1) For the carriage of baggage, other than small personal objects of which the passenger takes charge himself, the carrier must deliver a baggage check.

(2) The baggage check shall be made out in duplicate, one part for the passenger and the other part for the carrier.

(3) The baggage check shall contain the following particulars—

(a) the place and date of issue;
(b) the place of departure and of destination;
(c) the name and address of the carrier or carriers;
(d) the number of the passenger ticket;
(e) a statement that delivery of the baggage will be made to the bearer of the baggage check;
(f) the number and weight of the packages;
(g) the amount of the value declared in accordance with Article 22(2);
(h) a statement that the carriage is subject to the rules relating to liability established by the Warsaw Convention.

(4) The absence, irregularity or loss of the baggage check does not affect the existence or the validity of the contract of carriage, which shall none the less be subject to the rules of this Schedule. Nevertheless, if the carrier accepts baggage without a baggage check having been delivered, or if the baggage check does not contain the particulars set out at (d), (f) and (h) above, the carrier shall not be entitled to avail himself of those provisions of this Schedule which exclude or limit his liability.

SECTION 3 — AIR WAYBILL

Article 5

(1) Every carrier of cargo has the right to require the consignor to make out and hand over to him a document called an "air waybill"; every consignor has the right to require the carrier to accept this document.

(2) The absence, irregularity or loss of this document does not affect the existence or the validity of the contract of carriage which shall, subject to the provisions of Article 9, be none the less governed by the rules of this Schedule.

Article 6

(1) The air waybill shall be made out by the consignor in three original parts and be handed over with the cargo.

(2) The first part shall be marked "for the carrier", and shall be signed by the consignor. The second part shall be marked "for the consignee"; it shall be signed by the consignor and by the carrier and shall accompany the cargo. The third part shall be signed by the carrier and handed by him to the consignor after the cargo has been accepted.

(3) The carrier shall sign on acceptance of the cargo.

(4) The signature of the carrier may be stamped; that of the consignor may be printed or stamped.

(5) If, at the request of the consignor, the carrier makes out the air waybill, he shall be deemed, subject to proof to the contrary, to have done so on behalf of the consignor.

Article 7

The carrier of cargo has the right to require the consignor to make out separate waybills when there is more than one package.

Article 8

The air waybill shall contain the following particulars—

(a) the place and date of its execution;
(b) the place of departure and of destination;
(c) the agreed stopping places, provided that the carrier may reserve the right to alter the stopping places in case of necessity, and that if he exercises that right the alteration shall not have the effect of depriving the carriage of its international character;
(d) the name and address of the consignor;
(e) the name and address of the first carrier;
(f) the name and address of the consignee, if the case so requires;
(g) the nature of the cargo;
(h) the number of the packages, the method of packing and the particular marks or numbers upon them;
(i) the weight, the quantity and the volume or dimensions of the cargo;
(j) the apparent condition of the cargo and of the packing;
(k) the freight, if it has been agreed upon, the date and place of payment, and the person who is to pay it;
(l) if the cargo is sent for payment on delivery, the price of the cargo, and, if the case so requires, the amount of the expenses incurred;
(m) the amount of the value declared in accordance with Article 22(2);
(n) the number of parts of the air waybill;
(o) the documents handed to the carrier to accompany the air waybill;
(p) the time fixed for the completion of the carriage and a brief note of the route to be followed, if these matters have been agreed upon;
(q) a statement that the carriage is subject to the rules relating to liability established by the Warsaw Convention.

Article 9

If the carrier accepts cargo without an air waybill having been made out, or if the air waybill does not contain all the particulars set out in Article 8(a) to (i) inclusive and (q), the carrier shall not be entitled to avail himself of the provisions of this Schedule which exclude or limit his liability.

Article 10

(1) The consignor is responsible for the correctness of the particulars and statements relating to the cargo which he inserts in the air waybill.

(2) The consignor will be liable for all damage suffered by the carrier or any other person by reason of the irregularity incorrectness or incompleteness of the said particulars and statements.

Article 11

(1) The air waybill is *prima facie* evidence of the conclusion of the contract, of the receipt of the cargo and of the conditions of carriage.

(2) The statements in the air waybill relating to the weight, dimensions and packing of the cargo, as well as those relating to the number of packages, are *prima facie* evidence of the facts stated; those relating to the quantity, volume and condition of the cargo do not constitute evidence against the carrier except so far as they both have been, and are stated in the air waybill to have been, checked by him in the presence of the consignor, or relate to the apparent condition of the cargo.

Article 12

(1) Subject to his liability to carry out all his obligations under the contract of carriage, the consignor has the right to dispose of the cargo by withdrawing it at the aerodrome of departure or destination, or by stopping it in the course of the journey on any landing, or by calling for it to be delivered at the place of destination or in the course of the journey to a person other than the consignee named in the air waybill, or by requiring it to be returned to the aerodrome of departure. He must not exercise this right of disposition in such a way as to prejudice the carrier or other consignors and he must repay any expenses occasioned by the exercise of this right.

(2) If it is impossible to carry out the orders of the consignor the carrier must so inform him forthwith.

(3) If the carrier obeys the orders of the consignor for the disposition of the cargo without requiring the production of the part of the air waybill delivered to the latter, he will be liable, without prejudice to his right of recovery from the consignor, for any damage which may be caused thereby to any person who is lawfully in possession of that part of the air waybill.

(4) The right conferred on the consignor ceases at the moment when that of the consignee begins in accordance with Article 13. Nevertheless, if the consignee declines to accept the waybill or the cargo, or if he cannot be communicated with, the consignor resumes his right of disposition.

Article 13

(1) Except in the circumstancces set out in the preceding Article, the consignee is entitled, on arrival of the cargo at the place of destination, to require the carrier to hand over to him the air waybill and to deliver the cargo to him, on payment of the charges due and on complying with the conditions of carriage set out in the air waybill.

(2) Unless it is otherwise agreed, it is the duty of the carrier to give notice to the consignee as soon as the cargo arrives.

(3) If the carrier admits the loss of the cargo, or if the cargo has not arrived at the expiration of seven days after the date on which it ought to have arrived, the consignee is entitled to put into force against the carrier the rights which flow from the contract of carriage.

Article 14

The consignor and the consignee can respectively enforce all the rights given them by Articles 12 and 13, each in his own name, whether he is acting in his own interest or in the interest of another, provided that he carries out the obligations imposed by the contract.

Article 15

(1) Articles 12, 13 and 14 do not affect either the relations of the consignor or the consignee with each other or the mutual relations of third parties whose rights are derived either from the consignor or from the consignee.

(2) The provisions of Articles 12, 13 and 14 can only be varied by express provision in the air waybill.

Article 16

(1) The consignor must furnish such information and attach to the air waybill such documents as are necessary to meet the formalities of customs, octroi or police before the cargo can be delivered to the consignee. The consignor is liable to the carrier for any damage occasioned by the absence, insufficiency or irregularity of any such information or documents, unless the damage is due to the fault of the carrier or his servants or agents.

(2) The carrier is under no obligation to enquire into the correctness or sufficiency of such information or documents.

CHAPTER III

LIABILITY OF THE CARRIER

Article 17

The carrier is liable for damage sustained in the event of the death or wounding of a passenger or any other bodily injury suffered by a passenger, if the accident which caused the damage so sustained took place on board the aircraft or in the course of any of the operations of embarking or disembarking.

Article 18

(1) The carrier is liable for damage sustained in the event of the destruction or loss of, or of damage to, any registered baggage or any cargo, if the occurrence which caused the damage so sustained took place during the carriage by air.

(2) The carriage by air within the meaning of the preceding paragraph comprises the period during which the baggage or cargo is in charge of the carrier, whether in an aerodrome or on board an aircraft, or, in the case of a landing outside an aerodrome in any place whatsoever.

(3) The period of the carriage by air does not extend to any carriage by land, by sea or by river performed outside an aerodrome. If, however, such a carriage takes place in the performance of a contract for carriage by air, for the purpose of loading, delivery or transhipment, any damage is presumed, subject to proof to the contrary, to have been the result of any event which took place during the carriage by air.

Article 19

The carrier is liable for damage occasioned by delay in the carriage by air of passengers, baggage or cargo.

Article 20

(1) The carrier is not liable if he proves that he and his servants or agents have taken all necessary measures to avoid the damage or that it was impossible for him or them to take such measures.

(2) In the carriage of cargo and baggage the carrier is not liable if he proves that the damage was occasioned by negligent pilotage or negligence in the handling of the aircraft or in navigation and that, in all other respects, he and his servants or agents have taken all necessary measures to avoid the damage.

Article 21

If the carrier proves that the damage was caused by or contributed to by the negligence of the injured person the Court may, in accordance with the provisions of its own law, exonerate the carrier wholly or partly from his liability.

Article 22

(1) In the carriage of passengers the liability of the carrier for each passenger is limited to the sum of 8,300 Special Drawing Rights. Where, in accordance with the law of the court seised of the case, damages may be awarded in the form of periodic payments, the equivalent capital value of the said payments shall not exceed this limit. Nevertheless, by special contract, the carrier and the passenger may agree to a higher limit of liability.

(2) In the carriage of registered baggage and of cargo, the liability of the carrier is limited to a sum of 17 Special Drawing Rights per kilogramme, unless the consignor has made, at the time when the package was handed over to the carrier, a special declaration of interest in delivery at destination and has paid a supplementary sum if the case so requires. In that case the carrier will be liable to pay a sum not exceeding the declared sum, unless he proves that that sum is greater than the consignor's actual interest in delivery at destination.

(3) As regards objects of which the passenger takes charge himself the liability of the carrier is limited to 332 Special Drawing Rights per passenger.

(4) The sums mentioned in terms of the Special Drawing Right in this Article shall be deemed to refer to the Special Drawing Right as defined by the International Monetary Fund. Conversion of the sums into national currencies shall, in case of judicial proceedings, be made according to the value of such currencies in terms of the Special Drawing Right at the date of the judgment. The value of a national currency, in terms of the Special Drawing Right, of a High Contracting Party which is a Member of the Monetary Fund, shall be calculated in accordance with the method of valuation applied by the International Monetary Fund, in effect at the date of the judgment, for its operations and transactions. The value of national currency, in terms of the Special Drawing Right, of a High Contracting Party which is not a Member of the International

Monetary Fund, shall be calculated in a manner determined by that High Contracting Party.

Nevertheless, those States which are not Members of the International Monetary Fund and whose law does not permit the application of the provisions of paragraphs 1, 2 and 3 of Article 22 may at the time of ratification or accession or at any time thereafter declare that the limit of liability of the carrier in judicial proceedings in their territories is fixed at a sum of 125,000 monetary units per passenger with respect to paragraph 1 of Article 22; 250 monetary units per kilogramme with respect to paragraph 2 of Article 22; and 5,000 monetary units per passenger with respect to paragraph 3 of Article 22. This monetary unit corresponds to sixty-five and a half milligrammes of gold of millesimal fineness nine hundred. These sums may be converted into the national currency concerned in round figures. The conversion of these sums into national currency shall be made according to the law of the State concerned.

Article 23

Any provision tending to relieve the carrier of liability or to fix a lower limit than that which is laid down in this Schedule shall be null and void, but the nullity of any such provision does not involve the nullity of the whole contract, which shall remain subject to the provisions of this Schedule.

Article 24

(1) In the cases covered by Articles 18 and 19 any action for damages, however founded, can only be brought subject to the conditions and limits set out in this Schedule.

(2) In the cases covered by Article 17 the provisions of the preceding paragraph also apply, without prejudice to the questions as to who are the persons who have the right to bring suit and what are their respective rights.

Article 25

(1) The carrier shall not be entitled to avail himself of the provisions of this Schedule which exclude or limit his liability, if the damage is caused by his wilful misconduct, or by such default on his part as, in accordance with the law of the Court seised of the case, is considered to be equivalent to wilful misconduct.

(2) Similarly the carrier shall not be entitled to avail himself of the said provisions, if the damage is caused as aforesaid by any servant or agent of the carrier acting within the scope of him employment.

Article 26

(1) Receipt by the person entitled to delivery of baggage or cargo without complaint is *prima facie* evidence that the same has been delivered in good condition and in accordance with the document of carriage.

(2) In the case of damage, the person entitled to delivery must complain to the carrier forthwith after the discovery of the damage, and, at the latest, within three days from the date of receipt in the case of baggage and seven days from the date of receipt in the case of cargo. In the case of delay the complaint must be made at the latest within fourteen days from the date on which the baggage or cargo has been placed at his disposal.

(3) Every complaint must be made in writing upon the document of carriage or by separate notice in writing despatched within the times aforesaid.

(4) Failing complaint within the times aforesaid, no action shall lie against the carrier, save in the case of fraud on his part.

Article 27

In the case of the death of the person liable, an action for damages lies in accordance with the terms of this Schedule against those legally representing his estate.

Article 28

(1) An action for damages must be brought, at the option of the plaintiff, in the territory of one of the High Contracting Parties to the Warsaw Convention as amended by Additional Protocol No. 1 of Montreal 1975, either before the Court having jurisdiction where the carrier is ordinarily resident, or has his principal place of business, or has an establishment by which the contract has been made or before the Court having jurisdiction at the place of destination.

(2) Questions of procedure shall be governed by the law of the Court seised of the case.

Article 29

(1) The right to damages shall be extinguished if an action is not brought within two years, reckoned from the date of arrival at the destination, or from the date on which the aircraft ought to have arrived, or from the date on which the carriage stopped.

(2) The method of calculating the period of limitation shall be determined by the law of the Court seised of the case.

Article 30

(1) In the case of carriage to be performed by various successive carriers and falling within the definition set out in the third paragraph of Article 1, each carrier who accepts passengers, baggage or cargo is subjected to the rules set out in this Schedule, and is deemed to be one of the contracting parties to the contract of carriage in so far as the contract deals with that part of the carriage which is performed under his supervision.

(2) In the case of carriage of this nature, the passenger or his representative can take action only against the carrier who performed the carriage during which the accident or the delay occurred, save in the case where, by express agreement, the first carrier has assumed liability for the whole journey.

(3) As regards baggage or cargo, the passenger or consignor will have a right of action against the first carrier, and the passenger or consignee who is entitled to delivery will have a right of action against the last carrier, and further, each may take action against the carrier who performed the carriage during which the destruction, loss, damage or delay took place. These carriers will be jointly and severally liable to the passenger or to the consignor or consignee.

CHAPTER IV

PROVISIONS RELATING TO COMBINED CARRIAGE

Article 31

(1) In the case of combined carriage performed partly by air and partly by any other mode of carriage, the provisions of this Schedule apply only to the carriage by air, provided that the carriage by air falls within the terms of Article 1.

(2) Nothing in this Schedule shall prevent the parties in the case of combined carriage from inserting in the document of air carriage conditions relating to other modes of carriage, provided that the provisions of this Schedule are observed as regards the carriage by air.

CHAPTER V

GENERAL AND FINAL PROVISIONS

Article 32

Any clause contained in the contract and all special agreements entered into before the damage occurred by which the parties purport to infringe the rules laid down by this Schedule, whether by deciding the law to be applied, or by altering the rules as to jurisdiction, shall be null and void. Nevertheless, for the carriage of cargo arbitration clauses are allowed, subject to this Schedule, if the arbitration is to take place within one of the jurisdictions referred to in the first paragraph of Article 28.

Article 33

Nothing contained in this Schedule shall prevent the carrier either from refusing to enter into any contract of carriage, or from making regulations which do not conflict with the provisions of this Schedule.

Article 34

This Schedule does not apply to international carriage by air performed by way of experimental trial by air navigation undertakings with the view to the establishment of a regular line of air navigation, nor does it apply to carriage performed in extraordinary circumstances outside the normal scope of an air carrier's business.

Article 35

The expression "days" when used in this Schedule means current days not working days.

ADDITIONAL PROTOCOL TO THE WARSAW CONVENTION

The High Contracting Parties reserve to themselves the right to declare at the time of ratification or of accession that the first paragraph of Article 2 of this Convention shall not apply to international carriage by air performed directly by the State, its colonies, protectorates or mandated territories or by any other territory under its sovereignty, suzerainty or authority.

APPENDIX 6

THE WARSAW CONVENTION AS AMENDED AT THE HAGUE IN 1955 AND BY PROTOCOLS NOS. 3 AND 4

SIGNED AT MONTREAL IN 1975

The text is reproduced from the Second Schedule to the *Carriage by Air and Road Act 1979* enacted in the United Kingdom (1979 Chapter 28).

CHAPTER 1

SCOPE — DEFINITIONS

Article 1

1. This Convention applies to all international carriage of persons, baggage or cargo performed by aircraft for reward. It applies equally to gratuitous carriage by aircraft performed by an air transport undertaking.

2. For the purposes of this Convention, the expression *international carriage* means any carriage in which, according to the agreement between the parties, the place of departure and the place of destination, whether or not there be a break in the carriage or a transshipment, are situated either within the territories of two High Contracting Parties or within the territory of a single High Contracting Party if there is an agreed stopping place within the territory of another State, even if that State is not a High Contracting Party. Carriage between two points within the territory of a single High Contracting Party without an agreed stopping place within the territory of another State is not international carriage for the purposes of this Convention.

3. Carriage to be performed by several successive air carriers is deemed, for the purposes of this Convention, to be one undivided carriage if it has been regarded by the parties as a single operation, whether it had been agreed upon under the form of a single contract or of a series of contracts, and it does not lose its international character merely because one contract or a series of contracts is to be performed entirely within the territory of the same State.

Article 2

1. This Convention applies to carriage performed by the State or by legally constituted public bodies provided it falls within the conditions laid down in Article 1.

2. In the carriage of postal items the carrier shall be liable only to the relevant postal administration in accordance with the rules applicable to the relationship between the carriers and the postal administrations.

3. Except as provided in paragraph 2 of this Article, the provisions of this Convention shall not apply to the carriage of postal items.

CHAPTER II: DOCUMENTS OF CARRIAGE

SECTION 1 — PASSENGER TICKET

Article 3

1. In respect of the carriage of passengers an individual or collective document of carriage shall be delivered containing:
   a) an indication of the places of departure and destination;
   b) if the places of departure and destination are within the territory of a single High Contracting Party, one or more agreed stopping places being within the territory of another State, an indication of at least one such stopping place.
2. Any other means which would preserve a record of the information indicated in a) or b) of the foregoing paragraph may be substituted for the delivery of the document referred to in that paragraph.
3. Non-compliance with the provisions of the foregoing paragraphs shall not affect the existence or the validity of the contract of carriage, which shall, none the less, be subject to the rules of this Convention including those relating to limitation of liability.

SECTION 2 — BAGGAGE CHECK

Article 4

1. In respect of the carriage of checked baggage, a baggage check shall be delivered, which, unless combined with or incorporated in a document of carriage which complies with the provisions of Article 3, paragraph 1, shall contain:
   a) an indication of the places of departure and destination;
   b) if the places of departure and destination are within the territory of a single High Contracting Party, one or more agreed stopping places being within the territory of another State, an indication of at least one such stopping place.
2. Any other means which would preserve a record of the information indicated in a) and b) of the foregoing paragraph may be substituted for the delivery of the baggage check referred to in that paragraph.
3. Non-compliance with the provisions of the foregoing paragraphs shall not affect the existence or the validity of the contract of carriage, which shall, none the less, be subject to the rules of this Convention including those relating to limitation of liability.

SECTION 3 — DOCUMENTATION RELATING TO CARGO

Article 5

1. In respect of the carriage of cargo an air waybill shall be delivered.
2. Any other means which would preserve a record of the carriage to be performed may, with the consent of the consignor, be substituted for the delivery of an air waybill. If such other means are used, the carrier shall, if so requested by the consignor, deliver to the consignor a receipt for the cargo permitting identification of the consignment and access to the information contained in the record preserved by such other means.
3. The impossibility of using, at points of transit and destination, the other means which would preserve the record of the carriage referred to in paragraph 2 of this Article does not entitle the carrier to refuse to accept the cargo for carriage.

Article 6

1. The air waybill shall be made out by the consignor in three original parts.

2. The first part shall be marked "for the carrier"; it shall be signed by the consignor. The second part shall be marked "for the consignee"; it shall be signed by the consignor and by the carrier. The third part shall be signed by the carrier and handed by him to the consignor after the cargo has been accepted.

3. The signature of the carrier and that of the consignor may be printed or stamped.

4. If, at the request of the consignor, the carrier makes out the air waybill, he shall be deemed, subject to proof to the contrary, to have done so on behalf of the consignor.

Article 7

When there is more than one package:

a) the carrier of cargo has the right to require the consignor to make out separate air waybills;

b) the consignor has the right to require the carrier to deliver separate receipts when the other means referred to in paragraph 2 of Article 5 are used.

Article 8

The air waybill and the receipt for the cargo shall contain:

a) an indication of the places of departure and destination;

b) if the places of departure and destination are within the territory of a single High Contracting Party, one or more agreed stopping places being within the territory of another State, an indication of at least one such stopping place; and

c) an indication of the weight of the consignment.

Article 9

Non-compliance with the provisions of Articles 5 to 8 shall not affect the existence or the validity of the contract of carriage, which shall, none the less, be subject to the rules of this Convention including those relating to limitation of liability.

Article 10

1. The consignor is responsible for the correctness of the particulars and statements relating to the cargo inserted by him or on his behalf in the air waybill or furnished by him or on his behalf to the carrier for insertion in the receipt for the cargo or for insertion in the record preserved by the other means referred to in paragraph 2 of Article 5.

2. The consignor shall indemnify the carrier against all damage suffered by him, or by any other person to whom the carrier is liable, by reason of the irregularity, incorrectness or incompleteness of the particulars and statements furnished by the consignor or on his behalf.

3. Subject to the provisions of paragraphs 1 and 2 of this Article, the carrier shall indemnify the consignor against all damage suffered by him, or by any other person to whom the consignor is liable, by reason of the irregularity, incorrectness or incompleteness of the particulars and statements inserted by the carrier or on his behalf in the receipt for the cargo or in the record preserved by the other means referred to in paragraph 2 of Article 5.

Article 11

1. The air waybill or the receipt for the cargo is *prima facie* evidence of the conclusion of the contract, of the acceptance of the cargo and of the conditions of carriage mentioned therein.

2. Any statements in the air waybill or the receipt for the cargo relating to the weight, dimensions and packing of the cargo, as well as those relating to the number of packages, are *prima facie* evidence of the facts stated; those relating to the quantity, volume and condition of the cargo do not constitute evidence against the carrier except so far as they both have been, and are stated in the air waybill to have been, checked by him in the presence of the consignor, or relate to the apparent condition of the cargo.

Article 12

1. Subject to his liability to carry out all his obligations under the contract of carriage, the consignor has the right to dispose of the cargo by withdrawing it at the airport of departure or destination, or by stopping it in the course of the journey on any landing, or by calling for it to be delivered at the place of destination or in the course of the journey to a person other than the consignee originally designated, or by requiring it to be returned to the airport of departure. He must not exercise this right of disposition in such a way as to prejudice the carrier or other consignors and he must repay any expenses occasioned by the exercise of this right.

2. If it is impossible to carry out the orders of the consignor the carrier must so inform him forthwith.

3. If the carrier obeys the orders of the consignor for the disposition of the cargo without requiring the production of the part of the air waybill or the receipt for the cargo delivered to the latter, he will be liable, without prejudice to his right of recovery from the consignor, for any damage which may be caused thereby to any person who is lawfully in possession of that part of the air waybill or the receipt for the cargo.

4. The right conferred on the consignor ceases at the moment when that of the consignee begins in accordance with Article 13. Nevertheless, if the consignee declines to accept the cargo, or if he cannot be communicated with, the consignor resumes his right of disposition.

Article 13

1. Except when the consignor has exercised his right under Article 12, the consignee is entitled, on arrival of the cargo at the place of destination, to require the carrier to deliver the cargo to him, on payment of the charges due and on complying with the conditions of carriage.

2. Unless it is otherwise agreed, it is the duty of the carrier to give notice to the consignee as soon as the cargo arrives.

3. If the carrier admits the loss of the cargo, or if the cargo has not arrived at the expiration of seven days after the date on which it ought to have arrived, the consignee is entitled to enforce against the carrier the rights which flow from the contract of carriage.

Article 14

The consignor and the consignee can respectively enforce all the rights given them by Articles 12 and 13, each in his own name, whether he is acting in his own interest or in the interest of another, provided that he carries out the obligations imposed by the contract of carriage.

Article 15

1. Articles 12, 13 and 14 do not affect either the relations of the consignor and the consignee with each other or the mutual relations of third parties whose rights are derived either from the consignor or from the consignee.

2. The provisions of Articles 12, 13 and 14 can only be varied by express provision in the air waybill or the receipt for the cargo.

Article 16

1. The consignor must furnish such information and such documents as are necessary to meet the formalities of customs, octroi or police before the cargo can be delivered to the consignee. The consignor is liable to the carrier for any damage occasioned by the absence, insufficiency or irregularity of any such information or documents, unless the damage is due to the fault of the carrier, his servants or agents.

2. The carrier is under no obligation to enquire into the correctness or sufficiency of such information or documents.

CHAPTER III: LIABILITY OF THE CARRIER

Article 17

1. The carrier is liable for damage sustained in case of death or personal injury of a passenger upon condition only that the event which caused the death or injury took place on board the aircraft or in the course of any of the operations of embarking or disembarking. However, the carrier is not liable if the death or injury resulted solely from the state of health of the passenger.

2. The carrier is liable for damage sustained in case of destruction or loss of, or of damage to, baggage upon condition only that the event which caused the destruction, loss or damage took place on board the aircraft or in the course of any of the operations of embarking or disembarking or during any period within which the baggage was in charge of the carrier. However, the carrier is not liable if the damage resulted solely from the inherent defect, quality or vice of the baggage.

3. Unless otherwise specified, in this Convention the term "baggage" means both checked baggage and objects carried by the passenger.

Article 18

1. The carrier is liable for damage sustained in the event of the destruction or loss of, or damage to, cargo upon condition only that the occurrence which caused the damage so sustained took place during the carriage by air.

2. However, the carrier is not liable if he proves that the destruction, loss of, or damage to, the cargo resulted solely from one or more of the following:

a) inherent defect, quality or vice of that cargo;
b) defective packing of that cargo performed by a person other than the carrier or his servants or agents;
c) an act of war or an armed conflict;
d) an act of public authority carried out in connection with the entry, exit or transit of the cargo.

3. The carriage by air within the meaning of paragraph 1 of this Article comprises the period during which the cargo is in the charge of the carrier, whether in an airport or on board an aircraft, or, in the case of a landing outside an airport, in any place whatsoever.

4. The period of the carriage by air does not extend to any carriage by land, by sea or by river performed outside an airport. If, however, such carriage takes place in the

performance of a contract for carriage by air, for the purpose of loading, delivery or transshipment, any damage is presumed, subject to proof to the contrary, to have been the result of an event which took place during the carriage by air.

Article 19

The carrier is liable for damage occasioned by delay in the carriage by air of passengers, baggage or cargo.

Article 20

In the carriage of passengers, baggage and cargo, the carrier shall not be liable for damage occasioned by delay if he proves that he and his servants and agents have taken all necessary measures to avoid the damage or that it was impossible for them to take such measures.

Article 21

1. In the carriage of passengers and baggage, if the carrier proves that the damage was caused or contributed to by the negligence or other wrongful act or omission of the person claiming compensation, the carrier shall be wholly or partly exonerated from his liability to such person to the extent that such negligence or wrongful act or omission caused or contributed to the damage. When by reason of the death or injury of a passenger compensation is claimed by a person other than the passenger, the carrier shall likewise be wholly or partly exonerated from his liability to the extent that he proves that the damage was caused or contributed to by the negligence or other wrongful act or omission of that passenger.

2. In the carriage of cargo, if the carrier proves that the damage was caused by or contributed to by the negligence or other wrongful act or omission of the person claiming compensation, or the person from whom he derives his rights, the carrier shall be wholly or partly exonerated from his liability to the claimant to the extent that such negligence or wrongful act or omission caused or contributed to the damage.

Article 22

1. a) In the carriage of persons the liability of the carrier is limited to the sum of 100 000 Special Drawing Rights for the aggregate of the claims, however founded, in respect of damage suffered as a result of the death or personal injury of each passenger. Where, in accordance with the law of the court seised of the case, damages may be awarded in the form of periodic payments, the equivalent capital value of the said payments shall not exceed 100 000 Special Drawing Rights.
   b) In the case of delay in the carriage of persons the liability of the carrier for each passenger is limited to 4 150 Special Drawing Rights.
   c) In the carriage of baggage the liability of the carrier in the case of destruction, loss, damage or delay is limited to 1 000 Special Drawing Rights for each passenger.
2. a) The courts of the High Contracting Parties which are not authorised under their law to award the costs of the action, including lawyers' fees, shall, in actions relating to the carriage of passengers and baggage to which this Convention applies, have the power to award, in their discretion, to the claimant the whole or part of the costs of the action, including lawyers' fees which the court considers reasonable.

b) The costs of the action including lawyers' fees shall be awarded in accordance with subparagraph a) only if the claimant gives a written notice to the carrier of the amount claimed including the particulars of the calculation of that amount and the carrier does not make, within a period of six months after his receipt of such notice, a written offer of settlement in an amount at least equal to the compensation awarded within the applicable limit. This period will be extended until the time of commencement of the action if that is later.

c) The costs of the action including lawyers' fees shall not be taken into account in applying the limits under this Article.

3. The sums mentioned in terms of the Special Drawing Right in this Article shall be deemed to refer to the Special Drawing Right as defined by the International Monetary Fund. Conversion of the sums into national currencies shall, in case of judicial proceedings, be made according to the value of such currencies in terms of the Special Drawing Right at the date of the judgment.

Article 22A

1. a) In the carriage of cargo, the liability of the carrier is limited to a sum of 17 Special Drawing Rights per kilogramme, unless the consignor has made, at the time when the package was handed over to the carrier, a special declaration of interest in delivery at destination and has paid a supplementary sum if the case so requires. In that case the carrier will be liable to pay a sum not exceeding the declared sum, unless he proves that that sum is greater than the consignor's actual interest in delivery at destination.

b) In the case of loss, damage or delay of part of the cargo, or of any object contained therein, the weight to be taken into consideration in determining the amount to which the carrier's liability is limited shall be only the total weight of the package or packages concerned. Nevertheless, when the loss, damage or delay of a part of the cargo, or of an object contained therein, affects the value of other packages covered by the same air waybill, the total weight of such package or packages shall also be taken into consideration in determining the limit of liability.

2. The limits prescribed in this Article shall not prevent the court in an action relating to the carriage of cargo from awarding in accordance with its own law, in addition, the whole or part of the court costs and of the other expenses of the litigation incurred by the plaintiff. The foregoing provision shall not apply if the amount of the damages awarded, excluding court costs and other expenses of the litigation, does not exceed the sum which the carrier has offered in writing to the plaintiff within a period of six months from the date of the occurrence causing the damage, or before the commencement of the action, if that is later.

3. The sums mentioned in terms of the Special Drawing Right in this Article shall be deemed to refer to the Special Drawing Right as defined by the International Monetary Fund. Conversion of the sums into national currencies shall, in case of judicial proceedings, be made according to the value of such currencies in terms of the Special Drawing Right at the date of the judgment.

Article 23

1. Any provision tending to relieve the carrier of liability or to fix a lower limit than that which is laid down in this Convention shall be null and void, but the nullity of any such provision does not involve the nullity of the whole contract, which shall remain subject to the provisions of this Convention.

2. Paragraph 1 of this Article shall not apply to provisions governing loss or damage resulting from the inherent defect, quality or vice of the cargo carried.

Article 24

In the carriage of passengers, baggage and cargo, any action for damages, however founded, whether under this Convention or in contract or in tort or otherwise, can only be brought subject to the conditions and limits of liability set out in this Convention without prejudice to the question as to who are the persons who have the right to bring suit and what are their respective rights. Such limits of liability constitute maximum limits and may not be exceeded whatever the circumstances which gave rise to the liability.

Article 25A

1. If an action is brought against a servant or agent of the carrier arising out of damage to which the Convention relates, such servant or agent, if he proves that he acted within the scope of his employment, shall be entitled to avail himself of the limits of liability which that carrier himself is entitled to invoke under this Convention.

2. The aggregate of the amounts recoverable from the carrier, his servants and agents, in that case, shall not exceed the said limits.

Article 26

1. Receipt by the person entitled to delivery of baggage or cargo without complaint is *prima facie* evidence that the same has been delivered in good condition and in accordance with the document of carriage.

2. In the case of damage, the person entitled to delivery must complain to the carrier forthwith after the discovery of the damage, and, at the latest, within seven days from the date of receipt in the case of baggage and fourteen days from the date of receipt in the case of cargo. In the case of delay the complaint must be made at the latest within twenty-one days from the date on which the baggage or cargo has been placed at his disposal.

3. Every complaint must be made in writing upon the document of carriage or by separate notice in writing despatched within the times aforesaid.

4. Failing complaint within the times aforesaid, no action shall lie against the carrier, save in the case of fraud on his part.

Article 27

In the case of the death of the person liable, an action for damages lies in accordance with the terms of this Convention against those legally representing his estate.

Article 28

1. An action for damages must be brought, at the option of the plaintiff, in the territory of one of the High Contracting Parties, either before the court having jurisdiction where the carrier is ordinarily resident, or has his principal place of business, or has an establishment by which the contract has been made or before the court having jurisdiction at the place of destination.

2. In respect of damage resulting from the death, injury or delay of a passenger or the destruction, loss, damage or delay of baggage, the action may be brought before one of the courts mentioned in paragraph 1 of this Article, or in the territory of one of the High Contracting Parties, before the court within the jurisdiction of which the carrier has an establishment if the passenger has his ordinary or permanent residence in the territory of the same High Contracting Party.

3. Questions of procedure shall be governed by the law of the court seised of the case.

Article 29

1. The right to damages shall be extinguished if an action is not brought within two years, reckoned from the date of arrival at the destination, or from the date on which the aircraft ought to have arrived, or from the date on which the carriage stopped.

2. The method of calculating the period of limitation shall be determined by the law of the court seised of the case.

Article 30

1. In the case of carriage to be performed by various successive carriers and falling within the definition set out in the third paragraph of Article 1, each carrier who accepts passengers, baggage or cargo is subjected to the rules set out in this Convention, and is deemed to be one of the contracting parties to the contract of carriage in so far as the contract deals with that part of the carriage which is performed under his supervision.

2. In the case of carriage of this nature, the passenger or his representative can take action only against the carrier who performed the carriage during which the accident or the delay occurred, save in the case where, by express agreement, the first carrier has assumed liability for the whole journey.

3. As regards baggage or cargo, the passenger or consignor will have a right of action against the first carrier, and the passenger or consignee who is entitled to delivery will have a right of action against the last carrier, and further, each may take action against the carrier who performed the carriage during which the destruction, loss, damage or delay took place. These carriers will be jointly and severally liable to the passenger or to the consignor or consignee.

Article 30A

Nothing in this Convention shall prejudice the question whether a person liable for damage in accordance with its provisions has a right of recourse against any other person.

CHAPTER IV: PROVISIONS RELATING TO COMBINED CARRIAGE

Article 31

1. In the case of combined carriage performed partly by air and partly by any other mode of carriage, the provisions of this Convention apply only to the carriage by air, provided that the carriage by air falls within the terms of Article 1.

2. Nothing in this Convention shall prevent the parties in the case of combined carriage from inserting in the document of air carriage conditions relating to other modes of carriage, provided that the provisions of this Convention are observed as regards the carriage by air.

CHAPTER V: GENERAL AND FINAL PROVISIONS

Article 32

Any clause contained in the contract and all special agreements entered into before the damage occurred by which the parties purport to infringe the rules laid down by this Convention, whether by deciding the law to be applied, or by altering the rules as to jurisdiction, shall be null and void. Nevertheless for the carriage of cargo arbitration clauses are allowed, subject to this Convention, if the arbitration is to take place within one of the jurisdictions referred to in the first paragraph of Article 28.

Article 33

Except as provided in paragraph 3 of Article 5, nothing in this Convention shall prevent the carrier either from refusing to enter into any contract of carriage or from making regulations which do not conflict with the provisions of this Convention.

Article 34

The provisions of Articles 3 to 8 inclusive relating to documents of carriage shall not apply in the case of carriage performed in extraordinary circumstances outside the normal scope of an air carrier's business.

Article 35

The expression "days" when used in this Convention means current days not working days.

Article 35A

No provision contained in this Convention shall prevent a State from establishing and operating within its territory a system to supplement the compensation payable to claimants under the Convention in respect of death, or personal injury, of passengers. Such a system shall fulfil the following conditions:

a) it shall not in any circumstances impose upon the carrier, his servants or agents, any liability in addition to that provided under this Convention;
b) it shall not impose upon the carrier any financial or administrative burden other than collecting in that State contributions from passengers if required so to do;
c) it shall not give rise to any discrimination between carriers with regard to the passengers concerned and the benefits available to the said passengers under the system shall be extended to them regardless of the carrier whose services they have used;
d) if a passenger has contributed to the system, any person suffering damage as a consequence of death or personal injury of such passenger shall be entitled to the benefits of the system.

Article 40A

1. [*This paragraph is not reproduced. It defines "High Contracting Party".*]
2. For the purposes of the Convention the word *territory* means not only the metropolitan territory of a State but also all other territories for the foreign relations of which that State is responsible.

[*Articles 36, 37, 38, 39, 40, 41 and 42 and the concluding words of the Convention are not reproduced. They deal, among other things, with the coming into force of the Convention. The former Article 25 is superseded by Article 24.*]

ADDITIONAL PROTOCOL

(With reference to Article 2)

The High Contracting Parties reserve to themselves the right to declare at the time of ratification or of accession that the first paragraph of Article 2 of this Convention shall not apply to international carriage by air performed directly by the State, its colonies, protectorates or mandated territories or by any other territory under its sovereignty, suzerainty or authority.

APPENDIX 7

GUADALAJARA SUPPLEMENTARY CONVENTION (1961)

CONVENTION SUPPLEMENTARY TO THE WARSAW CONVENTION, FOR THE UNIFICATION OF CERTAIN RULES RELATING TO INTERNATIONAL CARRIAGE BY AIR PERFORMED BY A PERSON OTHER THAN THE CONTRACTING CARRIER*

THE STATES SIGNATORY TO THE PRESENT CONVENTION

NOTING that the Warsaw Convention does not contain particular rules relating to international carriage by air performed by a person who is not a party to the agreement for carriage.

CONSIDERING that it is therefore desirable to formulate rules to apply in such circumstances.

HAVE AGREED as follows:

Article I

In this Convention:

a) "Warsaw Convention" means the Convention for the Unification of Certain Rules Relating to International Carriage by Air signed at Warsaw on 12 October 1929, or the Warsaw Convention as amended at The Hague, 1955, according to whether the carriage under the agreement referred to in paragraph b) is governed by the one or by the other;

b) "contracting carrier" means a person who as a principal makes an agreement for carriage governed by the Warsaw Convention with a passenger or consignor or with a person acting on behalf of the passenger or consignor;

c) "actual carrier" means a person, other than the contracting carrier, who, by virtue of authority from the contracting carrier, performs the whole or part of the carriage contemplated in paragraph b) but who is not with respect to such part a successive carrier within the meaning of the Warsaw Convention. Such authority is presumed in the absence of proof to the contrary.

Article II

If an actual carrier performs the whole or part of carriage which, according to the agreement referred to in Article 1, paragraph b), is governed by the Warsaw Convention, both the contracting carrier and the actual carrier shall, except as otherwise provided in this Convention, be subject to the rules of the Warsaw Convention, the former for the

* ICAO Doc. 8181.

whole of the carriage contemplated in the agreement, the latter solely for the carriage which he performs.

Article III

1. The acts and omissions of the actual carrier and of his servants and agents acting within the scope of their employment shall, in relation to the carriage performed by the actual carrier, be deemed to be also those of the contracting carrier.

2. The acts and omissions of the contracting carrier and of his servants and agents acting within the scope of their employment shall, in relation to the carriage performed by the actual carrier, be deemed to be also those of the actual carrier. Nevertheless, no such act or omission shall subject the actual carrier to liability exceeding the limits specified in Article 22 of the Warsaw Convention. Any special agreement under which the contracting carrier assumes obligations not imposed by the Warsaw Convention or any waiver of rights conferred by that Convention or any special declaration of interest in delivery at destination contemplated in Article 22 of the said Convention, shall not affect the actual carrier unless agreed to by him.

Article IV

Any complaint to be made or order to be given under the Warsaw Convention to the carrier shall have the same effect whether addressed to the contracting carrier or to the actual carrier. Nevertheless, orders referred to in Article 12 of the Warsaw Convention shall only be effective if addressed to the contracting carrier.

Article V

In relation to the carriage performed by the actual carrier, any servant or agent of that carrier or of the contracting carrier shall, if he proves that he acted within the scope of his employment, be entitled to avail himself of the limits of liability which are applicable under this Convention to the carrier whose servant or agent he is unless it is proved that he acted in a manner which, under the Warsaw Convention, prevents the limits of liability from being invoked.

Article VI

In relation to the carriage performed by the actual carrier, the aggregate of the amounts recoverable from that carrier and the contracting carrier, and from their servants and agents acting within the scope of their employment, shall not exceed the highest amount which could be awarded against either the contracting carrier or the actual carrier under this Convention, but none of the persons mentioned shall be liable for a sum in excess of the limit applicable to him.

Article VII

In relation to the carriage performed by the actual carrier, an action for damages may be brought, at the option of the plaintiff, against that carrier or the contracting carrier, or against both together or separately. If the action is brought against only one of those carriers, that carrier shall have the right to require the other carrier to be joined in the proceedings, the procedure and effects being governed by the law of the court seised of the case.

Article VIII

Any action for damages contemplated in Article VII of this Convention must be brought, at the option of the plaintiff, either before a court in which an action may be brought against the contracting carrier, as provided in Article 28 of the Warsaw Convention, or before the court having jurisdiction at the place where the actual carrier is ordinarily resident or has his principal place of business.

Article IX

1. Any contractual provision tending to relieve the contracting carrier or the actual carrier of liability under this Convention or to fix a lower limit than that which is applicable according to this Convention shall be null and void, but the nullity of any such provision does not involve the nullity of the whole agreement, which shall remain subject to the provisions of this Convention.
2. In respect of the carriage performed by the actual carrier, the preceding paragraph shall not apply to contractual provisions governing loss or damage resulting from the inherent defect, quality or vice of the cargo carried.
3. Any clause contained in an agreement for carriage and all special agreements entered into before the damage occurred by which the parties purport to infringe the rules laid down by this Convention, whether by deciding the law to be applied, or by altering the rules as to jurisdiction, shall be null and void. Nevertheless, for the carriage of cargo arbitration clauses are allowed, subject to this Convention, if the arbitration is to take place in one the jurisdictions referred to in Article VIII.

Article X

Except as provided in Article VII, nothing in this Convention shall affect the rights and obligations of the two carriers between themselves.

Article XI

Until the date on which this Convention comes into force in accordance with the provisions of Article XIII, it shall remain open for signature on behalf of any State which at that date is a Member of the United Nations or of any of the Specialised Agencies.

Article XII

1. This Convention shall be subject to ratification by the signatory States.
2. The instruments of ratification shall be deposited with the Government of the United States of Mexico.

Article XIII

1. As soon as five of the signatory States have deposited their instruments of ratification of this Convention, it shall come into force between them on the ninetieth day after the date of the deposit of the fifth instrument of ratification. It shall come into force for each State ratifying thereafter on the ninetieth day after the deposit of its instrument of ratification.
2. As soon as this Convention comes into force, it shall be registered with the United Nations and the International Civil Aviation Organisation by the Government of the United States of Mexico.

Article XIV

1. This Convention shall, after it has come into force, be open for accession by any State Member of the United Nations or of any of the Specialised Agencies.

2. The accession of a State shall be effected by the deposit of an instrument of accession with the Government of the United States of Mexico and shall take effect as from the ninetieth day after the date of such deposit.

Article XV

1. Any Contracting State may denounce this Convention by notification addressed to the Government of the United States of Mexico.

2. Denunciation shall take effect six months after the date of receipt by the Government of the United States of Mexico of the notification of denunciation.

Article XVI

1. Any Contracting State may at the time of its ratification of or accession to this Convention or at any time thereafter declare by notification to the Government of the United States of Mexico that the Convention shall extend to any of the territories for whose international relations it is responsible.

2. The Convention shall, ninety days after the date of the receipt of such notification by the Government of the United States of Mexico, extend to the territories named therein.

3. Any Contracting State may denounce this Convention, in accordance with the provisions of Article XV, separately for any or all of the territories for the international relations of which such State is responsible.

Article XVII

No reservation may be made to this Convention.

Article XVIII

The Government of the United States of Mexico shall give notice to the International Civil Aviation Organisation and to all States members of the United Nations or of any of the Specialised Agencies:

a) of any signature of this Convention and the date thereof;
b) of the deposit of any instrument of ratification or accession and the date thereof;
c) of the date on which this Convention comes into force in accordance with Article XIII, paragraph 1;
d) of the receipt of any notification of denunciation and the date thereof;
e) of the receipt of any declaration or notification made under Article XVI and the date thereof.

IN WITNESS WHEREOF the undersigned Plenipotentiaries, having been duly authorised, have signed this Convention.

DONE at Guadalajara on the eighteenth day of September One Thousand Nine Hundred and Sixty-one in three authentic texts drawn up in the English, French and Spanish languages. In case of any inconsistency, the text in the French language, in which language the Warsaw Convention of 12 October 1929 was drawn up, shall prevail. The Government of the United States of Mexico will establish an official translation of the text of the Convention in the Russian language.

This Convention shall be deposited with the Government of the United States of Mexico with which, in accordance with Article XI, it shall remain open for signature, and that Government shall send certified copies thereof to the International Civil Aviation Organisation and to all States Members of the United Nations or of any Specialised Agency.

APPENDIX 8

AIR WAYBILL CONDITIONS

NOTICE CONCERNING CARRIERS' LIMITATION OF LIABILITY

IF THE CARRIAGE INVOLVES AN ULTIMATE DESTINATION IN A COUNTRY OTHER THAN THE COUNTRY OF DEPARTURE, THE WARSAW CONVENTION MAY BE APPLICABLE AND THE CONVENTION GOVERNS AND IN MOST CASES LIMITS THE LIABILITY OF THE CARRIER IN RESPECT OF LOSS, DAMAGE, OR DELAY TO CARGO TO 250 FRENCH GOLD FRANCS PER KILOGRAM, UNLESS A HIGHER VALUE IS DECLARED IN ADVANCE BY THE SHIPPER AND A SUPPLEMENTARY CHARGE PAID IF REQUIRED. THE LIABILITY LIMIT OF 250 FRENCH GOLD FRANCS PER KILOGRAM IS APPROXIMATELY USD20.00 PER KILOGRAM ON THE BASES OF USD42.22 PER OUNCE OF GOLD.

1. As used in this contract "Carrier" means all air carriers that carry or undertake to carry the goods hereunder or perform any other services incidental to such air carriage. "Warsaw Convention" means the Convention for the Unification of certain Rules relating to International Carriage by Air, signed at Warsaw 12 October 1929, or that Convention as amended at The Hague 28 September 1955, whichever may be applicable, and "French gold francs" means francs consisting of 65½ milligrams of gold with a fineness of nine hundred thousandths.

2. (a) Carriage hereunder is subject to the rules relating to liability established by the Warsaw Convention unless such carriage is not international carriage as defined within that Convention.
   (b) To the extent not in conflict with the foregoing, carriage hereunder and other services performed by each Carrier are subject to:
      (i) applicable laws (including national laws implementing the Convention), government regulations, orders and requirements,
      (ii) provisions herein set forth, and
      (iii) applicable tariffs, rules, conditions of carriage, regulations and time-tables (but not the times of departure and arrival therein) of such carrier, which are made part hereof and which may be inspected at any of its offices and at airports from which it operates regular services. In transportation between a place in the United States or Canada and any place outside thereof the applicable tariffs are the tariffs in force in those countries.

3. The first carrier's name may be abbreviated on the face hereof, the full name and its abbreviation being set forth in such carrier's tariffs, conditions of carriage, regulations and timetables. The first carrier's address is the airport of departure shown on the face hereof. The agreed stopping places (which may be altered by the carrier in case of necessity) are those places, except the place of departure and the place of destination, set forth in the face hereof or shown in carrier's timetables as scheduled stopping places for

the route. Carriage to be performed hereunder by several successive carriers is regarded as a single operation.

4. Except as otherwise provided in the carrier's tariffs or conditions of carriage, in carriage to which the Warsaw Convention does not apply carrier's liability shall not exceed U.S.$ 20.00 or the equivalent per kilogramme of goods lost, damaged or delayed, unless a higher value is declared by the shipper and a supplementary charge paid.

5. If the sum entered on the face of the air waybill as "declared value for carriage" represents an amount in excess of the applicable limits of liability referred to in the above notice and in the conditions and if the shipper has paid any supplementary charge, this shall constitute a special declaration of value and in this case carrier's limit of liability shall be the sum so declared. Payment of claims shall be subject to proof of actual damage suffered.

6. In case of loss, damage and delay of part of the consignment, the weight to be taken into account in determining the carrier's limit of liability shall be only the weight of the package or packages concerned.

Note: notwithstanding any other provision, for foreign air transportation as defined in the U.S. Federal Aviation Act, as amended, in case of loss damage or delay of a shipment or part thereof, the weight to be used in determining the carrier's limit of liability shall be the weight which is used (or *pro rata* share in the case of a part shipment loss, damage or delay) to determine the transportation charge for such shipment.[1]

7. Any exclusion or limitation applicable to carrier shall apply to and be for the benefit of carrier's agents, servants and representatives and any person whose aircraft is used by carrier for carriage and its agents, servants and representatives. For purposes of this provision the carrier acts as agent for all such persons.

8. (a) Carrier undertakes to complete the carriage hereunder with reasonable dispatch. Carrier may substitute alternative carriers or aircraft and may without notice and with due regard to the interests of the shipper substitute other means of transportation. Carrier is authorised to select the routing or to change or deviate from the routing shown on the face hereof. This subparagraph is not applicable to/from the USA.

(b) Carrier undertakes to complete the carriage hereunder with reasonable dispatch. Except within the USA where carrier's tariffs will apply, carrier may substitute alternate carriers or aircraft and may without notice and with due regard to the interests of the shipper substitute other means of transportation. Carrier is authorised to select the routing or to change or deviate from the routing shown on the face hereof. This subparagraph is applicable only to/from USA.

9. Subject to the conditions herein, the Carrier shall be liable for the goods during the period they are in its charge or the charge of its agent.

10(a) Except when carrier has extended credit to the consignee without the written consent of the shipper, the shipper guarantees payment of all charges for carriage due in accordance with the carrier's tariffs, conditions of carriage and related regulations, applicable laws (including national laws implementing the Convention), government regulations, orders and requirements.

(b) When no part of the consignment is delivered, a claim with respect to such consignment will be entertained even though transportation charges thereon are unpaid.

11. Notice of arrival of goods will be given promptly to the consignee or to the person indicated on the face hereof as the person to be notified. On arrival of the goods at the place of destination, subject to the acceptance of other instructions from the shipper prior to arrival of the goods at the place of destination, delivery will be made to, or in accordance with, the instructions of the consignee. If the consignee declines to accept the

1. This paragraph does not appear in all IATA carrier's air waybill conditions.

goods or cannot be communicated with, disposition will be in accordance with the instructions of the shipper.

12. (a) The person entitled to delivery must make a complaint to the carrier in writing in the case:

(i) Of visible damage to the goods, immediately after discovery of the damage and at the latest within 14 days from the receipt of the goods,

(ii) Of other damage to the goods, within 14 days from the date of receipt of the goods,

(iii) Of delay, within 21 days of the date the goods are placed at his disposal, and

(iv) Of non-delivery of the goods, within 120 days from the date of the issue of the Air Waybill.

(b) For the purpose of subparagraph (a) above complaint in writing may be made to the carrier whose air waybill was used, or to the first carrier or to the last carrier or to the carrier who performed the transportation during which the loss, damage or delay took place.

(c) Any rights to damages against the carrier shall be extinguished unless an action is brought within two years from the date of arrival at the destination, or from the date on which the aircraft ought to have arrived, or from the date on which the transportation stopped.

13. The shipper shall comply with all applicable laws and government regulations of any country to, from, through or over which the goods may be carried, including those relating to the packing, carriage or delivery of the goods, and shall furnish such information and attach such documents to this air waybill as may be necessary to comply with such laws and regulations. Carrier is not liable to the shipper for loss or expense due to the shipper's failure to comply with this provision.

14. No agent, servant or representative of carrier has authority to alter, modify or waive any provision of this contract.

15. If the carrier offers insurance and such insurance is requested, and if the appropriate premium is paid and the fact recorded on the face hereof the goods covered by this Air Waybill are insured under an open policy for the amount requested as set out on the face hereof (recovery being limited to the actual value of goods lost or damaged provided that such amount does not exceed the insured value). The insurance is subject to the terms, conditions and coverage (from which certain risks are excluded) of the open policy, which is available for inspection at an office of the issuing carrier by the interested party. Claims under such policy must be reported immediately to an office of carrier.

INDEX

Throughout the index, the suffix "n" following a page number signifies reference to the footnotes on that page. The suffix "&n" signifies reference to both the main text and the footnotes.

Added value: claim amount, 119
Adjusters *see* Claims adjusters; Loss adjusters
Agency, 46
  BIFA conditions, 55
Air carriage, statutory regulation, 61–62
Air waybills (AWBs), xvii
  conditions, 93–97
    full text (App. 8), 191–193
    notice of applicability of Warsaw, 93
    paragraph 1: definitions, 93
    paragraph 2: applicability of rules, 93
    paragraph 3: name and address on, 93
    paragraph 4: limitation of liability, 94
    paragraph 5: special declaration of value, 94
    paragraph 6: package weight limitation, 94
    paragraph 7: protection of agents, and others, 94–95
    paragraph 8: reasonable dispatch (avoidance of delay), 95
    paragraph 9: period of responsibility, 95
    paragraph 10: shipper's guarantee and payment of freight, 95–96
    paragraph 11: notice of arrival, 96
    paragraph 12: notice periods, 96
    paragraph 13: shippers' obligations, 96
    paragraph 14: authority to vary conditions, 97
    paragraph 15: transit insurance, 97
  "declared value for carriage", 75, 125
  defined, xvii
  description of commodity, 17
  Hague Protocol 1955 (Warsaw/Hague), 81–83
  insurance, 12–13, 97
  Montreal, 4
  non-payment of freight, 107
  simplification, 85
  in trucking, 104
  "unamended Warsaw", 66–67
Airline handling agreements, 99–102
  "hold harmless" agreements, 99–101
  wilful misconduct, 99
Airline master air waybills (MAWBs), xviii
  Guadalajara, 88
  title to goods, 108
Airlines
  claims handlers, 6
  movement of cargo, 2n, 3
Airports, movement of cargo, 2n, 3
Anger and aggression: claimants, 106
"Anonymising" packaging of cargo, 17, 18
"AOGs" (aircraft on ground), 121
"Assured", 9
Attitudes: claimants and respondents, 105–106
Aviation security laws, 30
AWBs *see* Air waybills

Back-to-back, defined, xvii
Bailment, 61
  liability in, 44
Bond-checks, 25
  damage noted, 28
Booking sheets, 37
Break-bulk agents, 2n, 3
British International Freight Association (BIFA): Standard Trading Conditions: full text (App. 2), 139–144
British International Freight Association (BIFA): Standard Trading Conditions (summarised), 53–59
  definition and application
    Condition 1: definitions, 54
    Condition 2: application and overriding law, 54
    Condition 3: authority to accept contract conditions, 54
    Condition 4: further authority to accept conditions, 54
  the company
    Condition 5: agency, 55
    Condition 6: acceptance of liability, 55
    Condition 7: contracts arranged by company as agent, 55
    Condition 8: freedom of choice for company, 55

British International Freight Association (BIFA): Standard Trading Conditions (summarised)—*cont.*
the company—*cont.*
Condition 9: use of associates, etc., 55
Condition 10: liens, 55
Condition 11: remuneration, 55
Condition 12: frustrated delivery, 56
Condition 13: (transit) insurance, 56
Condition 14: special delivery circumstances, 56
Condition 15: advice and information, 56
Condition 16: special cargoes, 56
Condition 17: dangerous goods, 56
Condition 18: declarations of value, 57
the customer
Condition 19: warranties, 57
Condition 20: dangerous goods, 57
Condition 21: against whom to claim?, 57
Condition 22: customer to indemnify company, 57
Condition 23: moneys owed to company, 57
Condition 24: customer guarantee of charges, 58
Condition 25: general average, 58
liability and limitation
Condition 26: diligence, 58
Condition 27: relief of liability, 58
Condition 28: delay, 58
Condition 29: limitations, 58–59
Condition 30: time limits for claims, 59
applicable law, Condition 31, 59
British International Freight Association (BIFA), xvii, 47
airline handling agreements, 100
house air waybills, 71
liability context: claims decisions, 103, 104
measure of damages, 118
notice of claim, 109
settlement amount and limitation, 124, 126
settlement criteria: proving liability, 112
time bars, 111

CAB (Civil Aviation Board), xvii, 73, 84
Cameras, damage photography, 26, 27, 28
Cargo
defined, xvii
and freight, 107
Cargo cover *see* Goods-in-transit insurance cover
Cargo handling agents, 2n, 3
Cargo irregularity report *see* CIR
Cargo owners
insurance cover, 12
loss control, 21–22
risk control, 18
Cargo-handling companies *see* GHAs
Carriage by Air Act 1932, 48, 64
Carriage by Air Act 1961, 48, 64, 82
Carriage by Air Acts (Application of Provisions) (Fourth Amendment) Order 1998, 64
Carriage by Air Acts (Application of Provisions) Order 1967, 64, 91
Carriage by Air (Parties to Convention) Order 1988, 64
Carriage by Air and Road Act 1979, 64, 82, 85, 87
Carriage by Air and Road Act 1979 (Commencement No. 2) Order 1997, 83
Carriage by Air (Supplementary Provisions) Act 1962, 88
Carriers
liability cover, 11–12
liability of, 69–80, 86–87
loss control, 15, 22–31
risk control, 15–16
see also Forwarders
CCTV, xvii
and pilferage of goods, 29–30
see also Cameras
Check-in sheets, 38
CIR (cargo irregularity report), xvii, 39
CITEJA, 61–62
Civil law, 61
Claim amount (quantum) *see under* Settlement criteria
Claim file, creating/administering, 33–42
claim number, 34–35
correspondence standards, 41–42
general principles
assumption of future litigation, 33–34
general construction of file, 34
housekeeping
chronology, 35
clarity of documents, 35–36
duplicated documents, 35
records to maintain, 36–40
see also Documents
reviewing and progressing, 40–41
diary v. database, 41
separate file/filing location, 34
Claim notices, 22, 39
Claimants, and respondents: attitudes, 105–106
Claims adjusters, 11
Claims decisions, 103–130
claimants and respondents: attitudes, 105–106
which liability context?, 103–105
air transportation, 104–105
trucking of air cargo, 104
see also Settlement criteria
Claims handlers, 1–2, 4, 6
integrity of, 34

"Claused" signature from driver, 28
"Clausing": proving liability, 116
CMR (Contrat de Transport International de Marchandise par Route), xvii, 71, 72, 73, 81, 103
Common law, 43, 53, 61
Computer database, 41
Computers and components, 16, 17, 31, 116
Consequential losses
  and CAB, 73
  claim amount
    delay, 120–121
    foreseeability, 121
    mitigation, 122
    proof, 120–121
  defined, xvii
  and delays, 21, 28
Consignees, 2&n, 3, 4
  insurance, 9
  jurisdiction: entitlement to claim, 110
  liability claims, 7
  risk control, 18
  title to goods, 108
  see also Importers
Consignment notes, RHA conditions, 50
Consolidation, 37
  defined, xviii
Consolidation manifest, 37
Consolidators, 2n, 3, 4, 5&n
  see also Forwarders
Contracting carriers, liabilities: Guadalajara Convention, 88–89
Contracts, 43
  regulation of
    by legislation, 48
    civil, 47
Contracts of carriage, xviii, 44, 45, 46, 108
Contractual relationships, 2–4
Contributory negligence *see under* Negligence
Correspondence standards, 41–42
"Courier" services, 20
Currencies, 119, 123
Customs/import agent, 2n, 3

Damage
  by staff, 100
  damage reports, 26, 39
  insurers, 26–27
  loss control, 26–28
  mitigation, 122
  noted at other times, 28
  on receipt
    from another depot in same company, 27
    from another party, 27
    from inbound aircraft, 27
  risk control, 19–21
  see also Perishable goods
"Damage and loss" report *see* CIR (cargo irregularity report)
Deadload weight statements, 40
Delay
  avoidance: air waybill conditions, 95
  and consequential losses, 120–121
  loss control, 28–29
  and perishable goods, 19&n, 20, 28–29, 117, 122
  in pursuit of claim, 112
  risk control, 19&n, 20–21
Delivery note, 39
Delivery signatures: proving liability, 116
Description of goods, risk control, 17–18
Documentation
  accuracy of: claim amount, 123
  errors and contributory negligence, 115
Documenting incidents, loss control, 22–23
Documents
  carriage of, 20
  ordinary, 39
  regular
    booking sheets, 37
    check-in sheets, 38
    consolidation manifest, 37
    damage report *see under* Damage
    delivery note, 39
    flight manifests, 38
    out-turn report, 38
    packing lists, 36–37
    pallet tags/pallet manifests, 38
    shipping invoices, 36, 37, 108
    tracing records, 38–39
    truck delivery notes, 37
    see also Air waybills (AWBs); Airline master air waybills (MAWBs); House air waybills (HAWBs); Notices of claim
  special, 40
  see also Claim file
"Dwell" time, risk control, 18

Electrical equipment/goods, 17, 116
"Escrow", 128
Exporters, 4, 5
  insurance, 9–10
  transit/cargo insurance cover, 12
  see also Shippers

Faxes, 21, 45
  filing of, 35
  tracing records, 38
Flight manifests, 38
Force majeure, 28, 113–114
Foreign currencies
  claim amount, 119
  settlement amount and limitation, 123
Foreseeability, and consequential losses, 121
Forwarders, 2n, 3, 4, 5&n, 6
  insurance cover, 12
  liabilities: Guadalajara Convention, 88–89
  liability cover, 11, 12

Forwarders—*cont.*
loss control, 15, 21, 22–31
risk control, 15–16, 17
see also Consolidators
Forwarding agents, 2n, 46
Fraud, RHA conditions, 51
Fraudulent claims, 105
Freight
defined, xviii
entitlement to claim, 107–108
non-payment, 107
payment of: air waybill conditions, 95–96
Freight charges, withholding of, 5&n, 6

Gatewhite v. *Iberia*, 108n, 127
General average, 46, 58
GHAs (general handling agents), airline handling agreements, 22, 99–101
Goods-in-transit insurance cover, 12
GSAs (general sales agents), 99
Guadalajara Convention, xviii, 63, 88–90, 110
full text (App. 7), 185–189

Hague Protocol 1955 (Warsaw/Hague), xix, 48, 63, 64, 85, 87, 91
amended articles, 81–85
Article 8: AWB particulars, 82
Article 9: effect of absence of AWB particulars, 82
Article 15: negotiable AWBs, 82–83
Article 22: limitation of liability, 83–84
Article 23: minimum levels of liability, 84–85
Article 25: intentional or reckless conduct, 85
Article 26: delivery and notices of claim, 85
full text of Warsaw Convention with Amendments (Apps. 4 and 6), 155–164, 175–184
settlement amount and limitation, 124, 125
see also Montreal Protocols
"Handling agents", 22
HAWBs *see* House air waybills
"Himalaya" clauses, 95
"Hold harmless" agreements, 99–101
House air waybills (HAWBs), xvii, xviii, 37, 88
insurance, 12–13
title to goods, 108
trucking of air cargo, 104

Importers, 2n, 3, 4, 5
insurance, 9–10
loss control, 15
transit/cargo insurance cover, 12
see also Consignees

Incorporation, importance of, 45
Inherent vice, 118
Insurance, 9–13
air waybill insurance, 12–13
damage to goods, 26–27, 28
"excess"/"deductible", 27
goods-in-transit cover, 12
late reporting of claim, 21
liability cover, 11–12, 13
need for, 10, 11–12
notification of loss, 23
origins, 46
RHA conditions, 52
settlement amount and limitation, 126
settlement of claim, 22
subrogation, xix, 109
transit: air waybill conditions, 97
transit: BIFA conditions, 56
Insurance brokers, 10, 23
damage to goods, 27
Insurance investigators, 31
Insureds, 9–10
Interest
claim amount, 120
settlement amount and limitation, 126–127
International Air Transport Association (IATA), xviii, 61, 65
air waybills, 71, 75, 78, 93
airline handling agreements, 99
non-payment of freight, 107
settlement amount and limitation, 125
trucking of air cargo, 104
IRP (irregularity report), 39

Jurisdiction
defined, xviii
entitlement to claim, 110
and legal proceedings: liability of carrier, 79

Labelling of cargo, 17, 19
Law
applicable law: BIFA conditions, 59
jurisdiction and legal proceedings: liability of carrier, 79
legal framework, 43–48
litigation: assumption of future, 33–34
litigation expenses: liability limits, 83–84
settlement criteria, 129–130
Lawyers, viii, 129–130
Liability
acceptance of: BIFA conditions, 55
of carrier, 86–87
Warsaw Convention 1929, 69–80
claims, 4
concept of, 7–8, 43
context: claims decisions, 103–105
of forwarder/contracting carrier: Guadalajara Convention, 88–89
insurance cover, 11–12, 13

Liability—*cont.*
insurers: loss control, 31
and limitation, BIFA conditions, 58–59
for loss and damage: RHA conditions, 51
proving *see under* Settlement criteria
"release of"/"discharge of", 128
see also Limitation of liability
Liability in bailment and transit
agency, 46
bailment, 44
importance of incorporation, 45
transit, 44
Limitation of liability
of air carrier, 69–80, 86
air waybill conditions, 94
evolution, 46–47
loss of, 76–77, 86–87, 100
non-Warsaw, 91
RHA conditions, 51–52
Warsaw Convention 1929 ("unamended Warsaw"), 74–75
Warsaw/Hague, 83–84
see also Settlement criteria (settlement amount and limitation)
Loss
of contracts: claim amount, 121
and damage, liability for (RHA conditions), 51
defined, 15n
of limitation, 86–87
risk control, 16–19
see also Consequential losses
Loss adjusters, viii, 11, 21
damage to goods, 27
insurance claims, 31
Loss adjustment, RHA conditions, 53
Loss assessors, 5
see also Recovery agents
Loss control, 15–16, 21–31
cargo owners, 21–22
carriers and forwarders, 21, 22–31
damage, 26–28
delay, 28–29
documenting incidents, 22–23
liability insurers, 31
missing during bond-check, 25
missing on picking-out, 25–26
missing on receipt
from another depot in same company, 24
from another party, 24
from inbound aircraft, 24–25
notifying insurers, 23
tallying of goods, 23, 24
theft, 29–31
Luxury goods, loss, 16

MAWBs *see* Airline master air waybills
Mis-loading to departing aircraft, 25, 26
Mis-routeing of cargo, 19
Mitigation, 15, 21–22
and claim amount, 121–122
consequential losses, 122
damage, 122
delayed perishables, 122
reasonableness of, 122
Montreal Protocols, xviii, 48, 63
Warsaw Convention, amendments to
Montreal No. 1, 63, 64, 65, 87, 124, 165–173 (App. 5)
Montreal No. 2, 63, 64, 80, 87, 155–164 (App. 4)
Montreal Nos 3 & 4, 63, 80, 84–86, 87, 88, 125, 175–184 (App. 6)

Negligence
of carriers and forwarders, 11
contributory negligence, 115–116
errors in documentation/handling instructions, 115
imprudent loading, 115–116
inadequate packing, 115
Warsaw Convention 1929 ("unamended Warsaw"), 74
defined, xviii
Non-Warsaw system, 71, 72, 87, 91
air waybill conditions, 94, 95, 96
settlement amount and limitation, 124, 125
Notices of claim, 22, 39, 78–79
entitlement to claim, 109–110
Guadalajara Convention, 90
Hague Protocol 1955 (Warsaw/Hague), 85
Notification of loss, to customer, 24, 25

Out-turn report, 38

Packages
limit: settlement amount and limitation, 125
weight limitation: air waybill conditions, 94
Packaging, risk control, 17, 18–19, 20
Packing
inadequacy of, and contributory negligence, 115
of perishables, 19
Packing lists, 36–37
Pallet tags/pallet manifests, 38
Perishable goods
delay, 19&n, 20, 28–29, 117, 122
packing of, 19
Personal effects/household goods, 123
Physical deformation, of cargo, 20
Pilferage, 36, 100
loss control, 29–31
risk control, 18–19
Police, theft reporting, 29, 30–31
Prima facie evidence, 116
defined, xviii
truck delivery notes, 37&n

Proof, consequential losses and claim amount, 120–121

Quantum
  defined, xviii
  see also under Settlement criteria, claim amount

Recovery agents, viii, 5
  see also Loss assessors
Regulation of contracts, 47–48
Reserve, defined, xviii
Respondents, and claimants: attitudes, 105–106
"Risk", 10
Risk control, 15–21
  damage, 19–21
  loss, 16–19
Road carriage, categories of, 72–73
Road Haulage Association Conditions of Carriage 1991: full text (App. 1), 131–137
Road Haulage Association Conditions of Carriage 1991 (conditions summarised), 49–53
  Condition 1: definitions, 49
  Condition 2: parties and subcontracting, 49–50
  Condition 3: dangerous goods, 50
  Condition 4: loading and unloading, 50
  Condition 5: consignment notes, 50
  Condition 6: transit, 50
  Condition 7: undelivered or unclaimed goods, 50
  Condition 8: carrier's charges, 51
  Condition 9: liability for loss and damage, 51
  Condition 10: fraud, 51
  Condition 11: limitation of liability, 51–52
  Condition 12: insurance, 52
  Condition 13: indemnity to carrier, 52
  Condition 14: time limits for claims, 52–53
  Condition 15: lien, 53
  Condition 16: unreasonable detention, 53
  Condition 17: computation of time, 53
  Condition 18: loss adjustment, 53
  Condition 19: impossibility of performance, 53
Road Haulage Association (RHA), xix, 47
  airline handling agreements, 100–101
  claim amount, 118
  liability context: claims decisions, 103
  notice of claim, 109
  proving liability, 112
  settlement amount and limitation, 124, 126
  time bars, 111

SDRs (Special Drawing Rights), 58–59, 71
  air waybill conditions, 94
SDRs (Special Drawing Rights)—*cont.*
  defined, xix
  liability limit, 74, 83, 86, 91
  non-Warsaw, 91
  settlement amount and limitation, 124
  trucking of air cargo, 104
Settlement criteria, 107–130
  claim amount (quantum), 118–123
    accurate calculation/supporting documents, 123
    added value, 119
    foreign currencies, 119
    interest, 120
    sound-arrived-value, 119
    subrogated claims, 119–120
    see also Consequential losses; Mitigation
  entitlement to claim, 107–112
    delays in pursuit of claim, 112
    freight, 107–108
    jurisdiction, 110
    notice of claim, 109–110
    subrogation, 109
    time bars, 111
    title to goods, 108–109
  lawyers and litigation, 129–130
  negotiation, 128
  proving liability, 112–118
    contributory negligence *see under* Negligence
    delivery signatures, 116
    force majeure, 113–114
      continuing duty of care, 114–115
    inherent vice, 118
    perishables: damaged by delay, 117
    transhipments and successive/preceding carriers, 113
    ULDs, 116–117
  settlement, 128–129
  settlement amount and limitation, 123–128
    air carriage
      declared value for carriage, 125–126
      Montreal Protocol No. 1, 124
      Montreal Protocol No. 2, 124
      non-Warsaw, 124
      package limit, 125
      unamended Warsaw, 124
      volumetric variance, 125
      Warsaw/Hague, 124–125
    BIFA, 124
    currencies, 123
    interest, 126–127
    limitation breaking, 126
    RHA, 124
    undesirable settlement practices, 127–128
    weight basis, 123–124
Shippers, 2&n, 3, 4
  insurance, 9
  liability claims, 7

Shippers—*cont.*
loss control, 15
see also Exporters
Shipping arrangements, risk control, 18
Shipping invoices, 36, 37, 108
SITA telex system, xix, 38n
Sound-arrived-value: claim amount, 119
Staff
hiring of, 22, 30
wilful misconduct, 99, 100
Subrogation
claim amount, 119–120
defined, xix
entitlement to claim, 109
receipts, 12

Tallying, 23, 24, 38
Telexes, 21, 35, 38
SITA, 19, 38n
Theft, 99–100
loss control, 29–31
risk control, 15, 16–19
"Third party notice": proving liability, 113
Time-bars, 53&n
entitlement to claim, 80, 111
Title to goods, 108–109
Tracing records, 38–39
Transit, liability in, 44
Truck delivery notes, 37
Truckers, 2n, 3
Trucking, of air cargo: claims decisions, 104

ULD (unit load device), xix, 19, 38, 40, 116–117
Underwriters, 10–11
"Unfair Contracts" legislation, 81
United Kingdom, 82
and Guadalajara Convention, 88
Hague Protocol 1955 (Warsaw/Hague), 85
Montreal Protocols, 85, 87
undesirable settlement practices, 127–128
Warsaw system, 64–65
categories of road carriage, 72–73
USA
defective air waybills, 67
and Hague Protocol, 48, 81, 82
settlement amount and limitation, 125, 127, 128
Warsaw system, 65, 85–86, 87
see also CAB (Civil Aviation Board)
"UTL" ("unable to locate"), 25

Vandalism, 100
"Vouchers", 123
"Voyage", 10

Warehouses
bond checks, 25
double-checking for loss, 24–25
loss control, 25, 26
and pilferage, 29, 30
and theft of goods, 18, 19
Warsaw Convention 1929 ("unamended Warsaw"), 48, 62, 63, 64, 65–81
full text (App. 3), 145–154
Chapter I: scope and definitions, 65–66
Article 1, 66
Article 2, 66
Chapter II
Article 5, need for and absence of AWB, 66
Article 6, number of copies, and signatures (AWBs), 67
Article 7, one AWB per package?, 67
Article 8, AWB particulars, 67
Article 9, effect of absence of particulars, 67–68
Article 10, consignor's responsibility, 68
Article 11, AWB particulars as evidence, 68
Article 12, right of stoppage in transit, 68–69
Article 13, acquisition of contract rights by consignee, 69
Article 14, consignor's and consignee's respective rights, 69
Article 15, limiting the effect of Articles 12, 13 and 14, 69
Article 16, consignor's responsibility for documents attached to AWB, 69
Chapter III: liability of carrier, 69–80
Article 17, passenger liability, 70
Article 18
categories of road carriage, 72–73
damage and loss liability, 70–73
Article 19, delay liability, 73
Article 20, carrier's defences, 74
Article 21, contributory negligence, 74
Article 22, limitation of liability, 74–75, 126
Article 23, minimum levels of liability, 75–76, 118
Article 24, permitted context for claims, 76
Article 25, deprivation of limitation, 76–77
Article 26, delivery and notices of claim, 77–79
Article 27, "death" of carrier, 79
Article 28, jurisdiction and legal proceedings, 79
Article 29, time bar, 80, 111
Article 30, successive carriers, 80

Warsaw Convention 1929 ("unamended Warsaw")—*cont.*
- Chapter IV: provisions relating to combined transportation, Article 31, 80–81
- Chapter V: general and final provisions, 81
- settlement criteria, 124

Warsaw Convention as amended by Montreal Additional Protocol No. 1 (App. 5), 165–173

Warsaw Convention as amended at the Hague 1955
- and Montreal Additional Protocol No. 2 (App. 4), 155–164
- and with Montreal Protocols Nos 3 & 4 (App. 6), 175–184

Warsaw system, 62, 63–90
- complication, 87
- concept of liability, 7–8
- defined, xix
- simplification, 86
- and USA, 85–86
- *see also* Air waybills (AWBs), conditions; Guadalajara Convention; Montreal Protocols; Non-Warsaw system; Warsaw Convention 1929 ("unamended Warsaw")

Warsaw/Hague and Montreal No. 2, full text (App. 4), 155–164

Warsaw/Hague and Montreal Nos 3 & 4, full text (App. 6), 175–184

Weather
- damage to cargo, 20
- and delay, 28

Weight basis, settlement amount and limitation, 123–124

Wetting, of cargo, 20

Wilful misconduct, xix

"Without prejudice": airline handling agreements, 101&n